PRAGUE: THE MYSTICAL CITY

BY THE SAME AUTHOR:

VIENNA, MY VIENNA

PRAGUE

THE MYSTICAL CITY

Joseph Wechsberg

THE MACMILLAN COMPANY
NEW YORK, NEW YORK

Copyright © 1971 by Joseph Wechsberg
All rights reserved. No part of this book may be
reproduced or transmitted in any form or by any means,
electronic or mechanical, including photocopying,
recording or by any information storage and retrieval
system, without permission in writing from the
Publisher.
The Macmillan Company
866 Third Avenue, New York, N.Y. 10022
Collier-Macmillan Canada Ltd., Toronto, Ontario
Library of Congress Catalog Card Number: 74-116785
First Printing
Printed in the United States of America

To Prague, with my love

PRAGUE: THE MYSTICAL CITY

Little Mother Has Claws

PRAGUE IS CALLED *Praha* in Czech, after *Prah*, "the threshold." The "a" at the end of the word denotes a woman's name: Prague is a feminine city. Not a glamorous young woman, like Paris, but *matička* (little mother) to her troubadours. Svatopluk Čech, the nineteenth-century poet, wrote:

> Praha! To jméno samo zpěv,
> Ten pouhý zvuk úchvatně
> Do strun české duše sáhá . . .
>
> (Praha! Your name is song,
> The very sound of it touches strongly
> The strings of the Czech soul . . .)

Many poets, before and after Čech, have agreed with him. Jaroslav Vrchlický calls Prague "the heart of the heart." Antonín Sova, a modern poet, writes, "In the depth of my soul / The echo of Prague lures me to her," and Josef Hora exclaims, "You are not mine—I am yours!"

Josef Kajetán Tyl, poet, playright and patriot—he was a leader of the Czech Renaissance movement against the Habsburg regime, in 1837—wrote, "Once in his lifetime every Czech must see Prague, once he must make a pilgrimage there as a Moslem goes to Mecca. He who dies without having seen Prague didn't know the focus of our national history and the cradle of our future." Fifty years later, toward the end of his life, the poet Julius Zeyer wrote that once more he wants to see Prague, "of which I often dream, as I saw her from Hradčany Castle—mystical, big, silent, in the haze of poetry, my Montserrat." To the Czechs Prague was always what Paris was to the French, "our *raison d'être* ... the fireplace of our national literature" (F. X. Harlas). The writers in the countryside of Bohemia, Moravia, Silesia, could never get away from the influence of Prague.

Men have been in love with Prague for a thousand years, often behaving irrationally, as people in love do. Detlev von Liliencron, the German *Junker* who became bewitched by Prague in 1866, during the Austrian-Prussian War, when he came there as a young Prussian officer and spent just one night in town, sleeping on a poolroom table, never forgot. Thirty years later, he wrote a German poem with the Czech title "Praha, Nazdar!" (Hail, Prague!) in which he said "Ganz Praha ist ein Goldnetz von Gedichten" (Whole Prague is a golden net of poems). Walking through the city he exclaimed, "Prague is more beautiful than my dearly beloved Palermo!" whereupon he confessed that he'd never been in Palermo. Goethe, with similar poetic license, called Prague "a truly royal and classical city ... unlike Berlin, which one sees only when one is inside, one sees Prague only from the outside or from above." But Goethe had never been in Prague though he made seventeen, well-publicized journeys to Karlsbad (Karlovy Vary) and other Bohemian spas. He'd often been invited to Prague by Carl Ludwig von Woltmann, the German historian, because "after Rome and Jerusalem, to which Prague is said to be similar in location, no other town is such a varied and strange historical document." Goethe wrote from Weimar, "Unfortunately the doctors send me to the restless Rhine stream; I would have a thousand times times preferred to visit the Moldau."

In Prague's Malá Strana district, an old house with a star above the entrance was shown "where Goethe might have lived, had he ever come to Prague." Goethe's poet friend Schiller, who had been in Karlsbad in the summer of 1791, didn't miss Prague, where his plays were very popular. His guide, Count Prokop Lažanský, showed Schiller the sights—the Old Town Square, where the Bohemian patriots had been executed in 1621, the Jewish Cemetery, and the Waldstein Palace that fascinated the author of the *Wallenstein* trilogy. "After a fortnight Herr von Schiller left the capital of Bohemia that he'd come to love," writes Josef Svátek.

Wilhelm Raabe, the German writer, called Prague "the mad, the solemn city, the city of martyrs, musicians and beautiful girls," and exclaimed, "Oh, Prague, what a piece of my free soul you took away from me!" Prague was always a city of martyrs. In 1815, Woltmann wrote to Goethe, "Germans and Czechs have built and again destroyed Prague out of national passion. . . ." Others, too. Not long ago, Ivo Fleischmann, a Czech poet now living in forced emigration, remembered Prague, "in the center of the ill-fated Bohemian rectangle whose geopolitical location was the source of the tragedy of a spirited nation." André Gide called Prague "the glorious, pain-filled and tragic city," and Ernest Denis, the French historian, noted that "every stone reminds you of heroic deeds. Nowhere else were passions more violent and battles more cruel." A monument of Denis, a friend of Masaryk's Czechoslovakia, was removed in 1938, after France (and the other Western powers) sold out Czechoslovakia in Munich. Earlier, in the same spot, there had been a statue of the Austrian Field Marshal Joseph Wenzel Radetzky that was removed in 1918, after the hated Habsburgs ceased to rule in Prague, although (and because) Radetzky was a native of Bohemia.

In 1826, Franz Grillparzer, the Austrian playwright, wrote that Prague reminded him of Venice, "because there is so much permanent here, the ancient next to the new," but that the Town Hall and the bridge towers reminded him of Florence. "The city somehow reconciled me with the Bohemian nation that I never liked," he admitted. "One really should never judge a nation before meeting it in its homeland." Chateaubriand called Prague "the celestial Jerusalem." Auguste Rodin called her "the Rome of the North." Fouquet said Prague was "queenly, indescribable, incomparable." Richard Wagner, an expert in romanticism, called Prague "romantic" and caused a sensation in 1863 when he conducted a concert on Sophie's Island, standing for the first time with his back toward the audience. Paul Valéry wrote, "There is no other place on earth where the great ensemble and the small detail are more beautifully blended." Guido Batelli compared the view of Prague to a symphony "in which all instruments merged their voices," and Bruno Walter wrote, "Walking through the old streets, I began to feel an intimate affection for the strangely overwhelming, romantically dark city."

"This is the Czech Athens," wrote L. E. Obolensky in 1899 from St. Petersburg which then was the Russian Athens. People have called her *Zlatá Praha*, the Golden Prague, though Prague is golden only in short, blessed

The Mystical City 5

moments—on a mild evening in spring or again in the fall, when the last rays of the setting sun caress the Gothic church towers and the cupolas of the Baroque palaces. They call her Prague of the Hundred Towers but there are one hundred and fourteen church towers, and a great many other towers in the city. (In the nineteenth century there were one hundred and eighty church bells in Prague.) Looking down from Hradčany Castle whose silhouette has dominated Prague for many centuries, the city's towers make you think of medieval knights guarding the Castle, with their spears pointing toward the sky.

Thomas Mann, whom Czechoslovakia made a citizen after the Nazis had deprived him of his citizenship, said that Prague was "one of the most magical cities on earth—in its old beauty she surpasses much of what is Italian." Egon Erwin Kisch once told Gustav Janouch, Kafka's friend, "Prague is different. Prague is a spell, something that holds you and always draws you back to her. One can't forget her." In 1902, Franz Kafka wrote, "Prague doesn't release you. This *Mütterchen* [little mother] has claws."

City-of-the-World

WRITING THE STORY of Prague is a thankless task. "When one reports the history of the Bohemian lands, one must not seek the approval of any of the nations, religions or social groups but will arrive at a useful achievement only by making everybody dissatisfied," writes Johannes Urzidil, the German writer from Prague who had many Czech and Jewish friends there, and later lived in America. "In no other city of Europe had two forces loved and hated each other as strongly as the Czechs and Germans in Prague, and in no other city in Europe had the Jews such an important task of mediating between them," writes Traugott Krischke, a German writer. The Czech poet, Gustav Janouch, in his *Conversations with Kafka* writes about Oskar Baum, the Jewish poet from Prague who went to German public school there. On the way home, the Czech and German boys often started to fight. During such a brawl a boy beat little Baum with his wooden pencase over the eyes. Baum later became totally blind. (I well remember him, a white-haired, smiling, kindly man, walking on the arm of his wife.)

"Oskar Baum, the Jew, lost his eyesight as a German," Kafka said to Janouch. "As something that he really never was, and which was never given to him. Perhaps Oskar is only a symbol of the so-called German Jews in Prague." The emphasis is on "so-called"—Kafka knew how to put a whole world into one word. Hugo Siebenschein, a literary critic, writes, "Kafka and his friends were Germans according to their language, and Jews according to their origin, but they refused not to love, or even to hate, the Czechs with whom they shared their hope of civilization."

Today Prague is a Czech city but it would be wrong to write the story of Prague as a Czech city, or as a German city, or as a Jewish city. Prague is all three. The city was over a thousand years old in 1968, the year of the unforgettable "Prague Spring," and also the year of the brutal awakening from the short dream of freedom. Prague always was either battlefield or symbiosis. No matter how one approaches the city, one becomes aware of a strange, many-

The Mystical City

faceted triality. Historically, culturally, linguistically, there are three peoples—Czechs, Germans, Jews. Spiritually, there is Judaism, Catholicism, Protestantism. Socially, there were for centuries the rulers (emperors or kings), the nobles (known as "the Estates"), and *misera plebs*. Architecturally, there is the Romanesque Prague, the Gothic Prague, the Baroque Prague. What came later cannot be compared with the greatness of the past.

Even topographically, there is the same strange triality, though Prague, like Rome, was built on seven hills. First, the Old Town on the right bank of the Moldau—the town of mystical legends, of the Old Jewish Cemetery, of Jan Hus preaching in Bethlehem Chapel, of defenestrations and executions. Second, Malá Strana, the old *civitas minor* on the left bank of the Moldau, underneath the Castle—the aristocratic enclave of Baroque palaces, monasteries and churches, of astronomers, adventurers and alchemists. Third, the New Town, the personal creation of Charles IV, who in 1438 "ordered himself a Gothic town as other men order a new suit" (Jacques Guenne, the French art historian), today the modern metropolis between Wenceslas Square and the National Theater.

I am using present-day Czech names for localities, streets and squares, except in certain cases where established English translations exist. "Old Town Square" means more to the reader than "Staroměstské Náměsti," and "National Theater" is clearer than "Národní Divaldo." I have not translated certain names where translations might be ambiguous. "Malá Strana" literally means "small side" ("Kleinseite" in German) but has been translated into "Lesser District" or "Little Quarter." I'll call it "Malá Strana" though historically one could plead for "Kleinseite." Some German names are used because they are better known in the English-speaking world than the corresponding Czech names. Concertgoers everywhere know Smetana's "Moldau," not his "Vltava." But I prefer Czech "Hradčany" to the German "Hradschin." *Hrad* is the Czech word for "castle," and the Prague Castle was built by the Czech Přemyslids. Confusion remains about many spellings. The composer Stamitz wrote his name in the German manner when he worked for the Duke of Mannheim but the Czechs now call him "Stamic." The Nostic dynasty, Bohemian nobles, are also known as "Nostiz" and "Nostitz." More important remains the fact that Franz Anton Reichsgraf von Nostitz began building the theater where Mozart conducted the world premiere of *Don Giovanni* in 1788, but he ran out of money and the Bohemian Estates had to finish the project. (Prior to the First World War, the boxes were inherited.) The street where Franz Kafka was born is called after Mordechai Maisel (or Meisel, Maisl, or Meisl), a rich man and former mayor of the Jewish town. Today the street is called "Maiselova."

In Prague, the change of a political regime was often reflected by the change of street names. Tolerance was never widespread in this city of cruel passions where the bizarre nomenclature reflects history. Sadova Silnice (Park Street), as it was originally called in 1875, in 1916 became Archduke Charles-Franz-Joseph Street, the following year Emperor Charles Street, and when the last Habsburg ruler lost his empire in 1918, it became Park Street again. In 1923, it was called "Hooverova," in honor of President Hoover, and in 1940, when the Nazis were in Prague, they renamed the street after Richard Wagner. In 1945, Wagner was out and Hoover was in again, but not for long. In 1947, Hooverova became Wilsonova, after President Wilson. And in 1952, the Communist regime renamed it Street-of-Victorious-February, "in memory of the failure of the reactionary putsch in February, 1948."

The large street leading up from the National Museum, at the very top of Wenceslas Square, to the district known once as Královské Vinohrady (Royal Vineyards), and later as plain Vinohrady, was originally called Cerno-Kostelecká, after a town in Bohemia. In 1884, it became Jungmannova, in honor of Josef Jungmann, a leader of the Czech national Renaissance. In 1920, after the First World War, it became Fochova, a gesture of gratitude to Marshal Foch and France, then Czechoslovakia's close ally. Came the Germans and renamed it Schwerinova, after a Count of Schwerin. In 1945, Schwerin was swept into the trash can of history, following the collapse of the Thousand-Year Reich, and once more the street was named after Marshal Foch. Not for long though; when the Communists took over in 1948, "Fochova" became "Stalinova," in honor of the *new* ally. In 1958, after Stalin was swept out of his mausoleum, "Stalinova" became "Vinohradská," the Vineyard Street. At this writing it is still called that. A nice name that won't offend anyone.

Many old houses in Prague still have their signs and names though they are not always clearly visible. Their origin is often mysterious; sometimes they are remembered in connection with certain people. The house where Mozart stayed is known as "At the Golden Angel"; the house where Egon Erwin Kisch was born is known as "At the Two Golden Bears" (a Gothic house restyled during the Renaissance); the house where three families of Prague violinmakers lived successively is known as "At the Three Fiddles," at No. 12 Nerudova Street. No. 25, with its lovely Baroque façade, bears the sign of a donkey in a cradle, and nearby is the rococo palace of the Bretfelds, where Mozart spent his first evening in Prague and met Casanova. No. 47, "At the Two Suns," is where Jan Neruda, the poet, who later gave his name to the street, lived during the last years of his life.

Some romantic names have survived below Hradčany, in the street called "Nový Svět" (New World), not meant as a synonym with America. This street was inhabited by poor people who lived off the crumbs that fell from the tables of the mighty ones in the Castle. Being poor, they gave their houses "golden" names: "At the Golden Horn," "At the Golden Star," "At the Golden Pear," "At the Golden Tree," "At the Golden Stork," "At the Golden Sun" and "At the Golden Plough," where the great violinist František Ondříček, who always ended his concerts with the national anthem, "Where Is My Home?" played on the G string, was born.

Nothing is clear and simple in Prague; everything is enigmatic and complex. The city's thousand-year-old history is constant flux and reflux, love and hatred, struggle and synthesis, contrast and symbiosis. Princes fight tribal leaders, kings fight the Estates, feudal rulers fight the upcoming bourgeoisie, the city fights the countryside, haves fight the have-nots. More recently, Czechs have fought Czechs. The social struggles have ended with the conversion of former have-nots into haves, and vice versa—but for how long? There are religious struggles throughout the centuries: pagans against Christians, Christians against "heretic" Christians, Utraquists against Jesuits, Christians against Jews. Architecturally, recent discoveries prove that the Romanesque Prague was superseded by the Gothic Prague, which in turn was systematically rebuilt by the Catholic Church into the Baroque Prague. Yet so strong is the *genius*

The Mystical City

loci that *all* styles become imbued with the spirit of Prague. The Prague Baroque cannot be mistaken for the Baroque in Italy or Vienna.

In 1930, Tomáš Garrigue Masaryk, the first President of the Czechoslovak Republic wrote, "Prague is a Czech city but it must also be a Czechoslovak city in which all inhabitants feel at home. It must become a city-of-the-world without losing its architectural, spiritual and cultural character." Earlier, Masaryk, the great humanist, philosopher and citizen-of-the-world had written, "Despite all enthusiasm for the Russians and all Slavs, despite all repugnance against the Germans, the Germans actually remain our teachers." František Palacký, the Czech humanist and nineteenth-century historian, called "the continuous contact of the Slav nation with the Roman nation and the German nation" the essentiality of Czech history. Much earlier, the seventeenth-century Moravian philosopher John Amos Comenius (Komenský) wrote in his *Panergesia*:

In truth Europe is separated from Asia, Asia from Africa, Africa from America and between empires and lands lie mountains and valleys, rivers and fields. One Earth, however, bears and nurtures us all, the same air embraces us, the same heavens rise above us, the same sun lights us all in our turn. We all live in one common habitation, one breath of life inspires us all. We are all citizens of one world—what then hinders us from gathering in one community, under the same laws? ... For one and the same thing is natural to all people: one system of the senses, reason, will, and all vital forces.

But the voices of humanism and wisdom have been rare in the chauvinistic wilderness. The last time all national groups got together in Prague was in 1859, at the centenary of Friedrich Schiller. The story of Prague depends on who writes it. The same historical event takes on a completely different aspect when it is "interpreted" by a liberal nineteenth-century German; a nationalistic Sudeten-German of the 1930s; an enlightened Czech historian prior to 1850; a Czech nationalist writing fifty years later; a liberal Czech during Masaryk's "First Republic" (now often derisively called "that bourgeois Republic"); a Prague Jew writing in German; a Prague Jew writing in Czech; a German writing during the Nazi occupation; or a contemporary Communist historian. ("From 1848 to 1939, each German writer in Prague had to decide whether he valued individual liberty more than national discipline," writes Paul Demetz, a German writer in Prague who valued individual liberty.) Max Brod, Kafka's closest friend, a Prague Jew writing in German who spoke Czech and loved Czech culture (he helped Leoš Janáček and translated Jaroslav Hašek before they were discovered by their own nation), calls Prague "a polemical city . . . where three nations fought each other: the Czechs as majority, the Germans as minority, and the Jews as minority within the German minority." An Italian writer, Orazio Pedrazzi, senses "the tragic soul of Prague, a city of contrasts . . . Polemical statues, polemical churches, polemical theatres, polemical universities, showing different cultures. Prague never smiles. Since the days of Hus, the Czech nation was always in a state of mobilization . . . But it is this fighting face that makes Prague so beautiful." Prague, the capital of Bohemia, which Goethe called "a continent in the middle of a continent."

The Czechs' "mobilization" for their national independence was always symbolized by their fight for their own language. Jan Hus, professor at the University of Prague who preached against the Pope and started the Hussite movement whose short glory helped the Czech nation to

The Mystical City 13

preserve its identity during centuries of defeat and Germanization, is now revered both as the great Reformer and a national hero because he preached in Czech, not in Latin, proving that Czech was not just "a language for the peasants." He also wrote grammatical works that saved both the language and the nation. Reading and writing has always been important in this country. In 1444, Aeneas Silvius Piccolomini, the Italian poet who later became Pope Pius II, wrote that the Czech people knew the Bible better than the Roman prelates. He asked his friend Tušek in Prague to buy him a Bible, "because I am tired of literature and want to look into the depth of the Scriptures ... Bibles are said to be rather inexpensive in Prague." A parchment Bible cost sixteen guilders, a paper Bible eight guilders. "Thus the later Pope bought his first Bible in Hussite Prague—a Bible which had perhaps belonged to a Tábor knight, the son of Satan," writes Josef Pekář, the Czech historian.

Occasionally, the desperate search for the Czech language led into dark side streets. On September 18, 1817, one Václav Hanka claimed to have found several pieces of old parchment underneath the church tower of Králový Dvůr in northeastern Bohemia. They contained fragments of old Czech epics and lyrical poems apparently going back to the late thirteenth century—welcome proof of the medieval existence of a Czech language and literature! It was just the time of the Czech national rebirth after two hundred years of Habsburg domination in Bohemia, and there arose enormous excitement about the manuscript. Josef Jungmann, educated on Voltaire, Wieland and Milton's *Paradise Lost*, declared that "a state cannot exist without nationality." Chateaubriand and La Motte-Fouquet wrote about the discovery, Jakob Grimm studied the translation and called it "original folk poetry," and Goethe translated the poem

"Kytice" ("Das Sträusschen," the small bouquet), "a Bohemian folk song."

The following year, the Czech Museum Society received from an anonymous sender, through the mail, fragments of the so-called Zelená Hora manuscript, epic songs about the foundation of Prague that had been—for reasons unknown—first published in Poland. Hanka, by that time a national hero and librarian at the National Museum in Prague, studied the manuscript and called it "authentic." But other people became suspicious. Abbé Josef Dobrovský, author of an old-Slavonic grammar, *Institutiones linguae Slavicae veteris dialecti*, expressed grave doubts about the manuscript (and was promptly labeled "a hypercritical traitor" by some ultra-nationalists). In the 1840s, the historians Pavel Josef Šafařík and František Palacký wrote learned apologies. The manuscripts remained a national symbol, and when a newspaper, *Tagesbote aus Böhmen*, printed a series of unsigned articles accusing Hanka of forgery, Hanka sued, and the paper's editor went to prison.

Then, in 1886, Tomáš G. Masaryk wrote a sociological examination of the manuscripts in his critical review, *Athenaeum*, and Jan Gebauer, a noted scholar, wrote a scientific philological analysis, proving beyond doubt that both the Králový Dvůr and Zelená Hora manuscripts had been forged by Hanka (who long ago had died a national hero and had been given a state funeral). For many years, Professor Masaryk was hated by the Czech nationalists for revealing the awful truth. Later, he again made himself very unpopular when he came to the aid of Leopold Hilsner, an impoverished Jew who was accused of the "ritual murder" of a girl near the Czech village of Polná. With no outside help whatsoever (such as Emile Zola had when he spoke up in favor of Captain Alfred Dreyfus in Paris) Masaryk proved Hilsner's innocence. When Masaryk became his country's first President in 1918, he adopted as his motto the old slogan of Jan Hus and King George of Poděbrady, *Pravda Vítězí*—Truth Prevails.

Around 1900, the language problem created a veritable inferiority complex among the Czechs. A French writer, André Chevadam, reported in 1902 that when educated people in Paris talked about Bohemia, they might say that "Budapest is a beautiful city," which created exasperation among the Czechs in Prague. They also complained because no one in Vienna, the capital, took real notice of them. In 1902, Max Graf, the Viennese critic, wrote, "If a kid breaks a glass window in Prague, the Viennese read about it a few hours later in their paper but no one in Vienna knows what a Czech poet or a Czech composer did in Prague." That year Guillaume Apollinaire came to Prague and was surprised when the first five people he met in the street didn't speak, or didn't want to speak, a word of German, only Czech. The sixth told him, in French, "Speak French, Monsieur, we hate the Germans more than the French hate them." The Czech word for "German" is *Němec*, from *němý*, "the mute one"— one who doesn't speak our language. The Czechs never forgave Shakespeare for placing Bohemia at the seashore in *A Winter's Tale*, and they were furious when Friedrich Hebbel, who should have known better, called the Czechs and "Polaks" *Bedientenvölker*, (nations of servants), "with the unkempt heads of caryatidys." They were not pleased when Jerome K. Jerome made fun of the Czech alphabet "which consists of 42 letters and reminds the foreigner of Chinese . . . Czech is not a language that one quickly comprehends." Today no one in Prague's ruling circles would like to remember that Karl Marx, in 1852, was quoted in *The New York Daily Tribune* as calling the Czechs "a dying nation . . . in a land that can only exist as part of Germany."

Czechs, Germans, Jews

THE CROSSROADS CITY of Prague, barrier between East and West, was divided by invisible and impenetrable walls. In 1900, less than half a million Czechs lived there, ten thousand Germans and twenty-five thousand Jews, of whom fourteen thousand spoke Czech and eleven thousand spoke German. The Czechs, who were not permitted to call themselves a nation, nevertheless said they were Czechs when asked about their "nationality." Most Germans in Prague, loyal to the Habsburgs, called themselves "Austrians." The Jews were allowed by regulations to fill out only the column headed "language" on official documents, and they wrote either "Czech" or "German." Only after 1918 was the Jewish "nationality" recognized by the First Republic.

Between the half million Czechs and the German-speaking people in Prague, of whom there were twenty-one thousand—some Germans, some Jews—no communication whatsoever existed. "There was no German-speaking proletariat in Prague," wrote Egon Erwin Kisch, the well-known Jewish reporter who wrote in German and early joined the Czech

Communist Party, died in Prague in 1948 and is now highly regarded by the present regime:

The Germans who accounted for five per cent of the city's population had two beautiful theatres, a large concert hall, two universities, five *Gymnasiums* [secondary-grade schools], two daily newspapers, big club localities, and an interesting social life. They had no private contact with their Czech fellow citizens. No German ever appeared at the Czech Burghers' Club. No Czech ever went to the German Casino, as their Deutsches Haus was called.

Czechs and Germans had their own banks (German Hypothekenbank vs. Czech Živnostenská Banka) and industries (Prager Eisen vs. Křižik), their own gymnastics societies (the Czech "Sokol" vs. the German "Turnverein"). When Emperor Franz Joseph I came to Prague to open the Chain Bridge, the Sokol members demonstratively made an "excursion" to nearby Kolín. The Germans made jokes about the Czech National Theater. "Why do they play every day? A Sunday afternoon performance would be enough for all the tailors, shoemakers, artisans and waiters who have a free afternoon."

When I first came to Prague in the 1920s, it seemed perfectly natural to me that each national group had its swimming pools, parks, playgrounds, restaurants, shops, coffeehouses. My innocence (which in retrospect seems rather stupidity) was shared by all my friends; we took complete segregation for granted. The Czechs had their *korso* (the popular promenade) in Národní Třída, and we in Graben, which no one would have called by its Czech name, Příkopy. As a student at the German University I didn't even know for over a year where the Czech University was. Prague's venerable Charles University, founded in 1348 by Charles

IV, had been split in 1882 into the Czech and the German universities of Prague. Each university had its own professors, institutes, laboratories, clinics, libraries, even its own observatory. The Germans had inherited the astronomical instruments once used by Johannes Kepler, the Czechs the equipment of Tycho de Brahe. Between the adjoining botanical gardens of the two universities a wall prevented the observation of plants in the other garden.

It seems grotesque now but it must have been worse prior to the First World War, according to reports of my older friends. Czechs and Germans had separate churches. A group known as Deutsche Fortschrittspartei, German Progress Party, showed its true colors by viciously attacking Richard Wagner, Oscar Wilde, Auguste Rodin. Prague's German soccer club, D.F.C. (Deutscher Fussball Club), never played against Slavia, the leading Czech club, but both played against the same league clubs outside of Prague, which created fascinating discussion about the "paper form" of both clubs: which one was better?

No Czech was ever seen in a German theater in Prague, and no German would go to a Czech theater. Prague's German newspapers might write about a premiere in faraway Vienna but ignored the guest performances of the *Comédie Française* at the Czech National Theater. Czech newspapers retaliated by taking no notice of Enrico Caruso's guest performances at the German Theater. When Czech and German actors in a fraternal spirit got together at a *Stammtisch* (the regulars' table) in a coffeehouse, they were reprimanded by the Czech *and* the German newspapers. The "liberal" German newspaper, *Bohemia*, had a strict rule against printing Czech names. (How liberal can you be?) A Czech girl whose name was Božena was rechristened

Theodora and thus lost her identity, and didn't recognize herself.

Even the coffeehouses where the intellectuals met were nationally segregated. In Vienna, the coffeehouses were separated by subtle literary, political and social distinctions: there were coffeehouses for expressionists and coffeehouses for naturalistic writers and artists, coffeehouses for conservative civil servants and liberal lawyers, and so on. In Prague, nationality was the only distinction. The Czechs met at the Národní Kavárna, across from the National Theater, while the German-speaking citizens congregated at the Café Continental in Graben. At the Café Louvre, a group of German philosophers met twice a month in a backroom facing a courtyard. At the Café Arco in Hybernská many writers enjoyed what chroniclers have called "the highly cultured atmosphere." The coffeehouse had its private library of "privately printed works." The headwaiter would approach a habitué, whispering, "I've got something for you, Sir, that is positively obscene." Among the "obscene" works (that would now be sold everywhere) were the works of Aretino, Franz Blei's *Der Amethyst*, an anonymous masterpiece called *The Marquise's Reading Manual* and that Viennese classic, *Josefine Mutzenbacher*, allegedly written by Felix Salten. To convey the impression of respectability, there was also an incomplete encyclopedia. Max Brod remembers the ambiance at the Café Arco as "scurrilous, frivolous-inquisitive, and youthfully lecherous, but also free and open to new ideas, people crowded in four rooms where the air was thick with smoke and the aroma of strong coffee."

The only ones who dared break out of the cultural ghettos and the confines of linguistic segregation were the writers of

Prague. Among Czech, German and Jewish writers (and some artists) there was stimulating contact and often close friendship. The city's Jewish poets, traditionally Prague's cultural mediators, became interpreters of Czech poetry and art. Friedrich Adler translated the work of Jaroslav Vrchlický; Hugo Salus promoted the music of Antonín Dvořák; Brod became interested in Smetana, whose "popular simplicity and profundity" he compared to Mozart, and he translated Janáček's *Jenufa* which became a worldwide success. Rudolf Fuchs translated the rhapsodic *Silesian Songs* of Petr Bezruč, the poet from Ostrava, and Werfel wrote the introduction. Otakar Březina, the Czech mystic and poet, was beautifully translated by the bilingual Jewish poet, Otto Pick, who also translated the works of František Langer and Karel Čapek. Another bilingual essayist, Pavel Eisner, translated the great Czech nineteenth-century writers Božena Němcová (whose *Babička*, Grandmother, is a classic), Jan Neruda and Karel Hynek Mácha.

"We were no longer unconditionally German in the political sense of our fathers, and we started contacts with older and younger Czech poets," writes Willy Haas, the Jewish-German literary critic who became Werfel's closest friend. Paul Demetz, Rilke's biographer, calls Rilke's friendship with the Czech poets "a way of escape for the German-writing poets of Prague. Here they found warmth . . . in Slav motives and themes."

René Rilke, who later called himself "Rainer Maria Rilke" and is now considered one of the great lyric poets of this century, came from a Sudeten-German family in Prague. His mother was a strong-minded woman and a terrible snob. "It was her greatest sorrow that she hadn't been ennobled," writes Demetz. She hated the Czechs, refused to learn the Czech language, and would not hang out the Czechoslovak

The Mystical City

flag on October 28, the country's Independence Day. Rilke started at the Piarists' Convent in Prague's elegant Panská, or Herrengasse, where I spent my early journalistic life on the editorial floors of the *Prager Tagblatt*, across from the Piarists' Convent; nearby was a tavern patronized by complaisant girls. At the age of nineteen Rilke published, and later renounced, his *Erste Gedichte*, First Poems. Later he wrote, edited and personally distributed a slim magazine, *Wegwarte* (Watchtower), which he sold at street corners, wearing either the black habit of an abbé with long locks, or dressed as a *Belle Epoque* dandy, wearing white gloves, lorgnette and an elegant walking stick. He called himself "a tragic outsider," and hated "the cold, philistine world of the Prague Germans." He didn't like to admit that he was admired by many poets in Prague, Werfel and Kafka among others. In spite of his mother's Czechophobia he became attracted by Czech language and culture. As a boy, he wrote from a holiday, "Here are three small girls, and although they are Czech, we understand each other well."

Rilke didn't speak Czech, but with a poet's somnambulistic instinct he sensed the sound and the rhythm of the Czech language so well that he once used the words of the Czech national anthem in one of his poems. He wrote poems about Jan Hus and the legendary Dalibor who played the violin in the Hradčany Castle Tower known as "Daliborka" where he was imprisoned, and about the playwright Josef Kajetán Tyl. Rilke's first love was Valerie David-Rhonfeld, the niece of the Czech poet Julius Zeyer whom Rilke addressed, "You are my master." He dedicated poems to Svatopluk Čech and Jaroslav Vrchlický, and in his novel *König Bohusch* (King Bohusch) he writes about the sad, dreamy people of Prague's mysterious Malá Strana. ("I know the heart of my dear little mother Prague," says Bohusch, "for this is her heart, Malá

Strana with Hradčany. The most secret things are always in the heart, and there are so many secrets in these old houses.")

König Bohusch retells the sensational assassination of Rudolf Mrva, a hunchbacked glovemaker whose body was found on Christmas eve, 1893, in a dark room in Malá Strana. The story has fascinated many Prague writers because of its cryptic elements. Mrva had been a member of an illegal Czech organization, called "Omladina" (Rejuvenation), which specialized in insulting the symbols of the Habsburg Monarchy in Prague, smudging the Austrian coat of arms, flinging dirt at the monuments of Emperor Franz Joseph I and Field Marshal Radetzky, and spreading such confusion that martial law had to be proclaimed in Prague. Suddenly the police managed to arrest the members of Omladina. It seems that Mrva, working for the police, had joined Omladina's terror group, "Subterranean Prague," and revealed the names of its members. A few days later, two men, called Doležal and Dragoma, who knew the secret code word, "the red-blue-seven," entered the hunchback's flat and stabbed the traitor to death. Ever since, folk songs have told the story of "the Prague Rigoletto."

Rilke regularly attended the Thursday evening meetings of the liberal-German "Assocation of Graphic Artists." (Its competitor was the "Concordia," which met at the "Deutsches Haus," or German House, also known as "Casino," though there was no gambling.) Rilke became a close friend of the Jewish painter and graphic artist Emil Orlik. Rilke admired Orlik because "he mirrored the world so honestly" and grasped "the essence of things"—which was exactly what Rilke tried to do in his poems. Orlik was a remarkable craftsman who could draw equally well with both hands and occasionally astonished his friends by "blindly" drawing, on a paper that he kept in his trousers pocket. His brother was a respected tailor. Well-dressed members of Prague's German society would irritate Orlik by asking him whether he was "the brother of the famous tailor," or where he had his "workshop." Orlik would angrily say, "I have a study—my brother has a workshop." The tailor admired his artist-brother and artists generally, and often made suits for them, at reduced prices, or even for nothing, becoming in his way part of Prague's cultural establishment. (Even in my Prague days, between the two World Wars, a successful tailor was more appreciated by the bourgeois society than a struggling poet or painter.)

Literature, the arts and love brought the nationalities together in Prague. "Our Czech girl friends loved Czech folk songs which they sang and taught us," writes Brod. "We began again to speak Czech, as we had done as children. We breathed more freely than before, and felt firm ground under our feet . . . We sensed (as the most liberal of our Czech men and women friends told us) that old Austria was unfortunately finished in Prague. It was the guilt of our fathers though they were not the main culprits. The guilty ones were the German nationalists in Aussig, Eger and Vienna, and we had as much reason to dislike these forerunners of Hitler as our Czech friends did." (Among the forerunners were two Sudeten Germans, Georg Ritter von Schönerer, later much admired by Hitler, and Karl Hermann Wolf. But there were also half-educated Czech lower-middle-class people who considered Prague's Jewish merchants and intellectuals their "rivals" and had their own anti-Semitic slogans.)

Willy Haas writes "I loved the poems of young František Šrámek . . . We had Czech girl friends and wives. Franz Kafka's love letters to Milena Jesenská, a gifted Czech writer, are a document of desperate love and also of the hopelessness of his bourgeois, Jewish, German existence." Kafka's deep feelings for Milena Jesenská lasted two years and ended in unhappiness. (She was the only one who translated some of his prose into Czech, while he was alive, and she wrote the only obituary after his death in a Czech paper, *Národní Listy*, of June 6, 1924. Milena Jesenská died in a German concentration camp.)

Kafka asked her to write to him in Czech because ". . . I never lived among the German people, German is my maternal language and thus natural to me, but Czech is closer to my heart . . ." In one of his letters to her he comments on the Czech word *nechápu* (I don't understand) that she wrote to him:

A strange word . . . it is so severe, indifferent, cold-eyed, parsimonious and above all nutcracker-like; three times in the word the jaws crack on each other, or more exactly: the first syllable attempts to seize the nut, it doesn't work, then the second syllable opens the mouth widely, wide enough for the nut, and the third syllable cracks it; can you hear the teeth?

Since the middle of the nineteenth century, the locally spoken German language in Prague had become a stagnating idiom that had no inner connection with the German spoken elsewhere. "One restricted oneself defensively to pure grammar, the sentences became stone, the verbal treasure got poor. Franz Kafka wrote this pure, hard, almost abstract language in which there were few words for color and warmth," writes Paul Demetz. Johannes Urzidil who spoke at Kafka's funeral (and who calls Prague "the lost beloved"), in his book *Da geht Kafka* (There Goes Kafka) analyzes the phenomenon of the poets in Prague who wrote in German:

We German poets wrote in the language in which we lived and which we spoke all day long. That went for Karl Egon Ebert, Rainer Maria Rilke, Egon Erwin Kisch. Between written poetry and spoken idiom there was no abyss . . . The complete coincidence of the daily language with the language of poetry is probably the strongest secret of form and effect of the Prague writers, especially of Kafka. Whoever heard him speak, now hears him down to the subtlest nuance in each of his lines. That is the secret of an inner identity that we *Prager* guarded as long as possible and which now disappears with the last ones of us.

The writers in Prague, Germans or Jews, who wrote in German, felt as though they were "sitting on a thin glacier with its rims slowly thawing." In Vienna and Berlin it was often said that "the best German" was written and spoken in Prague. Living in a linguistic ghetto, the German writers in Prague set their standards by the finest examples —Goethe, Moerike, and Adalbert Stifter who dedicated his beautiful *Witiko* over a hundred years ago "to the old, venerable city of Prague in faithful love." Few writers in Austria or Germany approach the sublime beauty of the language written by Rilke or Werfel or Kafka. Demetz writes that Rilke, "blessed and damned with a poor, grammatically precise but lifeless language in an isolated society, was intoxicated by Liliencron's poems."

There existed a local German dialect in Prague, called "Prager Deutsch" or "Böhmakeln," but it was used only by Czechs trying to speak German, or by comics imitating such people. They would use the double negation of the Czech language ("I don't have no money") and transitive words ("I bathed myself"), and it was also characterized by the Czechs' inability to correctly pronounce the umlauts *ö* and *ü*. It was popular in suburban comedy theaters and variety shows in Vienna and Germany making fun of Czech servants and tailors. The German-speaking people in Prague would never use it, not even as a joke; it just wasn't funny there. On the contrary, among German "society" in Prague it was extremely gauche to use such *Tschechismen*. The Prague Germans liked to be recognized by their rather hard accentuation, very different from the "softly" speaking Viennese and the "martial" dialect of the Berliners.

The Czechs in Prague had their linguistic problems, too. In 1874, Jan Neruda wrote, "In school, the boys from the countryside looked down upon us boys from Prague and laughed." In 1883, Jan Herben, a friend of Masaryk, wrote that the Czechs in Prague were proud of their German fellow citizens who spoke such good German "though the Czechs themselves spoke the most miserable [*nejmizernější*] Czech." Urzidil points out that

. . . almost all educated Czechs knew more about third-rate French writers than about their next-street neighbors, whose names might be Rilke, Kafka, Werfel or Brod . . . Somehow one could understand the Czechs' lack of interest because they were still drunk with, and perhaps awed by, their sudden national sovereignty. How could they know that the name of a German-Jewish writer would once be insolubly associated with the name of their charismatic capital, Prague? How were they to divine that once people everywhere would subconsciously associate "Kafka" with "Prague," that this historical city of European eminence would mean to many people so much because it happened to be the hometown of Kafka?

"Everything in Prague excites the fantasy but reason doesn't come off second-best; it must be wonderful to be born in this city, with its mysteries and miracles," wrote Friedrich Hebbel, the German poet, in his diary in 1854. It reads like an early answer to the question, often asked since—how was it possible that Prague produced so many great poets and writers in one generation, and became the center of German literature in Europe during the first quarter of our century? Certainly Prague's "mysteries and miracles" partly accounted for it; but there was another, negative reason. Oskar

Wiener, the friend of Liliencron and a member of the older group of Prague's German poets, wrote, "The German writers of Prague remained martyrs of being at home there. They remained sons of an isolated society surrounded by their Slav fellow citizens."

Kafka, Werfel, Rilke and others created in Prague in an atmosphere which Willy Haas called *"vis-à-vis de rien* . . . Around 1910 we read Kierkegaard and Pascal's 'Pensées.' They corresponded exactly to our vague existence that, seen from everywhere, seemed to be hanging in midair." The German and Jewish writers of Prague were "on a historical tilt," says Haas. "They strongly felt their sense of loneliness and isolation, of having no ground under their feet, as one feels in Kafka's despair, in Werfel's ecstasy." Many escaped out of the narrow ghetto of Prague—but they never forgot it. Long after Werfel had left Prague, he wrote about "the old Czech women"—the nursemaid Barbara, and Teta Linek, the cook, and many others:

> Ah, those old women
> always carry on their old hands
> The earthless, weeping
> dream light of the early day.

Heretics and Saints

PRAGUE REMAINS a mystical city although the present Communist regime tries hard to demystify it. "Social realism" does not recognize supernaturalism as a latent, powerful force; what cannot be rationally explained, simply doesn't exist. Mysticism, never mentioned in the works of Marx, Engels and Lenin, is "a decadent relic of the bourgeois past," hovering about dim churches, the statues of St. John Nepomuk, and above the gravestone of Jehuda Liva ben Bezalel, the "High Rabbi" Loew, who died in 1609 and is buried in the Old Jewish Cemetery. According to the old Prague legend, Rabbi Loew, a student of the Cabala, created the Golem, the clay robot which did all hard work, split wood, carried water and cleaned the streets. "Such self-built domestic servants are valuable," it says in the *Gallery of the Sipurim*, a collection of Jewish sagas and legends, published in Prague in 1847. "They need neither food nor drink, work all the time, and you can scold them without fearing that they will talk back at you." They won't quit either.

But mysticism was in the hearts of the Czech people long before the Golem. In 1100, Cosmas of Prague, the first Czech chronicler (whose *Book About Bohemia* begins: "According to the geometric division of the earth's surface, Asia covers one half, Europe and Africa the other half . . .") wrote down the oldest Czech legend of Libuše who had the gift of prophecy, and in the presence of her husband, Přemysl, declared that she had seen

> the town, whose glory reaches the stars, thirty miles from here, in a forest, washed by the waves of the Moldau . . . When you get there, you will meet deep in the forest a man who makes the threshold—*Prah*—for a house. And because even great rulers bow to the low threshold, you will call the town that you will build there Praha . . . All tribes of Bohemia and the rest of the world will honor Praha with their offerings.

Libuše also prophesied the arrival of the Jews in Prague. She told her son, Nezamyšl, that she had seen the Jews in her dream. One of Nezamyšl's descendants, Prince Hostivit, had an apparition of Libuše who told him "to summon the Jews that were expelled from Moscovia by the Wends."

In Prague, legend is built upon legend. In 929, the leaders of the Jewish Community decided to build a synagogue. As the workers excavated the ground, they found the remains of a wall, made of white, square stones, and a Holy Bible, written on parchment. Two wise men from Jerusalem who then happened to be in Prague said, "There must have been some Jews here at the time of the Second Temple who built a synagogue . . . We advise you to build your synagogue after the picture of the Holy Temple in Jerusalem. The Almighty will protect your house of worship against fire and water." Another legend claims that the Old-New Synagogue, now the oldest in Europe (it was called "Old-New" in the seventeenth century when the "New" Synagogue was built in the Jewish quarter), survived all conflagrations in the ghetto because two mysterious white doves would sit down on its roof whenever fire broke out in the neighborhood, to warn the people. (The mysterious white dove also appears in Wagner's *Lohengrin*, not exactly a Jewish legend.)

Another myth which I heard mentioned in Prague in the 1930s concerns a subterranean corridor "leading straight from the Old Jewish Town in Prague to Jerusalem." Such wishful dreams made life perhaps more tolerable in the crowded medieval ghetto. But no dove appeared on the roof of the Old-New Synagogue when the Nazis marched into Prague on March 15, 1938. And people who tried to run away didn't find a secret corridor (though some of them saved their lives by entering the subterranean corridor of a coal mine along the Czechoslovak-Polish border and getting out on the Polish side). In 1938, many people felt that the saga of the Old Jewish Town had come to its end.

And in 929, while the ground was broken for the Old-New Synagogue (other sources claim it was built as late as 1270), Prince Wenceslas was murdered by his brother, Boleslav I. (Wenceslas' grandmother was said to have been murdered by one of her daughters. Murder must have been the Přemyslid family syndrome.) "Good King Wenceslas" became a legend abroad, and a mystic cult at home. According to an essay, *The Prague Castle*, an official (1965) government publication,

the pious ideologists of the new [Přemyslid] state managed to turn this ruthless struggle for power to surprisingly good account: already in the second half of the tenth century a complete legend of martyrdom arose which explained the death of Wenceslas ... as a sacrifice in the interest of the Christian faith.

The tomb of Wenceslas in the south apse of the rotunda (today in St. Vitus Cathedral) became the focal point of the St. Wenceslas cult, "the most important Czech state cult of medieval times."

For pious-minded people the Castle of Prague was from that time much more than a fortified place and the seat of the reigning dynasty. It became for them above all the mystic shrine of St. Wenceslas, the protector of their country and of its feudal order. After all, the Castle is more effectively protected by the supernatural power of the saint than by the strongest ramparts ... The St. Wenceslas cult continued to influence the building development of Hradčany for centuries. Were we not to realize the strength and intensity of its operation, many things at the Prague Castle would be incomprehensible for us.

The St. Wenceslas cult has remained very much alive in Bohemia, notwithstanding the ironical or exasperated comments of present-day political historians. Even non-religious Czechs feel strongly about St. Wenceslas. In 1929, during

The Mystical City

the thousand-year celebrations in honor of the country's patron saint, Arne Novák wrote in *Lidové Noviny*, then the leading Czech newspaper, close to President Masaryk:

> Smetana, our national composer, wished that his opera, "Libuše," should be performed only "in great national moments." In such moments we should always make a pilgrimage to St. Wenceslas. Even the non-religious will realize that in the great St. Vitus Cathedral there began Gothic Christianity; and there the boastful Catholic Baroque filled the altars with its magnificence; and finally, spiritual romanticism brought there the neo-Gothic style. In all these spiritual manifestations our nation finds its mother tongue.

Lately, so many people have come to pray or place flowers at the foot of the statue of the Bohemian patron saint, on top of Wenceslas Square, that the authorities last year surrounded it with a scaffold, "to carry out some repairs," and later laid out a small lawn around it. People were not permitted to step on the grass. But the lawn couldn't keep the "St. Wenceslas cult" out of the heart of the people; it belongs to the multi-faceted mysticism of Prague that survived all regimes and all ideologies in the past thousand years.

It was at the statue of St. Wenceslas that the resistance of the Czechoslovak people was focused during the glorious week of August 21, 1968, when the whole nation, united as never before, rose morally and spiritually against the invading forces of the "fraternal" Warsaw Pact troops. Soon the statue was covered with don't-give-up posters. Every night the Soviets tore off the banners and slogans. Every morning young patriots put up new ones again. On the first day of the invasion, a fourteen-year-old boy was killed by the Soviet soldiers in front of the monument. Later, a seventeen-year-old girl was wounded there. Soon the space around the monument was covered with fresh flowers. "I saw a boy killed there who had carried our flag," a Czech recalls. "The Soviets pierced him with their bayonets."

All week long the marble socle accurately reflected the people's feelings. During the first days, there were fighting slogans saying that the word was stronger than the gun. A red-white-blue flag was put into the hands of the saint. Later, during the Moscow negotiations, the slogans were replaced with pictures of President Svoboda and Alexander Dubček, and with banners exhorting the leaders to remain firm. And after the delegation had returned from Moscow to Prague and the whole, terrible truth became known, the pictures disappeared, and then there was the black flag of mourning in the hands of St. Wenceslas. But underneath, it said, "We don't give up."

And in front of St. Wenceslas, on the morning of January 16, 1969, Jan Palach, a young philosophy student at Charles University, doused his clothes with gasoline and set fire to himself, as a protest against the occupation. It was perhaps the last gasp of the nation's spiritual solidarity and created an immense impact on the people. Historically, the death of Jan Palach, who is already one of his nation's martyrs, will continue to have a permanent meaning: life is not the most important human value.

In time of a national crisis the people of Prague instinctively turn for help to St. Wenceslas. If they have private worries, they are likely to go to Charles Bridge and light a candle at the statue of St. John Nepomuk. According to a Prague legend, Johannes de Pomuk (as he was then called), the general vicar of the Prague Archbishop, was tortured on March 20, 1393, by King Wenceslas IV "who burned him with a torch and ordered the dying man tied by his arms and legs." He had him dragged through the streets of Prague. At midnight Johannes was thrown from the stone bridge

The Mystical City

into the Moldau. The King, in a drunk, brutal mood, was furious because Johannes, the confessor of the Queen, "wouldn't reveal the confessional secrets." Ever since, John Nepomuk, as he was later called, remains the martyr of silence and of all who suffer in silence. The historical truth is different from the legend. The general vicar represented his Archbishop in a dispute with the King, who ended the dispute by having Nepomuk thrown into the river.

The canonization of Nepomuk, in 1729, created a furor that still hasn't quite died down. The Czech foes of the Jesuits have never retracted their accusation that the Church had to create a Czech saint in order to neutralize the memory of the "heretic" Jan Hus among the people of Bohemia. Everybody agrees that they succeeded. In 1800, Arthur Schopenhauer, then a boy of thirteen, wrote in a letter: "The *bygotted* [bigoted] inhabitants of Prague would consider it the worst sin to cross the bridge without doffing their hats." There are now more statues of St. John Nepomuk in Prague, and in Bohemia, than of any other saint; every little village has at least one. The last strophe of Rilke's poem "Heilige" (Saints) is dedicated to the many Nepomuks,

> Aber diese Nepomuken!
> Von des Torgangs Lucken gucken
> und auf allen Brucken spucken
> lauter, lauter Nepomucken!

and is an amusing assonance on the abundance of Nepomuks—nothing but Nepomuks everywhere. And the chronicler Johann Basilius Küchelbecker writes in 1730:

The inhabitants of this country . . . are very *superstitieux* and great connoisseurs of religious fables and tales. They revere their new saint, Johanne von Nepomuk, with countless masses and build for his glory the most beautiful altars, statues and monuments. You see his picture on all highways and it wouldn't be easy to find someone who doesn't wear a small Nepomuk, framed in glass, or made of metal, on his chest ... they think he will protect them against shame.

When Charles Patin, the noted French physician, was in Prague in 1695, he was told that Prague consisted of seven different towns and was "as wide as London was long ... The 1300 apothecaries of London proved the wealth of London, and the 2000 Jesuits did the same in Prague." Patin noted that the people were very religious and soon learned about "zeal":

I wouldn't believe anything that their zeal made them say. In a church they showed me three stones and a broken column that "the devil brought from Rome to deceive the priests." Then St. Petrus was said to have thrown the devil and his column three times into the sea. Thereupon they said, the devil became furious and broke the column. I remained silent which didn't please them at all. Then I said, I'd never heard such a thing though I considered myself well informed about the miracles of St. Peter. When did all this happen? "Many thousands of years ago," they said. "But," I said, "the Church exists only sixteen hundred years since Christ." "Yes," they said, "but the miracle is much older." I became so confused that I almost believed the Catholic Church to be much older. ...

Today many people in Prague take their worries and wishes to St. Thaddeus, whose face, exultant with pain and suffering, looks down on them in the small front-court of a church in Náměstí Republiky (Republic Square). People used to bring with them small, framed cardboard pieces on which they wrote their requests; there were so many of them that the saint was surrounded by a small picture gallery of secret wishes. Others prefer to light a candle which they place under a metal dome so that wind and rain won't blow it out. Or they go to pray before the Jezulátko, the small Jesus Child at the St. Savior's Church in Karmelitská Street in Malá Strana, which was brought there in 1628 from Spain. The Carmelites spoke of the miracles done by Jezulátko that "saved Prague from the pestilence and the Seven Years' War," and Jezulátko became the subject of books published in Würzburg, New York, Madrid and Genoa. Paul Claudel, who lived in Prague as a French diplomat, wrote a beautiful poem about "the Jesus Child watching until dawn over the small brothers." The small statue wears a different dress every day of the year. Jezulátko's dresses were donated by noble, pious ladies who had them made from their former wedding dresses, many of them decorated with precious stones and gold embroidery. Every morning a priest dresses the Jesus Child and puts the previous day's dress back into a vault. Unfortunately some people became more interested in the dresses than in Jezulátko. Thieves tried to steal a dress, and forty years ago a sacristan was murdered by a burglar. The mystical city was always a violent city.

The Golem

THE GOLEM is the most famous of Prague's mystical legends. *Golem*, a Hebrew word, means "germ," and also "formless," "mindless." The creator of the Golem was allegedly the High Rabbi Loew who lived in sixteenth-century Prague during the reign of Rudolph II of Habsburg, the mystic-minded, eccentric Emperor who became fascinated by the mysterious, occult atmosphere of Prague and moved his residence there from Vienna. (When Grillparzer planned a play about the strangest Habsburg of all, he wrote in his notebook, "The tragic idea would be that he senses the advent of a new era . . . and that whatever he does only serves to accelerate its advent."

The Golem is part of Prague's occult mood—a man-like figure of clay that was said to have become alive when the High Rabbi put the *shem*, a capsule containing the magic formula, into the Golem's mouth. At the beginning of the Sabbath, the High Rabbi would always take the *shem* out of the Golem's mouth, for the Golem must not remain alive during the Sabbath. One Friday evening (so the legend goes) the High Rabbi forgot to remove the *shem*. The Golem went beserk, "uprooting trees and creating terrible damage in the streets of the ghetto." The High Rabbi, summoned by the terrified inhabitants, found himself in the predicament of Goethe's *Zauberlehrling* (The Sorcerer's Apprentice). Fortunately, the Sabbath had not yet been consecrated at the Old-New Synagogue. There was still time! Rabbi Loew ran after the Golem and pulled the *shem* out of the robot's mouth. The clay figure fell to the ground and broke into many pieces. "Even today some pieces of the Golem are said to be kept in the attic of the Old-New Synagogue," we read in the *Gallery of the Sipurim*.

The Golem legend has fascinated mystagogues, cabalistic scholars, poets and historians ever since. As in the case of all legends in Prague, historical facts are blended with myths until truth and fiction can no longer be discerned. The destruction of the Golem is said to have happened after a midnight audience which Emperor Rudolph II granted to Rabbi

Loew, "on the 10th of Adar, 5352, after the Creation of the world." This audience actually took place on February 23, 1592. Isak Kohen, son-in-law of Rabbi Loew, notes in a manuscript that Rabbi Loew was taken one night to the Castle by Prince Bertier, where the two men talked for a while in a dim room. "Suddenly a curtain was pushed aside and the Emperor came in, asked my father-in-law several questions, and then retired again behind the curtain." In best *discrétion oblige* manner Kohen concludes, "The subject of the conversation must be kept secret as is the custom in Imperial matters." David Gans (1541–1613), the Renaissance astronomer and historian (his grave is in the Old Jewish Cemetery) who was Tycho de Brahe's friend, also reports about the audience with the Emperor.

Rabbi Loew kept the secret; mystics don't talk. But the meeting of the occult-minded Emperor with the cabalistic scholar must have created enormous excitement in the dark, crowded streets of the ghetto. Later sources claim that the "midnight audience" took place earlier. The Emperor, who was concerned about the Golem, is said to have made a deal with the High Rabbi: the Golem would have to disappear, and in return the Emperor would permit no more persecutions of the Jews, no accusations of "ritual murder."

Clemens Brentano, the Catholic romantic poet, wrote in 1814 in Vienna's *Dramaturgischer Beobachter:* "The Master who created the figure must extinguish from the word '*anmauth*' [truth], that he'd written on the Golem's forehead, the syllable '*an*,' leaving the word '*mauth*' [death], whereupon the Golem becomes a lifeless figure of clay." According to the Jewish legend, the matter was more complicated. After his return from the Castle, Rabbi Loew is said to have told "Joseph Golem" (the Golem had a first name!) that Joseph would no longer sleep in the courtroom but henceforth in the attic of the Old-New Synagogue. On Lag Be-omer, "the thirty-third day after Pessach" (Passover), High Rabbi Loew and two other men walked up to the attic, where the Golem had also been created.

"They were standing at the head of the sleeping Golem, their faces turned toward the Golem's feet . . . Then they walked seven times around the figure, speaking magic formulas. In one corner Abraham Chajim, the old temple servant, stood holding two burning candles. After the seventh rotation, all life had gone out of the Golem." Then the clay figure was clad in two *talesim* (prayer shawls) and concealed under a heap of books and parchments. The following day, the story was circulated in the ghetto that the Golem had escaped. No one was permitted to go up to the attic of the Old-New Synagogue. "But smart people knew that the lifeless figure of Joseph Golem was lying there."

Numerous books and publications about the Golem have since claimed that the clay figure remained concealed in the attic of the Old-New Synagogue—which must have been a paradise for cabalists, mystics and believers of the transcendental, especially at midnight, with the pale light of the moon falling in. Victor Hugo transferred the Golem saga from the early-Gothic attic of Prague's oldest synagogue to the French-Gothic towers of *Notre Dame de Paris*, where King Louis XI meets the great magician, Claude Frollo, who creates the frightening Quasimodo. The automaton falls in love with Esmeralda. (In some Prague legends, Joseph Golem became infatuated with Rabbi Loew's lovely daughter.) The death of Rabbi Loew is also surrounded by legends. He was so wise and learned that death was afraid to touch him. But one day the old Rabbi met a pretty young girl who offered him her rose and asked him to try its scent. The High Rabbi took the rose. Death, hidden in the flower,

The Mystical City

jumped out, and took Rabbi Loew away; a not-so-subtle reminder that even the wisest old men sometimes behave like fools when they meet pretty young girls.

In 1910, the celebrated Prague reporter Egon Erwin Kisch obtained permission to go up to the attic of the Old-New Synagogue, which wasn't easy. He had to climb up the iron clamps that had been fixed to the outside wall after 1883, by order of the Prague fire police, after the terrible fire of Vienna's Ringtheater that killed hundreds of people. It was an arduous journey. ("A tiler named Vondřejc had earlier fallen off the steep roof and was instantly killed.") Kisch was deeply impressed by the mystical atmosphere in the dim attic; what had begun as a journalistic stunt became a memorable experience.

"This is truly a place to create and bury the Golem, at moonlight," he wrote. Through the garret window he could see the Hebrew clock on the wall of the Jewish Town Hall. He noticed that the stones of the vault were "gray, geometric, regularly arranged in wave-like patterns, jagged and rough . . . If the clay figure is buried there, it will remain here until Doomsday. If one tried to exhume it, the synagogue might collapse." Kisch, a true child of Prague (he was born in a mystical house, "in an atmosphere of chiaroscuro," in nearby Leather Street), knew better than to destroy a cherished local legend.

That might be the end of the saga, except that yet another legend claims the Golem was taken from the attic a few nights after Rabbi Loew put it there, by one Abraham Secharja, servant at the nearby Pinkas Synagogue. (On Secharja's gravestone in the Old Jewish Cemetery it says that he died in 1602, "after thirty years in office"; again, there is some fact blended into the legend.) The clay figure was taken to a place fittingly called "Gallow Hill," in the suburb of Žižkov. (The spot is marked, with wheel and gallow, on a map of "Prage Bohemica, Metropolis Accuratissime Expressa 1562," that is kept at the Municipal Museum.) All public executions took place on Gallow Hill, the last in 1866, when Wenzel Fiala, a waiter, was guillotined for murdering his pregnant mistress, while a crowd looked on happily, and peddlers of *párky* (hot dogs) and "Turkish honey" did a land-office business. Later Gallow Hill became a disreputable place where couples sought brief solitude between ash cans and garbage dumps. If the Golem is buried *any*where, it might well be on Gallow Hill.

The most famous literary version of the old Jewish legend was written by Gustav Meyrink whose novel, *Der Golem*, published in 1915, made him world-famous. In Prague he was admired as the high priest of the town's literary mysticists. Meyrink was not from Prague, and he was not Jewish. (He actively promoted rumors that he was the illegitimate son of an illustrious member of the Wittelsbach dynasty in Bavaria.) Actually he was born, on January 19, 1868, in Vienna, in the "Blauer Bock" (Blue Buck) Hotel, as the illegitimate son of a Viennese actress, Maria Meyer. His father was Karl Freiherr von Varnbühler, an aristocrat from Wuerttemberg. Gustav Meyer grew up in Vienna, Hamburg and mostly in Prague. He became a private banker—a profession that may have a certain *mystique* and a great many mysteries but hardly any mysticism. That the *Herr Banquier* Meyer turned into the great expressionist of mysticism could happen only in Prague. Max Brod reports in his autobiography that Meyer was anonymously denounced to the authorities for doubtful business transactions and was arrested. His innocence was later established; a woman and a jealous man were involved; but though Banker Meyer was officially rehabilitated, he had lost the confidence of his clients and was ruined. He became a misanthropic, disillusioned man and began to write. (His bitterly sarcastic essay, *Prr-aha*, begins: "Rarely do the English or French know where Prague is located for they have chosen the better part, as the Bible says . . . The Moldau may appear to the innocent from abroad like the mighty Mississippi, but it is only four millimeters deep, filled with leeches.")

Nothing is known about the ability of Meyer, the banker, but he certainly emerged as a writer of considerable talent when he took on the name of Meyrink. The noted German magazine *Simplicissimus* began to print his bizarre stories. Around 1910, Gustav Meyrink was one of the most famous writers in Prague. It was then that he began to "discover" the esoteric sciences. He told his admiring friends that he was suffering from a "mysterious" disease. He had consulted the most famous doctors on earth, who couldn't help him. At last he was healed by a recipe which he'd discovered "in one of the old philosophical tracts of Paracelsus." Max Brod, a young admiring friend, described Meyrink as a slim and elegant-looking man, "like a retired army officer, with an arrogant face, and big, blue eyes filled with scorn." Meyrink called himself "a student of the secret sciences, theosophy, spiritism, and the phenomena of para-psychology, an expert of the exotic and the bizarre."

Meyrink's headquarters was a table in a corner of the chess room of the Café Continental, a coffeehouse in Graben (Příkopy) popular with Prague's German society. There the Master held court, surrounded by his novices, talking in a soft voice about the latest scandal in local society—Meyrink never forgave them for making him an "outcast," though he enjoyed playing the part—or discussing strange chemical formulas and mystical terminology. The novices were convinced that the Master was "haunted." Prague does that to people. Young Brod, who occasionally joined them, reports:

Among Meyrink's friends was a man who collected thousands of dead flies, and a second-hand bookstore dealer specializing in mysterious and incredibly rare books. A black raven with clipped wings was patrolling the pavement in front of the bookstore, and from the raven's behavior the dealer knew whether a customer entering the store was "an enlightened one." Everything connected with Meyrink seemed magically transformed: even the glass of water which the waiter brought, the coffee spoon, the small bowl with three lumps of sugar. The chess room had leather tapestries with red-and-gold lines on black ground: I thought of them as Turkish and Arabic designs. Late at night, when the coffeehouse was almost empty, filled with stale smoke and dust, we feared that a ghost would grasp the legs of the table and strangle our throats . . .

Meyrink lived in a deserted factory building near the gas works, and the novices were terrified at the thought that the Master's "divine spark" might set fire to the giant gas container. He received his friends in a dark library, talking vaguely about "manifestations of spiritistic powers," or showing them two intact, wooden, unbroken rings that "had been joined by the fourth dimension," which he'd received from the astro-physician Zoellner in Leipzig. Among Meyrink's prized possessions was a porcelain clock. The dial was set in a drum, which a devil kept between his knees while holding a hammer in his hand that seemed about to fall down any moment on the porcelain drum. Next to it was the painting of a pale man with a phosphorous-covered face surrounded by snakes. Meyrink called the figure "the guardian of the threshold."

After the success of *The Golem*, Meyrink moved from

The Mystical City

Prague to a pleasant villa on the shore of Starnberger Lake in Bavaria, where he lived happily with a wife and children. Young Brod visited him there and found him "healthy and sun-burned, much younger than in Prague where people always made life for one another more difficult." Yet years later Meyrink wrote, "There is no other city on earth which one likes to leave as happily when one lives there and none for which one is as homesick as soon as one has left it."

Among Meyrink's novices was Paul Leppin, the now forgotten poet of Prague's mystic Bohemia. Brod calls him "the true and chosen singer of dying Old Prague—of sinister streets, drunken nights, of tramps and empty faith in front of luxuriously Baroque statues of staints." His roots lay somewhere among Heine, Verlaine and young Rilke, and his verse had a rhythm of its own. A tall, thin man with a dead-white face and a big mouth, Leppin liked to demonstrate his permanent disgust of life. He was fascinatingly ugly, had to submit periodically "to the terrible malaria cure," spent his nights in small cafés, played the lute like the German poet Fritz Wedekind whom Leppin admired, and sang his own, mostly unprintable verse. Occasionally he led a strange procession of his friends on Sunday noon across Graben, the German *corso*. They wore dark suits, cut in Biedermeier style, very narrow around the waist, large black hats and each had a dark red rose in his hand.

The critics called Leppin the poet of sadness and sin, of wild protest and bizarre exultation. Leppin writes about "the old, decrepit house of my parents where I spent my childhood. Wooden stairs creaked on dark landings, *Pawlatschen* [backyard balconies] with shaky iron banisters ran along the rear, opening up into the courtyard where cats and barefoot children were playing . . . a milieu of sorry hardship and petit-bourgeois wilderness." He called his main work, *Severin's Walk into Darkness, ein Prager Gespensterroman* (a Prague ghost novel). Sample:

The twilight was getting dimmer as Severin turned through the tower entrance of Kleinseite toward the monument of Radetzky. Severin climbed up through Spornergasse to the Hradshin. The city he knew was different. Its streets led into nowhere. Evil was everywhere. Its heart beat between damp, treacherous walls. Night crept past blind windows and strangled the soul in its sleep. Everywhere the devil had set traps—in the churches and in the houses of the courtesans . . .

Leppin was the great "decadent neo-romantic." One of his early books was called *Glocken, die im Dunkeln rufen* (Bells That Call in the Darkness). He loved the churches of Prague and often praised them in his poems,

Nun bin ich verdorrt und von Sünde umstellt,
Aber die Kirchen von Prag sind die schönsten der Welt,

(Now I'm dried up and ensnared in sin
But the churches of Prague are the most beautiful in the world.)

Yet the poet who was "fascinating through his contradiction" (as he was described by Brod) also wrote frankly spiritistic prose. In his novel *Severin's Walk into Darkness* (Leppin, as so many writers in Prague, was obsessed by night, moonlight, darkness) he describes the home of one Herr Nikolaus, who is obviously modeled after Meyrink: "In his elegantly furnished apartment there were many strange, unusual things, bronze Buddhas with crossed legs, mediumistic drawings in metal frames, scarabs and magic mirrors, a portrait of Blavatsky, and a genuine confessional. It was rumored that in his room a man had died once under mysterious circumstances . . ."

The Mystical City

Leppin had great influence on the young Rilke and the neo-romantics. The younger generation (Kafka, Werfel, Urzidil, Brod) loved his poetic language but not his mystical prose. "The historical inheritance that Prague left to her poets was mystic ecstasy," writes Paul Demetz, Rilke's biographer. "In the shadow of the hundred towers emotions often came dangerously close to religious ecstasy." But Demetz correctly distinguishes between "the true mysticism of Franz Kafka or the magnificent poetry of Werfel," on the one hand, and the merely occult terror of Meyrink or the spiritualistic novels of Leppin and Otto Perutz, on the other hand.

In his novel *Nachts unter der steinernen Brücke* (At Night Below the Stone Bridge), which Perutz calls "a novel from the Old Prague," Perutz exhumes another old legend from Prague, about the sinful love between Emperor Rudolph II and Esther, the beautiful wife of Mordechai Maisel, the rich mayor of the Old Jewish Town. The Maisels had no children. Mordechai was a philanthropist, built two synagogues, a bathhouse and a hospital. He was also His Majesty's banker, often lending money to Rudolph. ("He knew the arrow that pierces even iron doors . . . the arrow was made of gold.") The High Rabbi Loew knew about the love affair between the Emperor and Esther, and was perturbed by it. Could it be that Esther, not the Golem, was the subject of his midnight audience with the Emperor? At night, the High Rabbi went down below the stone bridge (Charles Bridge) where earlier he'd planted roses and rosemary.

Black clouds raced across the sky, and the pale light of the moon shone on the pillars and arches of the stone bridge. The Great Rabbi stepped to the bank of the river and threw the rosemary into the water. It was carried away by the waves and disappeared. That night the epidemics of pestilence came to an end in the Jewish town. That night Esther, the wife of the Jew Maisel, died in her house in Three-Wells Square. That night, up in the Castle of Prague, Rudolf II, ruler of the Holy Roman Empire, roused out of his dream, cried out.

Perutz is better in his descriptive passages of Old Prague. "There was much to see in the Old Town of Prague . . . In Týn Church a colored baby was baptized, the child of a servant of Count Kinský, and many nobles attended the ceremony." (Next to Palais Kinský, Kafka's father later had his haberdashery warehouse.) In his epilogue, Perutz describes the Old Jewish Town of Prague around the turn of the century, when he was fifteen, a student at the Gymnasium:

. . . old, decrepit houses, about to fall down, with built-out fronts and small wings that blocked the narrow streets. Crooked streets where I could get lost when I wasn't careful. Dark entrances, dim courtyards. Broken walls and cavernous rooms, where pawnbrokers offered their wares. Cisterns and wells whose water was contaminated with the disease of Prague, and on each corner a dive [*Spelunke*] where Prague's underworld met.

Perutz remembers that once he went to see his tutor, Jacob Maisel, a student of medicine and member of the famous Maisel dynasty (there again is the fine thread between legend and fact). Maisel talked about the old houses that were systematically torn down to make room for modern buildings, among them the house of the High Rabbi Loew, which had lately served as storeroom of a manufacturer of boxes. Perutz and his tutor went there and found large holes in all the walls. "They didn't serve any mystical purpose," writes Perutz. "Rabbi Loew kept his cabalistic books there."

An earlier-generation mystic was Alfred Meissner, a liberal German writer and a close friend of Heinrich Heine in Paris. Meissner wrote a fine book about the great Jewish-

The Mystical City

German (or German-Jewish) poet in 1856. ("I loved Heine, the poet and the man; the kindness of his heart, so often questioned by everybody, was certain to me.") Meissner came from the Sudeten-German town of Teplitz, and studied at the Old Town Gymnasium, which was also Kafka's school. He later had great influence on Kafka; Brod calls him "the Old Master of Prague's literature." Yet the healthy German immigrant from Teplitz was completely bewitched by Prague's mystical magic:

Prague is really a chronicle in stone with beautiful illustrations and fantastic ornaments. The memory of Libuše in lonely Vyšehrad, the little chapel where Hus preached, the majestic Týn Church with Brahe's motto "Better to be than to seem to be," the Jewish cemetery sown with tombstones, and beyond the bridge the palace of the Friedländer (Wallenstein), the Alchemists' Street . . . the Wladislav tract of Hradčany with the large window through which two royal governors and their secretary were thrown out into the moat . . . all this and a hundred other memorable ruins, graves, houses, palaces I saw again and again, until the past became alive in my mind . . .

In Rilke's *Larenopfer*, his early poems about Prague, "the past became alive," as Meissner had said two generations earlier. Rilke became fascinated by Rudolph II, Jan Hus, Rabbi Loew. The eternal motif of death and All Saints' Day hovers about these poems. Even in his later years, when he left Prague, which had become too small for him, and lived in many places abroad, he always returned in his poetry to the cemeteries of Prague, the catacombs and convents. In his poem "Der Hradschin," he sings of the beauty of the Prague Castle, seen from Charles Bridge, which generations have associated with Prague (and which has sold more postcards from Prague than any other view):

> Und es grüssen selbst die eiligen
> Moldauwellen den Hradschin,
> von der Brücke sehn die Heiligen
> ernst auf ihn.

> (Even the Moldau's swiftly flowing waves
> salute the Hradschin,
> and from the bridge,
> the saints look gravely at the Castle.

Around the *fin de siècle*, the poets of Vienna, a scant two hundred miles away, sensed the imminent end of an era and the decadence behind the glitter. The writers of the "Young Vienna" School reacted with melancholy and symbolism (Hugo von Hofmannsthal), or with bittersweet irony (Arthur Schnitzler). But Prague with her black saints and black synagogues, her "deadly struggle with the angels," was light-years away from Vienna. There was no decadence in Prague (the exception of Paul Leppin confirms the rule), where life was mystical and polemical, but never charming and *gemütlich*. When Paul Leppin's and Liliencron's friend, the poet Oskar Wiener, who had just published a much admired ballade about the death dance of children in the Old Jewish Cemetery, was attacked during a public discussion for "the decadence of Young Prague," he shouted, "*Wir sind ja pumperl g'sund*" (Come, come, we're bursting with health), and everybody laughed.

Nowhere but in Prague would George Langer have been possible. He called himself Jiří (a Čzech name) Mordechai (a Jewish name) Langer (a German name); he was the younger brother of František Langer, the famous dramatist. Brod calls him "a bizarre personality, often provoking protest but also closer study among those who tried to look more deeply." Langer became disillusioned with the world around him, turned his back on Western-European culture and immersed himself in Eastern Galicia's Hasidism. He studied Hebrew and Aramaic, and became an authority on rabbinical and cabalistic literature. For years he lived among the Hasidim in Hungary and in the house of a "wonder rabbi" in Galicia. After his return to Prague, he wore—much to the dismay of his Czech-assimilated, bourgeois family— the long, black silk caftan and the broad felt hat of the Hasidim, looking not unlike one of the "Mastersingers" in the third act of Wagner's opera as they arrive on the festival meadow. No wonder. The Jews brought this hat from Nuremberg (which later became the city of Streicher's *Stürmer*) and other places in Southern Germany to Poland and kept it there, out of loyalty to "the old country."

Langer walked through Prague, a living rudiment of the Middle Ages. Like many mystics he was a somewhat paradoxical character. Brod writes that "Langer was less proud of his thorough knowledge of cabalistic science than of his mastery in ice skating, and often performed for my wife and me his beautiful figures in the Prague Ice Stadion." A genuine son of Prague, Langer wrote equally well in Czech, German and Hebrew. He wrote in German *Die Erotik der Kabala* (The Eros of the Cabala), and in Czech *Nine Gates, the Secret of the Hassidim*. The latter was later translated into German by Friedrich Thieberger, an excellent essayist who wrote a monograph on Rabbi Loew. Thieberger also happened to be the Hebrew teacher of Franz Kafka. Thieberger's sister, Gertrude, later became the wife of Johannes Urzidil. In 1969, Jaroslav Langer, a Czech writer whom Jiří Mordechai's brother František, the noted playwright, called his "adopted nephew," published in Vienna his essay *Franz Kafka's einziges erhaltenes Theaterstück*, (Franz Kafka's Only Preserved Play). Langer is trying to prove that

Ein Flug um die Lampe herum, of which no original manuscript exists, is an authentic work, and the only play, written by Franz Kafka. One character in the play is called Rabbi M., which may be a symbol for Jiří Mordechai Langer. Mystical Prague was, and still is, a small world. "If the play should have success," writes Heinz Politzer, Kafka's biographer and a friend of Max Brod, "it will be due to the name of Kafka whose bearer didn't write it. This contradiction and absurdity is the only trait that *Ein Flug um die Lampe herum* could have borrowed from Kafka."

In 1930, Langer published his journal *Imago*, a Freud-influenced, psychoanalytical investigation into Jewish phylacterics. Later he became a Hebrew teacher and taught Jewish religion in Czech schools. In 1939 he bought, for a small gold bar, passage on an illegal steamer to Palestine, where he soon died. One of his last Hebrew poems describes the death of Kafka, "the wedding of a pure soul with the infinite."

The strange atmosphere of what is now called Old Prague was perfect for the development of literary eccentrics, mostly in beer parlors and coffeehouses where they belonged, like the furniture and the mood. Werfel, Haas and Urzidil have written about Weissenstein Karl, a true bohemian and vagrant poet. Another local celebrity was Franta Sauer, whom Janouch describes as "half a former engine-fitter and half a former insurance agent, a Prague idler and practical joker with a serious note of social criticism." He was well-known in the lower-class taverns where he would help Jaroslav Hašek to peddle the cheap installments of the first edition of *The Good Soldier Švejk*.

At the turn of the twentieth century, the Jewish community in Prague was best known for its legends, sagas and

The Mystical City

monuments of the past. For almost six hundred years the Jews of Prague had been excluded from trade, the crafts and agriculture and restricted to live in the ghetto, whose entrances were closed on Friday night with heavy chains for twenty-four hours. The Jews had to make a precarious living as small artisans, money changers, hired laborers. During the Hussite era, the restrictions were briefly lifted, only to be re-introduced in 1434, after the end of the Hussite movement. Not till late in the eighteenth century did Emperor Joseph II, the Emancipator, give the Jews greater freedom.

But though most people in the ghetto were poor—wealth was concentrated in the hands of a few families, such as the Maisels—there was a lively spiritual, literary and artistic life. In 1512, the Gersonides, who had come from the Provence, set up in Prague the first Hebrew printing plant in Central Europe. The ghetto was a center of rabbinical thought; great scholars, such as David Oppenheim, poet, bibliophile and interpreter of the Cabala, had been Chief Rabbi in Prague; also great scholars were Ezekiel Landau, Solomon L. Rapoport, Marcus Hirsch and Nathan Ehrenfeld. Heinrich Brody published an anthology of Hebrew lyrical poems from the Spanish epoch. The ghetto had physically disappeared after the modern town-planning law of 1893, but the atmosphere of the Jewish Prague remained unique in Europe. The Jews of Prague took the legends and the memories for granted. Walking past the Jewish Town Hall in Maiselova, they hardly looked at the old clock with the Hebrew dial and the hands moving in an anti-clockwise direction which so fascinated Guillaume Apollinaire and other visitors in Prague. The scarlet flag with the embroidered Shield of David in the Old-New Synagogue was a museum piece for many local Jews who didn't know that it was a reminder of the courage of the Jews of Prague in the battle against the Swedes in 1632. One might go to the Old Jewish Cemetery in the company of visitors from abroad, but rarely alone.

On the whole, the Jews of Prague were economically secure after the beginning of this century. There were many doctors, lawyers, professors, bankers, merchants and industrialists among them who lived in large apartments or in beautiful villas far away from the dark houses of the former ghetto. Many were delighted with their official titles, "Imperial Councillor," or *Kommerzialrat*, "Commercial Councillor." They lived in a "liberal" atmosphere; many professors of the legal faculty of the German University were Jews. They were not very rich, as some Jewish families in Germany, but they lived well, and had time for their artistic or literary interests. Willy Haas remembers that his father "read Spinoza and Goethe, and owned precious first editions of Spinoza's work."

It was no accident that Jewish Prague became an early citadel of Zionism. "Prague was well-suited to revive the romantic longing for an individual past, for proud self-consciousness," Hans Tramer writes in *Prague—City of Three Peoples*. "In Prague, in the presence of the old palaces or the royal castles without a king, one could learn to appreciate the yearning and the dream of people for its mighty past and new future." There was not a large number of conversions to Christianity among the local Jews. In his autobiography, Brod describes how he and Kafka were slowly drawn from the German culture in Prague (which Kafka loved "in all sincerity and, so to speak, in innocence of heart") into the world of Jewish problems and eventually Jewish culture.

During the First World War, Prague which until then was considered a "provincial" city, compared to the Imperial capital of Vienna, suddenly emerged as the capital of German literature in Europe. Within a few years there appeared Meyrink's novels, Werfel's first volumes of poetry, Brod's *Tycho Brahe's Way to God*, the early books of Franz Kafka, Oskar Baum's *Die böse Unschuld* (Evil Innocence). Most among the German and Jewish creative artists were poets and writers; music remained the domain of the Czechs; and the only important Jewish painter was Eugen von Kahler, a fellow student of Paul Klee and Vassily Kandinsky at the Royal Academy of Munich. Kahler was also a gifted lyrical poet. Kandinsky calls him "the only Prague painter who could be counted among the representatives of a new trend in Prague painting. . . . The tender, dreamy, gay soul of Kahler that had something of a pure Hebraic resonance, an unquenchable mystic sadness, was repelled by one thing only—the ignoble . . . It seemed that a hidden aim had brought this soul along secret paths from Biblical times to our own . . ." Kahler died five days before the exhibition of the Blauer Reiter Group was opened in Thannhäuser's New Gallery in Munich, on December 18, 1911.

In 1890 Paul Cohen-Portheim, after a visit to Prague, wrote about "Hradčany with its legends, the house where Dr. Faust lives, the whole atmosphere of magic and mystic, of the supernatural and mysterious that is stronger here than in any other city . . ." Poets, artists and many sensitive people have always strongly felt "the magic and mystic" in Prague. The poets of Prague who wrote in German often revolted against the oppressive power of local mysticism. They felt isolated between the cemeteries and synagogues, the catacombs of Santa Maria della Victoria and the Alchemists' Street, the Faust House and the statues of ecstatic saints. Yet they always remained under the mystic spell of their native town. Rilke loved cemeteries; Werfel meditated in the

Stadtpark; Kafka walked through the quiet, narrow streets of Malá Strana and the Old Town. Hans Tramer calls their Prague "a strange kind of enclave. The character of the town, its culturally isolated existence, the inevitable contact with an intellectual elite that was nationally alien and spoke a different language, have all left their ineradicable and visible traces on the poetic works of many authors in Prague."

People in Prague have always loved poetry; they either read or wrote it. Two famous part-time poets were Friedrich Adler, a lawyer, who translated the beautiful poems of Jaroslav Vrchlický into German, and Hugo Salus, noted gynecologist, whose poem "Einfältiges Lied" was set to music in 1901 by Arnold Schönberg. Salus kept his collected poems on a shelf next to the white operating table in his doctor's office. Rilke professed his "enthusiastic" gratitude to the two poets who carried on a lifelong rivalry, and alternately read their poems at the "Concordia," a group of poets and artists that met regularly in the "German House," the meeting place of the older, liberal Germans and German-speaking Jews.

The family background of most of Prague's German-writing poets was similar. The fathers, or perhaps the grandfathers, had prospered in "the province," somewhere in Bohemia or Moravia, and had moved to the big city. Rilke's uncle was a court councillor; Werfel's father was a rich glove manufacturer; Brod's father was a high-ranking civil servant; Haas's father was a renowned lawyer; Kafka's father was a prosperous textile businessman. Their sons were solidly bourgeois, though many later revolted; but none wrote revolutionary poetry, as Bertolt Brecht did in Berlin. Vienna's neo-romanticism was closer to them than Berlin's naturalism.

"We were suspended in a vacuum—that was our curse and

also our blessing," remembers Willy Haas. "Everybody had to think for himself, to start at the very beginning, with the truth and the lie of our existence." Many became oppressed by the myths and legends, the dark symbols and invisible walls, and broke away. Rilke thought he would be happier abroad—but his memories always took him back to the mystical city. Kafka created his own world of reality-cum-metaphysics. And Werfel who went to Vienna, not so *gemütlich* after the First World War, found mysticism again in Lourdes and later in California, where he wrote *The Song of Bernadette* and remembered the lowly Czech servants of his Prague childhood.

The Czech Poets

IT WAS EASIER for the Czech poets in Prague. They too were caught in the web of the mystical and the supernatural but they could always find temporary escape in the healthy, tranquil countryside of Bohemia. The countryside was inhabited by sturdy Czech peasants who might have been the protagonists of Smetana's *The Bartered Bride*, with its songs and dances. They knew nothing about the Golem and Dr. Faust, though they too were not free from the mystic spell of St. Wenceslas, St. Nepomuk and all the other saints.

Julius Zeyer and Jakub Arbes were among the earlier Czech poets who heard the strange voices in the darkness around the palaces in Malá Strana and wrote about the old corners in forgotten cemeteries. Zeyer, in 1896, calls Prague "a big stone book, full of pathos and enigma . . . The chapel of St. Wenceslas at the Castle, Daliborka, Týn Church—they were not just buildings for me, but reached deep into the early conscience of my childhood . . ." Arbes was hypnotized by the painting of St. Xaverius in St. Nicholas Church in Malá Strana. F. X. Palko, the painter, had said shortly before his death that the picture showed "the secret of the redemption of millions of people." In *St. Xaverius*, Arbes writes, "The moment I looked at the painting I didn't see in the face of the dying man the fanaticism of a monk who renounces all earthly pleasures but the worst pain softened by the hope for redemption and strength of his faith . . ."

Later, Antonín Novotný, in *The Carmelites of Prague*, writes about the Convent of St. Joseph in Malá Strana where the Carmelites have been since 1655. Their first Abbess, Maria Elekta, was later sanctified after her grave was opened: and when they opened the grave, they were looking at a real miracle. The shroud in which Elekta had been buried was gone, but the body hadn't changed, lying before them as on the day of her death, though her eyes were darker . . .

Jan Neruda, the nineteenth-century creator of modern Czech prose, wrote about the mystic mood of Malá Strana where he'd been born and lived.

My dear, my golden Malá Strana, cradle of thoughts and dreams! The *Malostranák* [the citizen of Malá Strana] may be a little strange to you; he's certainly different in his thoughts and behavior. The secret life of the silent streets doesn't bother him, his walks always take him to some little corner, to the forgotten walls "At the Capuchins" where it is so quiet, or to the military cemetery . . .

The Mystical City

No one would believe how beautiful Prague is at night. People are asleep but the stones wake up, and the statues on Charles Bridge become alive . . . And the moon looks on until it is chased away by the jealous sun. The moon is getting around a good deal and sees a lot. And the moon told me that no city is as beautiful as Prague.

The Czech writers were fascinated by the "Faust House" in Charles Square, a beautiful sixteenth-century building where according to a later legend Dr. Faust lived. Again two facts are connected with the legend: in 1585, Edward Kelley, a former parish clerk from Lancaster, who came to Prague and became one of Rudolph II's most famous alchemists, bought the "Faust House" where Prince Wenceslas Opavský had already installed an alchemist's laboratory; and in 1770 one Ferdinand Antonín Mladota lived in the house "and carried on strange chemical experiments." Alois Jirásek, the author of *Old Czech Tales*, tells the story of Dr. Faust who "had lived in this house many, many years ago, read in conjuring books, called the devil and sold his soul . . . And in the end the devil took him along."

Alchemism created one of the ineradicable legends of mystical Prague—that Golden Lane, a miniature, fairy-tale street in Hradčany Castle, was the home of the local alchemists. Actually, many alchemists lived in Prague but not in Golden Lane (called "Goldsmiths' Street" until the end of the eighteenth century). After the great fire of 1541 that destroyed most of Malá Strana and the Castle, many poor people squatted in wooden dwellings under the Castle arches, among them a few goldsmiths. Later Emperor Rudolph II, a dedicated believer in alchemism, allotted the dwellings to his imperial archers. They must have been exceptionally short people. The houses, often rebuilt, are tiny. The rooms have a floorspace of six square yards and are so low that most people have to bend their heads as they step in. Prior to the Second World War, some famous fortunetellers lived there, among them Madame de Thèbes, who—not unlike the former alchemists—made gold out of people's ignorance by predicting their future and casting their horoscopes. Gustav Meyrink writes in *The Golem*,

> According to an old myth there is a house in Alchemists' Street that can be seen only during the fog, and even then only by Sunday children. It is called "The Wall at the Last Lantern." In daytime one sees only a gray, big stone . . . Underneath the stone there rests an immense treasure, the founding stone of a house laid by the Order of the Asiatic Brethren who allegedly created Prague . . . Methusalem himself keeps guard there to keep the Devil from conceiving a son with the stone, the so-called Armilos . . . who would have golden hair, crescent-like eyes, and arms reaching down to the feet . . .

Alchemism became a passion in sixteenth-century Prague, and the expensive hobby of the idle rich who spent good gold on phony experiments. Emperors, kings and princes sponsored adventurers and crooks who knew there was real gold in their patrons' exchequers. Ignaz von Münsterberg, the son of King George of Poděbrady, had his house alchemist installed in a laboratory in Kutná Hora. Wilhelm von Rosenberg spent a fortune employing several charlatans in his house. Johann von Hasenburg, President of the Prague Court of Appeals, supposedly an educated man, wasted a lot of good gold in order to make phony gold. A rich man, Wenzel Wřesowetz von Vřesowitz, kept the famous alchemist Claudius Syrrus in his house. To have one's own house alchemist was an important status symbol. More important,

The Mystical City

Wenzel also collected an important library which he left to the Malá Strana City Council. Three rich men—Korálek von Teschen, Johann Kaper von Kaperstein, and a famous doctor, Nikolaus Löw von Löwenstein—ruined themselves in their search for gold. In 1584, a *Magazine for Magicians* was published in Prague.

From all over Europe adepts of alchemy came to the Prague Castle to offer their services. Rudolph II, a superstitious man (once he asked for "moss which grows on the bones of convicts hanged on the gallows"), was no fool where alchemy was concerned. He named his personal physician—Thaddeus Hájek of Hájek, famous astronomer, doctor and mathematician—"examinator" of all would-be alchemists. Hájek set up an "Academy of Alchemists" in his house near Charles University, where he tested all applicants.

Still, strange characters managed to fool the good doctor. A Polish charlatan named Sendivoy, and an Englishman, John Dee, became intimates of the Emperor. Dee impressed everybody at the Castle when he declared that he could understand "the language of the birds" and pretended to know "exactly how Adam and Eve had spoken at the Garden of Eden." Present-day historians in Prague claim that he was really a spy sent by Elizabeth I to report on Rudolph II. He was succeeded by the formidable Kelley (both his ears had been cut off for forgeries committed in England), who passed Hájek's "tests" in Prague. A French medical man, Dr. Barraud, declared, that Kelley had transformed with one drop of blood-red oil "a pound of molten mercury into pure gold." After "producing" gold at the Emperor's court laboratory, Kelley was awarded the title "Knight of Imana." Kelley married a rich Prague girl and invested his wife's money in a brewery, a mill and a couple of houses, among them the "Faust House." Obviously, Kelley was a *smart* alchemist, who considered real estate a better investment than unreal gold. Unfortunately, his luck ran out when Emperor Rudolph II was told by members of his court camarilla that Kelley "had discovered the recipe for the stone of wisdom," whatever *that* was, and had not given it to the Emperor, who needed it badly, since his empire was disintegrating under the impact of the Reformation. Kelley got into a fight with the Emperor's chamberlain Hunkler, was arrested, sent to the tower of Castle Křivoklat, and all his papers, recipes and mixtures were confiscated.

The royal alchemists tried to get the secrets out of Kelley's papers and failed. Sensing his advantage, Kelley asked for his release so he could continue his "experiments." In an effort to break out of Castle Křivoklat, he used rope for his escape down the Castle moat. The rope broke, and Kelley fell down and broke his leg. His rich wife left him, he couldn't pay his debts (apparently the making of gold was not as easy as he had pretended), and in the end he poisoned himself. This pleased the Jesuits, who considered the alchemists nothing but crooks and often exposed them.

(Contemporary writers also take a skeptical view of alchemists. Anna Tučkova and Alois Svoboda wrote, "Everything we learned in school about the laws of chemistry and physics was against the possibility of anybody turning baser metals into gold by means of a powder; we might have been readier to believe if the amount of pure gold had not always been so many times the quantity of powder used, in the belief that the powder might have been a gold compound from which the gold could be disengaged by chemical reaction." They quote a smart Westphalian alchemist whom Rudolph tried to lure to Prague: "If I really knew how to make gold by artificial means, I should have no need of the Emperor. Since I do not know how to do this, the Emperor has no

The Mystical City

need of me. There is no reason why I should enter his services.")

There were amusing alchemists like Dr. Dobranský, the Rector of the University of Prague, who admitted that it wasn't fitting for scholars to search for gold made of baser metals, and switched to more practical problems, trying to make a mixture to grow thick hair (out of boiled fir cones), to keep game fresh in summer by putting it in cooled aspic, and other useful things. (Modern physicists make beta active gold by sending streams of neutrons through mercury. The result is the active isotope of gold 198—ordinary gold is 197—that will disintegrate after two days.)

My favorite alchemist is Rodovský of Hustořany who looked for gold and instead came up with a recipe for "aqua vitae," the water of life that is popular as *eau-de-vie* with the French, as *Aquavit* with the Norwegians, and as *Akvavit* with the Danes. Rodovský's recipe makes good sense. "Take good wine" (I like the emphasis on *good*) "and distill it at least fourteen times. It will be stronger than at the beginning. Keep it safe as gold and use it against the ills listed below, that you may enjoy a long life." The long list contains many diseases, from "afflictions of liver, lungs and stomach" to "leprosy, vertigo, stink from the nostrils, and loss of memory." Rodovský wrote several volumes about what he called "the hermetical sciences." And his book, written in 1600, *Cooking, or a Book About Different Foods Which Are to Be Prepared in a Useful and Tasty Way*, is one of Europe's first cookbooks. Another valuable document from those days is Suetonius' *Cosmopolitae novum lumen chymicum*, published in Prague in 1604.

In 1902, Guillaume Apollinaire, the poet of haunting melancholy, after a visit to Prague wrote *The Wanderer of*

Prague, the beautiful story of his walk through the mystical city in the company of Isaak Laquedem, also called Buttadio, Boudedeo, Juan Espera-en-Dios or—Ahasver:

We went to hear the clock strike the hour from the tower of the Old City Hall. Death, pulling the bell cord, shook its head . . . We entered an inn where music was being played. Laquedem ate, without sitting down, and wandered through the place. The musicians played and collected some money. Meanwhile the room was filled with the guttural sounds of the guests, Czechs with ball-like heads, round faces and Ascension-noses . . . In the dome's chapel where the kings of Bohemia are crowned and where St. Wenceslas became a martyr, Laquedem showed me the walls covered with jewels, agates, and amethysts.

The Czech poet Jiří Mašek, who writes about "the half-sleep and the half-dream," describes his meeting with the eternal Jew in the Old Jewish Town. Vilém Závada has mystical visions about "the midnight city," life in Prague at night, with "the burned-out people and unhappy desperadoes." In the poem "The Siren" he feels caught in the labyrinth of the ghetto,

where at night the girls stand on the slippery threshold, where strangers discover Prague in the darkness, where they sense the romanticism of a damned world.

To the Czech poets Prague is often a city of tragedy. "O Prague, stone-heart of my country! How hard did you fall! Come back, come back! A gray cloud, formed by the tears of your sons, hangs over you!" exclaims Karel Hynek Mácha. They love Prague at dusk, when the evening bells ring from Hradčany. In "Stars over Prague," Jiří Karásek ze Lvovic sings:

> In the dark houses people have lost themselves.
> My soul, rest at least for a little while,

The Mystical City

> Now, in the loneliness,
> Carry the burden of your sorrows.

In "Fights and Fates," the poet Antonín Sova writes about "Prague, Eternal Sentry":

> O city down there: how many times
> did I die in you, rise from the dead
> ....
> how many times, in ruin,
> without a word, without a shout,
> did I sail with you, dead, in
> a quiet, dead stream . . .

"In the poems of our lyrical poets Prague is often a city of tears," writes Jan Šnobr. "They see Prague as an oasis of beauty, but also of melancholy unreality." Death, graves, cemeteries are always present. The great modern poet Vitězslav Nezval wrote a beautiful poem, "Epitaphs." There is more darkness than light in the poems of Jiří Wolker, Jaroslav Seifert, Jaroslav Bednář. Konstantin Biebl reveals the soul of Prague in his poem "The Condemned" about a murderer's last night and last thoughts before his execution. Some, like Ladislav Dymeš, cannot stand it any longer, feeling as oppressed as their German and Jewish fellow poets, longing for the "bright, peaceful countryside." And the great poet Josef Hora, in "The Working Day," asks:

> I don't know, Praha,
> Whether I love you more
> Or hate you more.

The Czech writers of Prague received powerful impulses from their German and Jewish fellow writers, who were in turn influenced by them. Karel Čapek, in his play *R.U.R.*, revives the old Golem legend—the robots rebelling against their master. Čapek was a mystic and symbolist-at-heart. (He was also the friend of Masaryk, the realistic philosopher, who spent nearly every Friday evening in Čapek's villa in the company of poets and writers—the *pátečnici*, or Friday men—where he felt more at home than in his splendid residence in Hradčany Castle.) In 1948, Karel Čapek shared the fate of his great friend and was condemned to official oblivion.

Nowadays Čapek is again reluctantly recognized. The critic Alexander Matuška compares him to Georges Duhamel. Čapek differentiated between "man alone" and "man in the crowd." He considered the individual to be "human" and the crowd "bestial." (No wonder he wasn't very popular during the dark age of Stalinism.) Duhamel said, "Perhaps mankind will once become worthy of man." Čapek wrote, "Man's whole misfortune is the fact that he was obliged to become mankind." In *Sloupkový Ambit* he writes:

Ora pro nobis, pray for us, it says in the litanies to the saints. But the saints and martyrs of this world don't pray for us in heaven but on earth; they pray in their hearts for mankind not to lose its faith. *Morere pro nobis*, die for us, when it will again be necessary to give a supreme example of love and courage in the midst of all the evil that torments mankind. *Revive pro nobis*, return for ever among us: for it is our fate to suffer much and often to lift our eyes to the shining face of man.

These words (which might have been written by Kafka) reveal a philosophy different from the optimism of Julius Fučík, the official poet laureate of the People's Republic of Czechoslovakia. In his *Reportage Written Under the Gallows*, the gifted young writer from Prague, who was tortured and killed by the Gestapo, writes, "Once more I repeat:

we've lived for the joy, for the joy we went into the fight, and for the joy we shall die. Thus there should never be mourning conected with our name."

Čapek went the opposite way. "We should start at man's last breath to understand what his life was like, to learn about the significance of what he experienced," he wrote in *Meteor*. He was a cosmopolite, *horribile dictu*, who was convinced that Czech art "always elaborated on European art." "Frankly speaking, we are not a country which abounds to any great extent in new ideas and trends," he wrote in 1936, two years before his death. He lived in seclusion but he listened to the world and its voices, and in his mysteries, moralities and utopias he showed—like Kafka—a remarkable gift of prophecy. He foresaw the apocalypse of the Second World War—a merciful fate made him die a few months before the Germans occupied his country—and he worried about "the white disease" long before the effects of radiation began to worry us. "We may not agree with him," concludes critic Matuška, "but the Second World War proved that he was not mistaken in his warnings."

In 1913, in a study on the American way of life published in the magazine *Přehled* (Survey), Čapek wrote:

The spirit of America, infinitely more human than we think, gives birth to a spiritual man, complete and well-balanced, a finished human being. His harmony is entirely different from the ancient symbiosis between beauty and goodness, but all the same harmonic in the equilibrium of his thought and action. The progress in which the typically non-conservative American believes is guided by the mind . . . This is the true example that America provides and that Europe disregards . . .

Kafka

FRANZ KAFKA was born on July 3, 1883, at the corner of No. 5, Maiselova, "U Radnice" (At the Town Hall). The house was badly damaged during the fighting in the spring of 1945, and later rebuilt. Only the old entrance was left. In the summer of 1965, a memorial sculpture, showing Kafka's head, made by Karel Hladik was put up on the corner of the house. Stepping out of the entrance, Kafka might have turned right, toward the Old Jewish Town and would reach the Old-New Synagogue or the Old Jewish Cemetery in a couple of minutes. Turning left, he was practically in Staroměstské Námestí, the Old Town Square, which has more historical associations for the people of Prague than any other place.

Some sixteen feet below the level of the present-day pavement there was the ancient East-West trade road, going back to the pre-Christian era, that led from Byzantium to the later Frankish Empire. In 1419, the first Prague defenestration at the Old Town Hall marked the beginning of the Hussite wars. The Hussite movement later led toward the Reformation. In 1437, Jan Roháč z Dubé, the last great Hussite warrior, was executed in front of the Town Hall. In 1458, George of Poděbrady, the newly elected King of Bohemia, was led across the square toward Čeletná. Frederick of the Palatinate, the "Winter King," crossed Old Town Square, on his flight, following his defeat at the White Mountain. The next year, in 1621, twenty-seven Czech nobles and burghers were executed in front of the Town Hall. (The spot is marked by crosses in the pavement at the foot of the tower.) "The Prague executioner beheaded twenty-four men, using four swords . . . then the remaining three, who had been condemned to death by hanging, had their arms bound behind their backs . . . within four or five half-hours the executioner put an end to twenty-seven lives," it says in an old chronicle, *Pragerische Execution.* During World War I, on the morning after the unveiling of the Jan Hus Memorial in the center of Old Town Square, a mysterious carpet of roses, which the people of Prague had silently woven during the night, was spread all over it. Shortly before the Revolution in October, 1918, demonstrators tore down the pillar of St. Mary's. (In Prague it was always claimed that the meridian of Prague followed the line of the shadow thrown by St. Mary's pillar at noon.)

Early in May, 1945, an S. S. unit, in a perverted, final act of hatred, brought up a tank and fired a shell from close range into the *Orloj* (horologe), the astrological clock of the Old Town Hall, a Czech national symbol. It had been finished around 1480 by Hanuš Růže, an Utraquist professor of Charles University, and its calendar plaque, showing the signs of the Zodiac, medallions of the months and country scenes, was painted by Josef Mánes. (The present plaque is a copy; the original is at the Municipal Museum.) Kafka, as so many other people, often stood there waiting for the clock to strike the hour. The little windows open, the small statues of the Apostles and of Christ file past the windows, Death tolls a tiny bell, the old man nervously shakes his head, he doesn't want to die yet. Death reverses the hourglass. There follow the figures of a Turk, a miser with his purse, who thinks you can take it with you, a dandy adjusting his costume. The windows are closed but up in the gable a tiny window opens and a cock appears and crows.

It is hard to believe that in 1787, when the Old Town Hall was rebuilt, the clock was almost sold as scrap metal, and was saved only by the intervention of Anton Strnad. Kafka loved the astronomical clock, and the *Orloj* returned his affection. After Kafka's coffin had been lowered into his parents' grave at the modern Jewish Cemetery at Strašnice, exactly at four o'clock, on May 11, 1924, family members and friends, among them Max Brod, returned to Kafka's home. In Old Town Square, Brod noticed that the Town Hall's *Orloj* had stopped—exactly at four o'clock . . .

Old Town Square remains the focus of Prague's history. It is closer to the hearts of the people than the magnificent but somewhat remote Hradčany Castle. "There are few squares on earth that can compete with Old Town Square in Prague, magnificent palaces surround it, strange houses whose builders must have enjoyed their own imagination, the Old Town Hall with its serious-cheerful loggia and astronomic clock, the grandiose Týn Church with its two towers stretching toward the sky . . . and the pavement that drank noble and ignoble human blood," wrote the poet Hugo Salus whom Kafka admired.

(After the Soviet troops occupied Prague, late in August, 1969, no one was able to go to Old Town Square. The Russians, probably instructed by some local "advisers," completely blocked off the square with tanks and antiaircraft guns. In front of the Kinský Palace there was a large banner, "Russian Art of the 1920s," publicizing a show that had recently been opened. Now there were tanks in front of the banner. Some youthful Czech photographers made pictures of the "new" Russian art. "Perhaps it was

The Mystical City

just as well we couldn't demonstrate at the Jan Hus monument," one said. "It's easy to get up on the monument, and lie there, and that might have created trouble.")

Kafka loved the Old Town Square and spent a considerable part of his short life in and around it. He went to the Old Town Gymnasium, on the second floor of the Kinský Palais. Among his classmates were Hugo Bergmann, who became a philosopher and Rector of the University of Jerusalem, and Emil Utitz, professor of philosophy in Halle and Prague. At various times Kafka lived in nearby Celetná, in a narrow, twisting building near Týn Church; in 36, and Pařížská from where he could see the Russian Church. Later, in Bílková, and in Dlouhá (Long Street), he was within a short distance of the Old Town Square.

The relationship between Kafka and Prague is still the subject of much research and the question is often asked whether Kafka's genius would have developed if he hadn't been born and lived in Prague. He often refers directly to Prague in his *Diaries* but never in his novels. He doesn't write about the people of Prague the way Thomas Mann, whom Kafka much admired, writes about the people of Luebeck. "But anyone able to recognize the reality in a surrealist picture will recognize the reality of Prague in the work of Kafka," writes Hugo Siebenschein. (When I first read *The Trial*, I was rather young and had not been in Prague; the book never made me think of Prague. Rereading it again after having lived in Prague for years, I realized that *The Trial* was the deeper truth about Kafka's city, seen with a poet's inner vision. Without trying to photograph Prague, Kafka relived the city's inner, secret life and created a permanent picture that cannot be seen with one's eyes, only felt with one's soul.)

The deepest truth of Kafka's work is as unfathomable as

the innermost mysteries of Mozart's music. Both Mozart and Kafka have been defenseless against their posthumous interpreters who often "interpret" by trying to blend their own thoughts into the work of a genius. Goethe, much interpreted and much abused, once wrote ironically in "Zahme Xenien,"

> Im Auslegen seid frisch und munter!
> Legt ihr's nicht aus, so legt was unter,

which, somewhat freely translated, means

> Don't hesitate when you interpret,
> Elucidate, or Mistranslate.

Max Brod, Kafka's closest friend and biographer, writes in *Streitbares Leben* (Polemical Life):

It is difficult and superfluous to comment on Kafka. Every reasonable reader feels that in Kafka's work an extremely precise realism is combined with another element that in each line borders upon the sphere of what cannot be said and can only be spiritually comprehended. Kafka's teachers were the Bible, Goethe, Kleist, Flaubert and Kierkegaard. He himself considered as the highest form of poetry a work that expresses in every syllable something real and, at the same time, something that cannot be put into words . . . He didn't retire into the ivory tower, he didn't evade life . . . yet on the other, the metaphysical side of his life there was his painful perception of divine matters, the pure, the perfect, the absolute.

Willy Haas (at this writing one of the last surviving contemporaries of Kafka in Prague) writes in 1960 in his *Erinnerungen* (Memoirs),

When I read the works of Kafka I read them as one reads the completely familiar panorama of one's own youth. I recognized every corner, every dusty corridor, every lascivity. Kafka certainly said everything that we never said, were never able to say. I believe I can read his books as in a dream. I don't understand that one word is needed to explain them . . . That's why I don't understand all the essays that were written about Kafka's work, since every word that is added is superfluous and only camouflages what is on the surface . . . *I cannot understand how anyone can understand him who wasn't born in Prague, around 1880 or 1890.* His strangely mute, allegorically realistic deeper meaning [*Tiefsinn*] is the reason that those who don't really know the enormously suggestive foreground world won't understand the milieu of "The Trial" and "The Castle" that exists only in this local microcosmos; and thus the most abstruse misunderstandings were born . . .

and he continues,

The special situation of the Old Town of Prague, the traces of the former ghetto, the narrow, crooked streets, the dim churches and synagogues, the dusty office buildings, the banks of the Moldau and the Baroque gardens . . . all this helped to form the atmosphere in the tortured visions of Kafka.

Gustav Janouch writes in his *Conversations with Kafka* that they once talked about Meyrink's *The Golem* and that Kafka said:

In all of us there are dark corners, mysterious corridors, blind windows, dirty courtyards, loud dives and closed taverns. We walk through the broad streets in the newly built quarters of the city but our steps and glances are unsure. In our inside we are still trembling as in the old streets of the misery [*Elend*]. *The unhealthy Old Jewish Town is much more real for us than the hygienic new town around us.* Wide-awake we walk through a dream: ghosts of long-gone days.

This is the answer to the enigmatic question of Franz Kafka and Prague. Or when Kafka writes about the building of the Tower of Babylon in "Das Stadtwappen" (The Coat of Arms):

Every national group wanted to have the nicest living quarters which created arguments that ended in murderous fights. These fights never stopped. They offered new grounds to the leaders that the tower should be built very slowly or rather only after conclusion of a peace treaty. But one didn't spend all the time fighting, in the intervals one made the town more beautiful, which however caused new envy and new fights. Thus passed the time of the first generation but none of the succeeding ones was different, only the workmanship got better, and with it the eagerness to fight. The second or third generation already realized the senselessness of the sky-tower-building, but by that time one was too much attached to each other to be able to leave the town. All sagas and legends of the town express the longing for the day (as was predicted) on which the town will be smashed to pieces by a giant fist—with five blows quickly succeeding each other. Therefore the town has the fist in its coat-of-arms.

Kafka's *Diaries* are running footnotes to his daily, humdrum life in Prague. After graduating from the Old Town Gymnasium, a very strict school, Kafka studied law at the German University, just two minutes away from Old Town Square. (A quarter of a century later, when I studied law in the same lecture halls and seminary rooms, I came to dislike the vaulted corridors, dark courtyards and old stone stairs very much. It was cold and damp in winter. In springtime the smell from the toilets hovered over the venerable Alma Mater that Charles IV had founded right here in 1348, the first in Central Europe. Since then, no repairs whatsoever seemed to have been carried out inside. We students wished it would have more comfort and less history.)

The Mystical City

In 1906, Kafka became a doctor of jurisprudence, was addressed as "Herr Doktor," which pleased his parents more than it pleased him, and did his "unpaid" year as a court clerk, to gain a short breathing spell. (The cross-examinations in his novels *America* and *The Trial* show how much practical experience he gained in court.) He didn't want to be a "Herr Doktor." He wanted to write. "Writing is a form of prayer," he confides to his *Diary*. He was looking for a single-shift job that would be over by two in the afternoon, so he could spend the rest of the day thinking, reading, writing. His friends envied him when he found such a job at the nearby "Workers' Accident Insurance Institute," in Poříč Street. He was assigned to the department that studied the prevention of accidents, and in 1909 wrote an article for the *Annual Report of the Accident Institute*, which his boss painstakingly corrected. (Brod later spoke to Kafka's former boss, who had no idea that his erstwhile hireling had become a world-famous writer. Kafka would have appreciated this bit of irony.) The atmosphere of the Insurance Institute later appears in several chapters of *The Trial* and *The Castle*. Brod remembers how one day in 1909, "Herr Doktor" Kafka read to him the beginning of a short novel called "Preparations for a Wedding in the Country." On a rainy afternoon a man named Raban (Kafka?) walks to a small railroad station. Very little happens—and also very much. "It was extraordinary," Brod writes. "I got the impression that there was no ordinary talent speaking, but a genius."

Much of his life Kafka had to do things which he didn't like to do. Once he writes in his *Diary*, "After studying since six o'clock in the morning, I noticed how my left hand clasped the fingers of my right hand for a few moments, as though it had pity for them." Later, he was very unhappy in his job. ("Here in the office, for the sake of such a miserable, official document I must rob a body that is capable of such happiness of a piece of its flesh." Or, "The tremendous world I have in my head! But how can I release it and release myself without tearing apart?" And finally, "I lead a double life from which perhaps the only way out is madness.")

One is reminded of the letter that Mozart wrote to his father, Leopold, when he refused to take on pupils. "You must not think it is laziness—no!—but because it is utterly against my genius, against my way of life. You know that I am so-to-speak soaked in music, that I am busy with it all day, that I love to meditate, to study." Mozart had more determination than Kafka, who went on wasting his precious little strength doing things he hated; later he had to work in his father's factory, which he hated even more.

But there were also happy days: excursions into Prague's vicinity to Senohraby, walking in the woods with Brod, Werfel and Felix Weltsch, one of his closest friends who later became an eminent philosopher, or reading to each other poems at the banks of the Sazava river. ("The train leaves at 6:05," Kafka once wrote to Brod. "At 7:45 we'll start toward Davle where we'll eat a goulash at Lederer's. At twelve we'll have lunch at Štěhovice. From two to a quarter to four we shall walk through the woods to the rapids where we shall row a bit. At seven, we'll take the boat back to Prague . . .") Kafka loved the swimming schools at the banks of the Moldau. On August 12, 1911, he writes in his *Diary*, "The time that passed during which I wrote not a single word was very important for me because I stopped being ashamed of my body in the swimming schools of Prague, Königsaal and Černošice."

On October 1 of the same year he writes about his visit to the Old-New Synagogue on the eve of the Day of Atonement,

The Mystical City

Muted murmurs. Churchlike interior. Three pious, apparently Eastern Jews. In socks. Bent over their prayer books, wrapped in their prayer scarves, looking very small. Two are crying, moved by the High Holiday . . . In the Pinkas Synagogue I was much more impressed by the Jewishness . . .

Edison told in an interview in America about his journey through Bohemia that he believed there is a higher development there (wide streets in the suburbs, small gardens in front of the houses, new factories) because emigrés return from the United States bringing back new aspirations . . .

According to the Cabala, the pious ones are given on each Friday a new, heavenly, more tender soul that stays with them until Saturday night . . .

Werfel's poems yesterday filled my head with steam. For a moment I was afraid my exultation would drive me into madness.

Kafka often describes his walks through Prague in his *Diaries*. "With Ottla [his sister], fetched her from the English lesson. Across Quai, stonebridge, Malá Strana, new bridge, back home. Exciting statues of saints on Charles Bridge. The strange summer evening light while the bridge is as empty as at night." There is a definite rhythm in his walks. On May 4, 1913, he notes, "By accident, walked in the opposite direction up to Hradčany and Charles Bridge." He often went to read and relax in the Chotek Gardens and writes about "the pleasure of sitting yesterday in Chotek Park and today in Charles Square reading Strindberg's 'Am offenen Meer.'"

After looking at Oskar Kokoschka's expressionist painting of Prague, Kafka said to Janouch, "On the picture the roofs fly away. The church coupolas are umbrellas in the wind. The whole city is about to fly off. But Prague remains

—despite all inner discord. That is the wonderful thing about Prague." And at a very difficult time of his life, when Fräulein F. B. from Berlin whom he loved refused to marry him, he asks himself, "What will you do? Leave Prague? React to the worst human damage with the strongest means of reaction?" He loved Prague but not Vienna ("which I hate and where I would be very unhappy"). Demetz writes, "Kafka's love for his city burns like a permanent, faithful fire that dies out only with the return of the dead poet into the walls of the Jewish Cemetery." And Dagmar Eisnerova says, "Prague, unnamed, is the city of Kafka's 'The Trial.' ... In the chapter 'At the Dome' there are important details, especially the silver statue of the Saint—the tomb of St. John Nepomuk. ... Franz Kafka lived, suffered and fought in Prague."

Kafka wrote only in German but spoke good Czech. "His language had an inner tension ... each word was a stone; his language resembled his hands; he had strong hands with long fingers," remembers Janouch. Once he and Janouch were laughing at his office, when Janouch's father, who also worked at the Insurance Institute, came in and asked whether his son was bothering "*Doktor* Kafka." "No," Kafka said and laughed, "we're talking about devils and demons." But the next moment he might say something like, "People —like our parents and those we love and fear—must die to be really understood." Or, "We Jews are already born old ... I am as old as the Eternal Jew."

They were talking about Karl Brand, a young German-Jewish poet, who had spent much of his time at the Café Arco, and died at the age of twenty-seven of tuberculosis. Kafka said, "Among the century-old Jews at the coffeehouses, Brand lost his way and died. And what else could he have done? The coffeehouses are the catacombs of the

Jews of our time, without light and love. Not everybody could stand them." Kafka couldn't, and when his friends asked him to come there, he often found an excuse.

Kafka's friends and biographers point out the specific isolation, the "border situation" of a Jewish poet, born in Prague as a citizen of the Habsburg Monarchy, who was educated in German and surrounded by Czechs and died as a citizen of the Czechoslovak Republic. Emil Utitz, the philosopher, Kafka's onetime classmate, writes:

> All of us sensed the invisible border around us and our artificial situation . . . We talked about everything, naturalism, secession, symbolism, socialism, Zionism, nationalism, about the individual and the collective, about religion and atheism . . . I understood only much later that Kafka in his soul lived through the border situation with more strength than the rest of us. His whole life was a process that he carried on within himself. On the outside, he was the quietest and the most indomitable of us. There was nothing conspicuous about him. He dressed neither as a poet nor as a bohemian. He was always clean and orderly, never shabby and never elegant. When I think back, I see the picture of a tall, slim, boyish young man, who was so quiet and polite, who happily recognized other people's merits, and always remained a little remote . . .

Rudolf Fuchs, the poet and translator, once told me how he met Kafka in the street the day after Fuchs's poem "House of Gentle Peace" had been published by the *Prager Tagblatt* (where Brod, Fuchs and I, among others, were working in the 1930s). Kafka had praised the poem, but Fuchs himself no longer liked it; it was an old piece. "I expressed some doubt about the sincerity of Kafka's praise," Fuchs said. "I was ashamed and delighted, when Kafka quoted the whole poem by heart."

Once Kafka compared the Jews and the Germans. "The

Jews had their Temple," he said to Janouch. "The Germans had their God that grows iron. *Their* Temple is the Prussian General Staff." Both laughed and then Kafka said that he meant it quite seriously. Another time he called Heine "an unhappy man. The Germans accuse him of being a Jew and he is a German, even a German who is in conflict with his own Jewishness. That is the typical Jewish in him." On September 14, 1915, he writes how he went to see a famous wonder rabbi in Žižkov, a workers' district of Prague, accompanied by Max (Brod) and Georg (Langer):

... an inn. Upstairs completely dark, one walks like a blind man with outstretched hands. A room with pale twilight, white-gray walls, filled with women and girls. White handkerchiefs, bloodless faces. Next room. Everything black. Filled with men and younger people. Loud praying. We creep into a corner. "All rabbis look wild," says Langer. The rabbi in his silk caftan. Unreal. One sees his white underdrawers. ...

Kafka loved especially Malá Strana and the quiet streets below the Castle. In the winter of 1916–17 he lived in a tiny house, No. 22, in Golden Lane, "the alchemists' street." The house had a small room and a very small kitchen. Brod writes, "Franz didn't choose this place at all from any mystic or romantic inclination, or at least any such inclination was not the deciding factor, except perhaps subconsciously, in the form of his love for Old Prague. The main reason was his need for a quiet place where he could work." Kafka was extremely sensitive to noise.

He wrote to Fräulein F. B. when he was looking for an apartment, "We saw a few places in Malá Strana, and all the time I was thinking, if only there were some spot in a quiet attic corner in one of the old palaces where one could at least stretch out in peace." Later a rental agent showed him "a flat in one of the most beautiful palaces . . . Two rooms and a hall, half of which has been turned into a bathroom. Six hundred crowns a year. It was a dream come true. I went to see it. The rooms were beautiful, red and gold, as in Versailles. Four windows looking out on a quiet, hidden courtyard, one window facing the garden. The garden! You can hardly believe your eyes. Through a semi-circle flanked by caryatids you see stone-stairs, leading in zig-zag to the great garden . . . a broad balustrade rising gradually, in sweeping curves to a gloriette." Unfortunately the place had "one small fault." The owner, a young man, had put in expensive improvements and wanted the new tenant to share the expenses. Instead Kafka rented a flat in the Schönborn Palais (today the United States Embassy, property of the U.S. Government) that was nice but couldn't be heated.

In May, 1946, in a secret, national election, 38 per cent of the population of Czechoslovakia gave their votes to the Communist Party, making it the strongest in the country. The country was not "taken over" by the Communists; there was no revolution; it was an orderly, democratic procedure; the people voted for the Communists, and Klement Gottwald, the protégé of Stalin, became Prime Minister. In May, 1948, not less than 89.3 per cent of the electorate voted for the (Communist-dominated) National Front candidates. President Dr. Beneš relinquished his office in June, and Gottwald became his successor. "In this month, also, the National Assembly ratified the new Constitution which affirmed that Czechoslovakia was a People's Democracy on the road to socialism," writes Miloš Kratochvil.

Somewhat later—no one will ever know exactly when and

how—Franz Kafka joined the distinguished company of unpersons led by former President Masaryk. His books were put on the index, his works disappeared from the bookstores, and his name from the mouths of cautious citizens who didn't want to get in trouble.

During the dark days of Stalinism it wasn't advisable to mention Kafka—famous all over the Western world—in his hometown. From one of Kafka's former residences in 36, Pařížská Street, not far from the Old-New Synagogue, one had a splendid view of Prague's monumental Stalin statue, largest on earth, built of the same expensive sandstone of which, centuries earlier, the "exciting statues of saints on Charles Bridge" (I'm quoting Kafka) had been made. In 1946, the French magazine *Action* asked, "Faut-il brûler Kafka?" (Must one burn Kafka?), after Kafka's books had already been burned by the Nazis.

The rediscovery of Franz Kafka in Communist Czechoslovakia was as sudden and bewildering as his earlier disappearance. In 1963, Professor Eduard Goldstücker of the University in Prague, a leading Kafka expert, said:

It is a fact that Marxist research dealt with Kafka's work only in the past few years. The impulse was given by the results of the Twentieth Party Congress of the Communist Party of the Soviet Union which realized that the antagonistic systems of today's world must co-exist. . . . Franz Kafka whom the world considers one of us, became in Czechoslovakia, and not only here, a victim of what is known as the consequences of the personal cult . . . We must not condemn under the undefined conception of "decadence" summarily all artistic currents creating works that run counter to our methods and our spirit.

Goldstücker made these astonishing revelations at a scientific conference taking place in Liblice, near Prague, in May, 1963, shortly before Kafka's eightieth birthday. It was "the first meeting of Marxists dedicated to a writer whose work is characterized by deep contradictions," and proceeded to find "the ideological clarification of the literary-scientific problems connected with Kafka's work." Translated into plain English this meant that the Czechoslovak Government, no matter how its members may have felt about Franz Kafka (President Antonín Novotný was not exactly known as a friend of writers, poets and philosophers), could no longer prevent the official rehabilitation of Kafka.

(Goldstücker was sentenced to death during the Stalinist regime, was saved by the intervention of Khrushchev, and stayed in jail for years. In 1968, he was elected president of the courageous Czechoslovak Writers' Union that spearheaded the spiritual liberation preceding the "Prague Spring." In 1969, after the downfall of Dubček, he was expelled from the Communist Party. He now lives as an exile in England. Kafka wouldn't have been surprised.)

In her opening speech, the Czech writer, Marie Majerová, claimed Kafka as "a *Pražan* [a citizen of Prague] and a Prague poet . . . without the sets of Old Prague and her thousand-year-old stones there wouldn't be the atmosphere of 'The Trial' and 'The Castle.' He is a unique and inimitable poet . . ." Paul Reiman noted that Kafka's father had been a "capitalistic exploiter" and that Kafka hated his father "not so much as a person but in a social function." Reiman asked for a "kind, sympathetic [*liebevoll*] review of Kafka, in the sense of Karl Marx's slogan, *nihil humani a me alienum pato.*" Goldstücker said, "In the literature prior to the First World War we could hardly find a non-proletarian author who states the proletarian cause with such partiality," and compared Kafka's relationship to socialism and the working class with the characteristics that Marx and Engels in their

Communist Manifesto give to the representatives of critical-utopian socialism and communism, for whom the proletariat exists only as the "most suffering social class."

František Kautman analyzed Kafka's relationship to the Czech nation, Czech literature, Czech language. Kafka was bilingual, spoke Czech with the servants at home and with the employees in his father's factory. At a time when no German would go to the Czech National Theater, Kafka often went there. He was familiar with German translations, of Machar, Bezruč, Březina, Šrámek and other Czech poets, and had friendly connections with some contributors to the *Modern Revue*. "Kafka," wrote Pavel Eisner, the bilingual Prague critic, "had to live in the three-fold ghetto of the Prague Jews—the self-centered attitude of the tribal ghetto, the ghetto of society, and the ghetto of the poet's soul . . . He didn't find it easy to break out of his isolation, remained concentrated within himself and his work."

By this time the rehabilitation of Kafka had been "scientifically" established. It was reported that Kafka had often visited the meetings of the Czech "anarchists" and enjoyed their stormy debates. And he would attend political meetings and listened to the speeches of Kramář, Klofáč, Soukup and, above all, Masaryk. The experts agreed on many parallels between Kafka and Jaroslav Hašek, the author of *The Good Soldier Švejk*. Kautman said:

Both comprehend the absurdity of external, visible reality. Hašek's and Kafka's worlds are absurd, though each in its own way. In "Švejk" the absurdity of orders and commands is the basic motive. But many of Kafka's officials, judges, characters observe the laws ad absurdum by fulfilling their duties . . . Tragic situations suddenly turn into comical ones and vice versa . . .

The Czech literary critic Jiří Hájek said, "In our society Kafka becomes the passionate appeal for all that is human within us." He characterized the difference between Kafka and the Marxists "not, as some Marxist critics claim, that Kafka didn't realize the historical revolutionary role of the working class and that we know it. The difference is that we have the power, while he and his protagonists were powerless, that we are able to change the relations between things, while he could only point at their untenability with all his despair." And the Austrian Communist critic and writer, Ernst Fischer, ended his paper with an appeal to the conference, "to save Kafka from the region of the cold war, not to reserve his work for the commentators but to give it to the readers," and he exclaimed, "I appeal to the socialist world: Get Kafka's work back from involuntary exile! Let's give him a permanent visa!" (Because of his sympathies for the Dubček regime, Fischer was expelled by the Communist Party of Austria late in 1969.)

One year later, on June 23, 1964, Max Brod said in an address at the Kafka Exposition in Prague:

Franz Kafka's entire life was a search. What was he searching for? I believe that all his life he was searching for one thing— the purity of the soul, the absolute, uncompromising, unegotistical purity—justice. As a true son of Prague, Kafka had his roots in the soil of Prague. His poetic soul was charmed by the mystical magic of the Old Prague and the mixture of her people. As a true son of Prague, he had his roots in Czech and German culture, and also in the very ancient Jewish culture. In the Jewish ethics and traditions he found a way to his search . . . Irony, humor and paradox—these were the essentials of his art. He was, in spite of his skepticism, cheerful, he loved life. A modern interpretation makes him a decadent, a desperate romanticist somewhat in the style of Edgar Allan Poe, a weakling who evaded life. But Franz, for more than twenty years my best friend, whom I saw often twice a day, was full of life, active, a positive human being. He was interested in everything: sports, theatre, cinema, animals, the circus. He was simple in his feelings though his mind often walked labyrinthic, enigmatic paths. He loved the life of the artists and the life of the simple people. And he loved Prague.

Probably the most beautiful poem about Prague was written neither by a great Czech poet nor by the two great German-Prague lyrical poets, Rilke and Werfel. Kafka wrote it in a letter to a friend. It is simple and true as a folk song and fulfills Kafka's ideal (I'm quoting Brod) of "the highest form of poetry that expresses in every syllable something real and at the same time something that cannot be put into words":

> Menschen, die über dunkle Brücken gehen,
> vorüber an Heiligen
> mit matten Lichtlein.
> Wolken, die über graue Himmel ziehen,
> vorüber an Kirchen
> mit verdämmernden Türmen.
> Einer, der an der Quaderbrüstung lehnt
> und in das Abendwasser schaut,
> die Hände auf alten Steinen.

> (People who walk across dark bridges,
>   past saints
> with dim, small lights.
> Clouds which move across gray skies
> past churches
> with towers darkened in the dusk.

One who leans against the granite railing
gazing into the evening waters,
his hands resting on old stones.)

Charles Bridge Revisited

I FELL UNDER the spell of the mystical city long before I went there. I read Gustav Meyrink's *Der Golem* when I was fourteen or fifteen and was going to school in my hometown in Moravia. During the following nights I didn't want to go to bed because I was afraid to dream of the Golem and the dark streets of the Prague ghetto. (I didn't know that Kafka had said, "The atmosphere of the Prague Jewish town is wonderfully described in *Der Golem*.") I was fascinated by Meyrink's descriptive passages:

Showers beat over the roofs and run down the faces of the houses like streams of tears . . . Sometimes a soft trembling shakes the walls that cannot be explained. In my dreams I often listen to these houses with their spooky doings, and I discovered with fearful astonishment that they were the real, secret rulers of the street. Sometimes they give up life during the day but take it back at night. In daytime they may lend life to the people living there but in the evening they demand it again, with usurious interest.

(Many years later I read in Max Brod's autobiography, published in 1960: "Once in a while I can still hear the soft beating of subterranean drums underneath the hills of Prague, when we approached the black city district at dusk. I never found an explanation for this strange phenomenon.")

There is an unforgettable mood accompanying Pernath as he walks up to Hradčany:

I walked through the arches of the square-stone arcades in the Old Town Square, past the brass fountain, with its Baroque railing full of icicles, and across the stone bridge, with its statues of saints, and of John Nepomuk. The river underneath was foaming wrathfully against the piers. Doorways received and again released me, palaces with carved, arrogant portals passed by, there were lion's heads with heavy bronze rings. Snow—soft as a polar bear's white fur. High, proud windows, its cornices glistening with ice, looked up indifferently toward the clouds. And as I walked up the countless granite steps toward Hradčany, each as wide as four human bodies, the city with its roofs and gables receded in a haze. . . .

Much earlier, when I was a little boy, our old, pious cook, Marie, had told me the story of St. John Nepomuk who "refused to betray the confessional secrets of the Queen, the King's wife, to cruel King Wenceslas," and had been thrown off Charles Bridge, one night in 1393, into the dark waters of the Moldau, while the King's halberdiers pushed back the people with their spears. "And when the holy man disappeared in the waves, five small blue flames appeared on top of the water," Marie said, crossing herself.

I wondered what the confessional secret might be, but I was afraid to ask. Little did I know that Johannes de Pomuk, was drowned probably because he'd infuriated the irascible King by installing a new abbot at Kladruby Monastery. Many historians now agree that the legend of the "confessional secret" was later created; confession was the Jesuits' most effective weapon during the Counter-Reformation. Also,

Johannes de Pomuk was no "holy man" when he was drowned, for he was not canonized until 1729. But I could almost see the flames dancing on top of the dark waves, and I was as deeply impressed by what seemed a miracle as Marie, or millions of other people in Czechoslovakia. I concluded that anything might happen in Prague where flames were dancing on the water of the Moldau and where Rabbi Loew held court among the tombstones in the Old Jewish Cemetery—just a stone's throw away from the river.

After graduating from the local Gymnasium it was decided at home that I would study law at Prague University. There was a strange, unwritten law in our town that the oldest son of "a good family" had "to become a doctor," and the easiest way of becoming one was to study law in Prague. I reluctantly agreed, provided I could also study music in Vienna, and "something" (I didn't know myself what it would be) at the Sorbonne in Paris. My earlier interest in Prague and her miracles was gone. I spoke German with my family at home and Czech with Marie, the cook, and I thought it was about time to go to Paris and speak an "elegant" language. (I was not narrow-minded, though, in the choice of my early girl friends. Some were German, Sudeten German to be exact, and some were Jewish, and some of the prettiest, sexiest ones were Czech.)

Fortunately one didn't have to remain in Prague in order "to become a doctor." Medical students had to be there all the time, but students of jurisprudence needed only the professors' signatures to prove that they had attended the prescribed lectures and seminars. One could buy the signatures, at five crowns a piece, from the *Pedell* (the proctor's man). Naturally, one had to pass the examinations, which meant a sustained effort every two or three semesters. But aside from that no one asked where you lived and what you were doing, and I spent only a few weeks in Prague, and left for Vienna, and then for Paris.

I believe it was on my second or third visit to Prague, some time in 1928, when it happened. The German University was located in Železná, a short walk from the Old Town Square. I got used to walking around Old Town Square. (If Kafka hadn't died in 1924, I might have met him there; of course, I wouldn't have known him. He was hardly known outside the small circle of his devoted friends.) Like so many people, before and after, I became mesmerized by the atmosphere, history and architecture of the Old Town Square. Jacques Guenne, the French art critic, writes:

Does not Old Town Square where fell the heroes, offer a summary of the history of the styles, with the Gothic Town Hall where Renaissance motives are not wanting, with the ogival jewel, the Church of Týn, henceforth liberated from the Chalice of John Hus, with the elegant Kinský Palace, with the Church of Saint Nicholas, whose façade is of the most lithe Baroque, with the modern dwellings which can be seen at the corner of Pařížská?

King John of Luxemburg had given permission to the burghers of the Old Town to build a Town Hall from the proceeds of the wine tax, which made wine-drinking a patriotic, popular activity. I saw the old Romanesque cellars below the Town Hall. I loved the arcades in the square, with their meter-thick walls and irregular stone floors which must have been already there when the Bohemian nobles were executed in 1621. Now there were beerhouses and sausage shops under the arcades; in one shop the *vuršty*—thick, juicy, hot sausages—would fairly explode in your mouth when you bit into them. I would walk toward Pařížská, which leads past the Old-New Synagogue, toward the Moldau; in Prague,

The Mystical City

everything is concentrated in a small space—history, architecture, mysticism. I walked into the old synagogue down below street level, but didn't stay there long. I was instinctively apprehensive of the eerie dimness, the soft murmur of pious men, the small slits in the walls through which, it was said, women were only permitted to look in; they were excluded from the synagogue itself.

In 1930, I was "promoted" as doctor *juris utriusque* at the Gothic Chapel of the Carolinum, after solemnly swearing *"spondeo ac polliceor"* (I vow and I promise). For a few months, I worked as a court apprentice. (It so happens that I graduated at the Chapel and worked at the court building where Kafka did his "unpaid year." And when I had a much-hated job at the law offices of Adler & Pick, I happened to be just around the corner from Poříč, where "Dr. Kafka" had been so unhappy as an employee of the Workers' Accident Insurance Institute.) I much admired Max Brod, the music critic of the *Prager Tagblatt* for which I began to write, but we always talked about music, rarely about writing. Brod would come up to our penthouse apartment, with its fine view of the Moldau and Hradčany. We played violin sonatas together. Brod was an excellent pianist, playing the difficult piano parts of the sonatas by Brahms, Debussy and César Franck with rhapsodic sweep. He told me about Leoš Janáček, whose music I didn't know. Brod was surprised. "But he died in your hometown, Ostrava, at the Sanatorium Klein, in 1928," he said with slight reproach. Today I wish I had gone to see Janáček. Some day he may be recognized as the greatest composer of my homeland, and one of the greatest on earth.

About that time I once walked on a dark, foggy November afternoon across Charles Bridge. I had been at one of the Ministries in Malá Strana, doing an errand for a client of our law office, and I was frustrated because once again I had failed to extricate the client's file that was hidden under a pile of other files in the dusty office of a dusty bureaucrat. The poor man worked in a tiny room with bars in front of the window, as in a prison cell; no wonder he was lonely and didn't want to miss the company of his beloved files.

I crossed Malá Strana Square and Mostecká and walked toward the bridge. In the middle of it, candles were burning at the foot of the dark statue of St. John Nepomuk. The fog had formed tears on his face, and the holy man seemed to be crying. I expect no one to believe it, but it was true; such things do happen in Prague. I had often walked across the bridge, paying no attention to the saints. In Prague one was always in the company of saints; after a while one didn't notice them any more.

That afternoon an old woman was kneeling and praying in front of St. John Nepomuk. She made me think of Marie, our pious old cook, and I stopped. A wet mist came up from the river, and from Kampa Island, underneath the bridge. People called Kampa "Pražské Benátky," "the Prague Venice," with its silent palaces facing the canal, and the boats on the dark water. I looked down, and I thought this might indeed be a little-known corner of Venice. I had been in Venice several times but I'd never walked down to Kampa Island, which today is the choicest residential district in town, a mark of real status; famous artists and national prize-winners live there. Nearly every house has its legends. Kampa was once the domain of the washerwomen and their gossip. At least one of them, Marta Sporer, who did the washing for Emperor Rudolph II and was known for the excellence of her work, was visited by the Emperor in her lovely house called "The White Swan." She was said to be a very attractive woman.

Turning around I looked back at the Malá Strana bridgehead. Behind, its outlines blurred in the fog, was the cupola of St. Nicholas Church, and farther up the Castle. The bridge was almost empty. Once in a while a pedestrian hurried by, his coat collar turned up, looking neither right nor left at the black statues on both sides. The old woman kept praying. She got up, crossing herself, exactly as Marie had done, when she'd told me the story of John Nepomuk, and then she walked away. I looked across the railing into the dark river—perhaps to see the blue flames dancing on the waters that Marie had told me about. (Somewhere I'd read that in the early years of this century somebody had seriously suggested removing the stone statues and replacing the stone railing of the bridge with an iron railing in order to extend the width of Charles Bridge by a few inches. Fortunately, the foolish notions were ignored. The stone railing is now being repaired—even stones get old—and the statues of the saints have been cleaned and restored. The bridge has been closed to all traffic, thank God. Only pedestrians may cross it, as at the time when it was built, and there are always local people and strangers who love to walk there slowly and happily, feeling comfortable being surrounded by all the saints, with the magnificent view of Hradčany in the rear. At certain moments, when the light is right, this is the most beautiful bridge on earth.

"The head of the legendary saint with its stars truly touches the transcendental," wrote Erich Bachmann. The five stars around the head of St. John Nepomuk (*Tacui*—I Was Silent) were there. Sometimes a couple of them would be missing. Students were said to steal them as good-luck charms prior to examinations. Near the Old Town Bridge Tower was the Cross with gilded Hebrew letters. In 1696, a Jew had scoffed at the Cross, was sentenced to pay a fine, and now the letters say, "Holy, Holy, Holy God!"

I walked through under Peter Parler's beautiful Bridge

Tower. I turned left at the monument of Charles IV and walked along Křižovnická toward the Old-New Synagogue. I stepped down the stairs through the vestibule with the two tax collectors' niches. (On Easter Sunday, 1389, "neither fathers nor mothers nor their children" were spared in a pogrom, reported by the poet Abigdor Karo, whose tombstone is the oldest in the Old Jewish Cemetery. "My soul laments the men that fell, the women and the old men, and all the congregation. They that had fled into the synagogues; even they were destroyed in the house of God by the bloody sword of the enemy . . .") No dark statue has been set up to remind posterity of the event, and the martyrs have not been canonized; but they remain forever remembered in the words of a poet.

I stayed there for a while, and then I walked up and out again, past the Jewish Town Hall and the clock with the Hebrew dial. I was suddenly very conscious of walking through the former ghetto. It was dark. I went on, through Maisel Street, toward the Old Town Square. I walked slowly, at peace with myself. It was like coming back to a place I'd wanted to revisit for a long time. It was strange because I had never been in Maisel Street before.

Scenes from History

THE EARLIEST DESCRIPTION OF Prague was written exactly one thousand years ago by Ibrahim Ibn Jacub, an educated Jew of Spanish-Arab origin, long believed to have been a

The Mystical City

merchant who came to Bohemia to buy slaves for the Caliph of Cordoba. Recent research, however, proved that Ibrahim's report was not a mere traveler's account, as had been assumed, but a diplomatic memorandum written in the second half of the tenth century for the Caliph, ruler of the Pyrrhenean peninsula. It was published in the *Book of Voyages and Countries*, edited by the renowned Cordoba geographer-philosopher, Abu Obaid al Bakri. (The book was discovered toward the end of last century in the imperial library in Constantinople.) Ibrahim reports that Fraga (*sic*) is "made of stone and lime and is the biggest merchant center, where Russians and Slavs come from Cracow with goods. From Turkey come Muslims, Jews and Turks also carrying merchandise and coins, and export slaves, tin and various furs."

In 965, Ibrahim, accredited ambassador of Caliph Al Hakam II to the German Emperor, Otto I, visited Utrecht, Paderborn, Mainz and Prague. Historians remained doubtful about his report because they couldn't imagine so many buildings being "made of stone and lime" in Prague at that early time. The only known stone buildings were inside the Castle. Modern research takes a less skeptical viewpoint of Ibrahim's report. The proximity of the Great Moravian Empire, a powerful state extending in the eighth century from the Baltic all the way to Moravia, Bohemia and Austria, with many stone dwellings that have now been found by the archeologists, makes it highly probable that they existed in Prague too. Prague was an important market center. Ibrahim called Bohemia "the best country of the north, and the best supplied with food stuffs," and he wrote that

> you can buy for one *kinshar* [a silver coin used at the tenth-century exchanges of Christian Europe] as much wheat as a man will need for one month, and for the same price as much barley as an animal transport will need for forty days, and further, for one *kinshar* ten hens. In the city of Fraga one makes saddles,

bridles and thick shields. In the country of Bujima [Bohemia] scarves are sold of thin linen, made to no practical purpose. The price is always ten scarves for one *kinshar*. These are used for exchange amongst themselves as well as for business. They have chests full of them; they buy wheat, slaves, horses, gold, silver, and everything else with it. It is strange that most inhabitants have brown or dark hair; the blond type is rare.

Ibrahim ends with a statement that is now much quoted by Czech historians, "The Slavs are courageous and brave, and were they not split up into several tribes and groups, no nation could overcome them by force."

Prague's early history reaches back into the early stone age, when the first settlers, members of an unknown tribe, lived on the hills overlooking the Moldau where they felt secure against attacks. During the later stone age they had settlements all over the heights, in the form of a large P, which Prague's mystics have interpreted as a symbolical monogram of the future capital of Bohemia. Traces of stone-age civilization have been found on the heights of Hradčany, Vyšehrad, Libeň, Bubeneč and Střešovice, where people lived long before "Praha," down by the river, became settled. Gradually people dared descend toward the Moldau. There was a ford near today's Rudolphinum and another between today's Charles Bridge and Mánes Bridge. Merchants from abroad stayed at the settlement before fording the river, to barter goods and catch their breath. Prior to the Christian era, Celtic and Teutonic tribes lived here. There was the short-lived empire of the Marcomanni and Quadi, and at the end of the first century A.D. the Roman Empire advanced its northern frontier toward the Danube. An inscription on a rock below Trenčín Castle in Western Slovakia reports of the victorious battle fought by the Second Roman Legion in

172 under Emperor Marcus Aurelius who completed his *Meditations* on the bank of the river Hron. He died eight years later in Vindobona.

Dramatic events occurred around Prague but, as an anonymous chronicler complains, "there was none in these days to set down in writing the deeds of their time." The first Slav tribes probably came from the region beyond the Carpathians. The tribe of the Czechs became installed on territory formerly occupied by the Boiens; other Slavs settled in Slovakia and Moravia. Then came the rise of the Great Moravian Empire, so powerful that both the Franks in the West and the Byzantines in the East tried to conquer it. The Byzantine Emperor Michael III sent two educated Greek monks, Constantine (Cyril) and Method, to spread the gospel to the Slavs. They were brothers from Salonika and prepared themselves for their task by creating, from the Greek alphabet, special characters for the Slav sounds and translating from the Bible some passages into Old Slavonic. They also introduced native language into the prayer books. (The Popes later forbade the use of Slav prayer books.) The Great Moravian Empire broke up around 907 after an invasion of the Magyars, but the Cyrillic alphabet has remained to this day, in Russia and Yugoslavia. Cyril and Method are venerated as the patron saints of Moravia.

During the past fifteen years, new archeological discoveries have shed more light on the foundation of Prague. The "stone book" of Hradčany, the Prague Castle—its history and architecture that can be read in the various strata of stone —proves that a fortified castle had been built there in the second half of the ninth century. "Prague is a sarcophagus of past centuries, petrified history, the heart of the Czech nation turned to stone," wrote Ferdinand Gustav Kühne. Hradčany is younger than the settlement down by the river. Centuries earlier, in the vicinity of today's Old Town Square, the two great European trade routes crossed each other—the north-south "amber" route and the West-East route between the Frankish Empire and Byzantium. The two routes crossed exactly where today's Rudolphinum (which was built in the 1880s as a concert hall, later served as the Parliament during Masaryk's Republic and now is again a concert hall, known as "House of the Artists") stands. There the caravans of Frankish, Byzantine, Arab and Jewish merchants forded their goods across the river. The nearby Jewish ghetto became a bartering place for agricultural products, textiles, leather goods and slaves.

Only later were the two castles of Prague built, overlooking the river: Hradčany and Vyšehrad ("The High Castle"), which lost much importance after the tenth century, and is now mainly a national symbol, the Czech pantheon where the nation buries its great dead. (The graves of Smetana and Dvořák are there; of the poets Karel Hynek Mácha, Julius Zeyer, Josef Hora and Vitězslav Nezval; of the writers Božená Němcova, Jan Neruda and Karel Čapek; of the painter Mikoláš Aleš; of the sculptor Jan Myslbek; of the violinist Jan Kubelik; and of many others.) The castles were built to protect the growing trade center of Prague which, in turn, owes its importance to the river. The Czechs say that it was the Moldau that founded Prague. They have a deep mystical love for their river, which flows through the entire length of Bohemia, from north to south. The people of Prague never get tired of watching the wild ducks and sea gulls on the Moldau embankment, sitting or flying there, always in pairs.

The first rulers of the Slav tribe of the Czechs were the ambitious Přemyslids who subjugated other tribes and gave the whole country the name "Čechy" (the Latin name was

"Bohemia.") Modern Czech historians assume that the Přemyslids were "inspired" to create their own state by the example of the Great Moravian Empire. Prince Bořivoj began the bloody struggle for unification, "with much internecine conflict." His son Spytihněv permanently transferred the residence of the Czech princes from Levý Hradec, about six miles north of Prague, to the Castle of Prague. The Czech princes soon attained a strong position in the German Empire and became members of the curia of seven electors who chose the Emperor.

The Czechs had been a heathen tribe until Prince Bořivoj and his wife Ludmila in 875 were baptized by Method in Velehrad, Moravia. The first church was built in Levý Hradec; the next up on Castle Hill in Prague, near the old heathen place of sacrifice, was consecrated to the Virgin Mary. (Remains were discovered in 1950, in the lowest stratum of masonry of the little Romanesque church below the Castle's western tract.)

Prince Wenceslas, who reigned from 892 to 929 and is now revered as Bohemia's patron saint, was not a warrior but rather a skilled politician. Realizing that his country was unable to contend with the German Empire he concluded a peace treaty with Henry I and received a precious relic, the arm of St. Vitus (who later became the patron saint of neighboring Saxony). To enshrine the relic, Wenceslas built a Roman rotunda; its foundations were later discovered under the present Chapel of St. Wenceslas. Wenceslas was murdered by his brother Boleslav I who disapproved of the Good King's friendly politics toward the German Empire.

During the next two centuries, the Přemyslids were involved in numerous fights against the Poles and the Magyars; one of them, Vladislav II, helped Frederick Barbarossa in the conquest of Milan. In 1212, Přemysl I was recognized as King of Bohemia by both the Pope and the German Emperor; the double-tailed lion in the Czechoslovak coat of arms dates from that time. The Czech kingdom prospered but today Marxist historians take a dim view of that era. ("The leading positions in the administration, trade and economic life of the royal towns were occupied by the wealthy burghers and patricians of German origin, and a tiny minority dominated the Czech people," writes Miloš Kratochvil. "The Czech inhabitants were craftsmen, less wealthy burghers, laborers and the poor. This created . . . a future discord capable of producing an explosion.")

King Přemysl Otakar II who ascended the throne in 1253 made his empire as big as later Austria-Hungary was. He extended his rule all the way to the Adriatic, conquered Austria, Styria, Carinthia. (He also founded Malá Strana, Prague's most aristocratic district, whose Baroque beauty has survived all of Přemysl Otakar's former acquisitions.) His prestige was great in Europe. Dante saluted him in the seventh canto of his "Purgatorio" as the future liberator of Italy, and the Austrian poet, Franz Grillparzer, made him the hero of his play, *König Ottokars Glück und Ende*. His luck ran out when he refused to recognize Rudolph von Habsburg whom the German princes had elected emperor. Přemysl Otakar was defeated on the Marchfeld, near Vienna, in 1278, and lost his life. (The Poles helped him; the Magyars had deserted him.) It was one of the decisive battles in European history, and made Vienna, not Prague, for the next seven hundred years the capital of a Central-European empire. The tragedy of Bohemia began on the Marchfeld: ever since, the Habsburgs wanted to dominate a Prague that might threaten the position of Vienna. The whole history of the Czech nation is an endless struggle

The Mystical City

against the Habsburgs, and often also against the Church that was allied with the Habsburgs.

Přemysl Otakar's successor, his son Wenceslas II, built himself a huge Slav empire—Bohemia, Moravia, Silesia, Hungary and Poland—but when *his* son, Wenceslas III, succeeded him in 1305 at the age of seventeen and was assassinated a year later, the dynasty died out. After much rivalry and fighting, John of Luxemburg (whose wife was a Přemyslid princess) became King of Bohemia in 1310. A busy warrior, he spent little time in Bohemia. But he succeeded in getting his son Charles elected as Holy Roman Emperor. Charles IV did more for Prague than any other man, before or after him, and made Prague, "his jewel," one of the world's fascinating cities. The people of Prague revere him as the real founder of their city. During his rule, Prague became the cultural center of Europe, and Hradčany the continent's largest, most powerful fortress.

Hradčany Castle, an immense conglomerate of historical epochs and architectural styles, has remained the seat of power in Bohemia from its foundation to this day. The President of the Socialist People's Republic of Czechoslovakia now resides there. Kings, emperors, architects, sculptors and painters had a hand in forming it but History remains its chief builder. The country's entire past is reflected in Hradčany. ("At certain times the dark shadow of a harsh and soulless imperial bureaucracy fell over the Castle," I read in a new history of the Castle.) The dark shadow is there again, though the bureaucracy is no longer "imperial."

The ground plan of Hradčany preserves the characteristics of the old Slavonic tribal strongholds. The inner ward was reached through a larger outer ward. Where tourists now

step through the main gate, there was a deep ditch with a
bridge that can be seen in older pictures. A baker had his
bakery oven there and the smoke from the chimney was said
to irritate the feudal inhabitants of the Castle. The ditch was
not filled until toward the end of the eighteenth century.

The oldest buildings on the Castle grounds were built in
Romanesque style. Around 1200, Prague was already a large
town with over fifty stone churches and houses, two castles,
a stone bridge and many works of art; the Romanesque style
lived longer here than in Western Europe and was followed,
after 1230, by the early Gothic. The center of the Castle was
then the Romanesque basilica that Spytihněv had built on
the site of Wenceslas' modest rotunda. (The Wenceslas cult
had already become so strong that the rotunda became too
small for the crowds that came to pray here.) Nearby was
the grave of St. Adalbert, a former bishop of Prague who
died "as a martyr" on a missionary expedition to the Baltic
and was canonized. There were other churches inside the
Castle—the Chapel of St. Maurice, the Church of St. George,
the small Church of the Virgin. Hradčany was becoming a
small town of sacred buildings. And then Charles IV made
his entrance at the Castle.

He had grown up in Paris where he changed his Czech
first name "Václav" (Wenceslas), which was hard to pronounce for the French, to "Charles." His teacher was Pierre
Roger, later Pope Clemens VI. He was educated according to
the French *studium generale*, had studied the centralism of
the French kings, and learned a lot about practical politics
during a long stay in Italy. He was only eighteen when he
came to Prague but he must have been an unusual young
man, and he decided to bring the French-Gothic culture to
his court in Prague and make it a sort of Central-European
Paris. He didn't get along with his father, who still lived in

the Medieval Age while Charles sensed the ideas of a new era. He forbade searching for "hidden treasures" in churches or in the Old-New Synagogue, as his father had done when he needed money. (Usually, all males in the ghetto were arrested and released only after paying ransom, a popular method of collecting money.)

Charles understood the national complexity of Bohemia; he made it quite clear that he needed them all—Czechs, Germans, Jews. His coronation procession moved from Vyšehrad to Hradčany, the two great castles of the Czechs, but later he had his wedding meal in Old Town Square where the German burghers had their houses. In his decrees he talks of "the sweet, tender sound of the Czech language, the noble Slav idiom," and at the same time negotiates with the German Hanse, and he also tries to establish a new trade route from Venice to Bruges, by way of Prague. Charles IV sensed that Prague was the heart of Europe—centuries before modern statesmen and military strategists knew it.

Charles IV is not popular with modern (Communist) Czech historians. An official publication, *The Prague Castle*, calls him "an ardent propagator of the St. Wenceslas state cult . . . His religious fervor was deeply tinged with mysticism and a strong sense of dynastic tradition." Charles was a mystic among mystics and "the embodiment of medieval feudalism," as they now say. He also remains the great national king to the Czech nation. He was, and still is very popular. Some admire him for his robust constitution; he survived four wives, including Elizabeth of Pommern, a strong woman who was said to be able to bend a sword in her hands. The people of Prague remember Charles IV as they walk through the squares and streets of the New Town he founded, past the churches and convents he built, and across the magnificent stone bridge named after him.

He was a passionate builder and a visionary: a perfect combination. "It was in the happy time of the Middle Ages, only just free from barbarism, but still lacking the hustle of Modern Times," writes Jacques Guenne. Charles IV called his builders and ordered a Gothic town the way other mortals order a new suit. When he first saw Hradčany, which had been devastated in 1303 by a terrible fire, he immediately planned its reconstruction *ad instar domus regis Franciae*, "after the example of the King of France." He ordered a new royal palace built, with a beautiful chapel patterned after Sainte-Chapelle in Paris. And he vowed to build a dome "that would equal the largest in the Occident" on the site of the old Romanesque basilica. In France and Germany, the great cathedrals were built with the help of powerful guilds and religious fraternities; in Prague, the great Gothic Cathedral of St. Vitus is the personal conception of Charles IV. He summoned the French architect and master-builder, Matthias of Arras, from Avignon, who began the work in 1344 and directed it for eight years. (Remains of the old rotunda are still beneath the floor of the Cathedral.) After Matthias' death, the Emperor showed again his amazing flair for gifted artists when he assigned an unknown, twenty-three-year-old German sculptor and builder, Peter Parler of Gmünd, to become Matthias' successor. Peter Parler did for the Gothic Prague what Johann Bernard Fischer von Erlach later did for the Baroque Vienna: he brought a foreign style to Prague which under the powerful influence of the *genius loci* became an indigenous style. The dreams of Charles IV, the great mystic, often touched the sky, and Peter Parler sensed it: the Gothic style made the city the "Prague of the Hundred Towers." ("They built edifices for the sake of spires, towers, belfreys and watch-towers," writes Guenne.)

The immense Gothic tower at the southern end of the

The Mystical City

Cathedral, the visible symbol of the silhouette of Hradčany —and of Prague—remains the subject of much speculation among the experts. Why did Parler sacrifice the symmetry of the ground plan when he placed the tower in a position contrary to the philosophy and the tradition of Gothic church architecture? Parler's sketches no longer exist. One doesn't know whether the position of the tower was his idea or the Emperor's. There are experts in today's Prague who believe that Charles IV wanted to create a "symbolic" tower in Hradčany which had no donjon, as other medieval fortresses —replacing, so to speak, the tower's defensive function by a mystical power. Thus the foundations of the tower are close to the sacred spot where the remains of St. Wenceslas, Bohemia's patron saint, were buried—the spiritual heart of the great Cathedral. ("For us who belong to the scientifically-minded twentieth century . . . a symbolic tower, on an ideal, mystical plane may seem altogether fantastic yet it fully corresponded to the mentality of medieval people in the thrall of religious notions," writes Václav Formánek.)

Another question remains unanswered: what would the St. Vitus Cathedral's appearance be if it had been finished according to the original designs of Peter Parler? It took over six hundred years to build St. Vitus Cathedral and it still isn't completed. The western part was built by architects of the nineteenth and twentieth centuries. Many people sense that the western part doesn't have the daring and originality that distinguishes Peter Parler's best work.

During his last eight years, Matthias of Arras built eight apsidal chapels and an arcade resting on nine pillars, raising the building to the height of the lower cornice of the triforium. Peter Parler completed the remaining part below the triforium, and did all the work from the triforium upward. There is an unmistakable difference in the style of the two masters. The pillars of Matthias are distinguished works of art but betray an academic sense of exactness. He was very much concerned with detail and sometimes there is a certain sharpness in his work. Parler's pillars show boldness of imagination and vitality of spirit. They seem to have a secret life of their own, as so many great sculptures. Parler was more concerned with power and sweep than with detail and execution. His shafts climb up beside the pillars to the top of the vault, cutting through the horizontal cornices. His windows have chamfered corners and beautifully designed tracery. The sexpartite vault conveys a sense of the dynamic. He was a very great builder, and his portrait sculptures— Charles IV, his four wives, other members of the Luxemburg dynasty, Matthias of Arras and Peter Parler himself, looking quite pleased with his work—are among the great works of European sculptural portraiture. And St. Wenceslas Chapel, which Parler built from 1362 to 1364, is one of the finest achievements of Czech Gothic.

In 1354, Charles IV had written to Archbishop Arnošt of Pardubice, "I think you will not find a town or a city in Europe, with the exception of Rome, where the pilgrim will see more relics than in the metropolitan Cathedral of St. Vitus." He was a passionate collector who often demanded relics and liturgical vessels as gifts; and who dared refuse the Emperor's request? Perhaps he had more enthusiasm than taste; he occasionally became the victim of forgers. But he assembled the largest part of the St. Vitus Treasure, which is the richest collection of relics in Central Europe. (In 1961, the present regime deposited the "artistically most valuable items" at the Castle Chapel of the Holy Rood that was built in 1753 by Anselmo Lurago, leaving "relics of saints and objects of no artistic value" at the Cathedral, which may not have been the intention of Charles IV.)

The Mystical City

The St. Vitus Treasure contains, among hundreds of items, relics of the Bohemian patron saints—the skulls of St. Wenceslas and St. Adalbert, the helm of St. Wenceslas, the sword of St. Stephen, the mitre of St. Adalbert, a Gothic silver statue of St. Ludmilla, a Gothic gold coronation cross, a French ivory statuette of Our Lady, the golden Zavis Cross, with fine thirteenth-century, Byzantine enamel work, "the veil of St. Mary" (No. 80,b), "part of Christ's Cross" (No. 83), "the sponge that was given to Christ on the Cross to quench His Thirst," "the staff of Moses," and numerous monstrances and chalices, as well as "curiosities from the domain of zoology." One of the greatest Czech relics, preserved at the tomb of St. John Nepomuk, is the Saint's tongue encased in a monstrance-like reliquary.

Perhaps the most valuable parts of the Treasure are the Bohemian coronation jewels: the royal crown in its original leather case, orb and scepter, and the coronation robe of red brocade. Charles IV founded the cult of the sacred Bohemian crown which was made to order in 1346 from the old coronation jewels. He was the first man to wear it, and he made a reliquary of it. In the top of the sapphire cross a thorn is inserted that is said to come from Christ's Crown of Thorns. Charles dedicated the crown to St. Wenceslas on whose skull it now lies. The crown weighs five pounds, is adorned with ninety-one precious stones and, according to the guides who take you around St. Vitus, is "as valuable as the whole Cathedral." Charles designed the ritual for use of the crown which may be removed only for the coronation of a new king, never longer than for one day. A fee of 200 talers must be paid for the benefit of the Cathedral Chapter. The last coronation took place on September 7, 1836, when Ferdinand V, the Emperor of Austria, known as *der Gütige* (the Good One), had himself crowned as King of Bohemia. Ilsa Barea calls him "mentally backward, feeble-minded if kindly; his condition was no secret." In the 1860s, the northern part of the Castle was restored for the projected coronation of Franz Joseph I which never took place though, because it would have given Bohemia at least temporarily the right of self-government. Vienna was against it.

An old Czech myth says that no man except the future king must place the Czech crown on his head. This makes the coronation valid. Anyone else who dares set the Bohemian crown on his head will die an unnatural death. When Reinhard Heydrich, the hated "Reichsprotektor," visited St. Vitus and heard about the myth, he laughed and put the crown on his head. Several weeks later, in June, 1942, Heydrich was assassinated outside of Prague, whereupon Hitler ordered the village of nearby Lidice "erased" in a wholly arbitrary and "terrifying demonstration of the strength of the Third Reich." The village's entire male population, a hundred and ninety-two men and boys, from sixteen to eighty-four, were shot.

Originally, the coronation jewels were kept in an underground chamber near the grave of St. Wenceslas. During the Hussite wars they were transferred to Karlštejn Castle and were shown to "the noblest personages" only with permission of the Bohemian Estates. When they were brought to Prague for a coronation, they were accompanied by the highest dignitaries of the realm, and, just to be safe, by two hundred riders. During the Thirty Years' War, the jewels were taken to a secret hiding place in the collegiate church of České Budějovice. Ferdinand III of Habsburg, after his coronation in Prague, took them to Vienna where they were exhibited at the Schatzkammer of the Vienna Burg. Another Habsburg ruler, Leopold II, returned them to Prague, at the urgent request of the Bohemian Estates. The coronation jewels were deposited in the chamber of the Golden Gate where, at this writing, they still are. The safety measures are regulated by ancient custom: the chamber is closed with seven locks, each of which is opened by a key kept by the President, the Lord Mayor of Prague, the Archbishop and so on. In the case of an impending attack on the Castle, the jewels will be taken to the underground vaults below the old Soběslav Palace.

Work in St. Vitus Cathedral never comes to an end. Prior to the Second World War, the modern Czech painter Max Švabinský painted the middle window at the eastern end illuminating the choir. Švabinský loved to go to the Old Jewish Cemetery for meditation and inspiration. A modern Prague mystic, he felt equally at home near the austere stone sarcophagus of the High Rabbi Loew (1609) and near the pompous silver Baroque tomb of St. John Nepomuk in St. Vitus Cathedral, made in the 1730s by Joseph Emanuel Fischer von Erlach. A present-day restoration problem concerns the fourteenth-century mosaics of Venetian origin above the Cathedral's original main entrance, on the wall containing the Golden Portal. It shows the Casting of the Damned into Hell, the Resurrection, and Charles IV, kneeling in the company of several saints. (The Emperor loved a little publicity, and we must not blame him.) The colors of the mosaics have turned dull, and experts are trying to protect them against the vicissitudes of the climate.

On a wooded hill overlooking the lovely valley of the Berounka river, a short ride from Prague, Charles IV built himself the Castle of Karlštejn, his strange retreat with a French donjon and French-Gothic chapels on the upper floors, a shrine for his sacred relics in whose miraculous power he believed. The walls of his private chapel are covered with amethysts, carnelians and other precious stones that shimmer in a mystic half-dimness, and the ceiling is covered with large frescoes. "All over the earth no other castle contains such treasures," Beneš von Weitmühl, the Emperor's historian, wrote with more enthusiasm than accuracy.

At the same time, the improbable mystic personally conceived and designed the New Town of Prague, which he called "the work of Our hands," between Cattle Market (now Charles Square) and Horse Market (now Wenceslas Square). "No doubt, Wenceslas Square made Prague a European capital though it was probably more beautiful as a provincial square," writes Wilhelm Hausenstein. Charles IV designed the system of longitudinal blocks with cross streets that still exists. It was walled toward east and south, with five gates leading out. It was to be a Czech town. Special decrees promised civic liberties to new settlers. The ground would become the property of the inhabitants; for the first twelve years everybody was freed from taxation, "provided the settler started to build one month after receiving the ground, and would have his house ready within eighteen months." A very modern inducement; and it was also decreed that no property could be mortgaged higher than half its value. The great mystic was a gifted town planner. Jews from the ghetto in the Old Town were not permitted to move into the New Town, but Jews from abroad were welcome. These inducements attracted many people. Eleven years after the foundation of the New Town there were over a hundred butchers there. The citizens of Prague were given many privileges. They could travel to all towns in Germany and to Venice without paying customs duties. Prague was the first town in Central Europe with paved streets that were

The Mystical City

regularly cleaned; since 1340, the whole town had a contract with one Jindřich Mithard "to clean the streets before All Saints' Day and keep them clean thereafter." At the end of Charles's reign, Prague had become a city of forty thousand people and had over four thousand houses. (After the devastation of the Hussite wars, in the sixteenth century, there were less than two thousand nine hundred houses.) A chronicler noted that Charles IV "loves this town more than all other places in his Empire."

In 1348—the very year he founded the New Town—Charles also founded Prague University, one year after Pope Clemens VI, Charles's former teacher, had agreed that in Prague, after the example of Bologna and Paris, *"studium generale vigeat in qualibet facultate."* In 1344, the Emperor had persuaded the Pope to make Prague the seat of an Archbishop—an ambition that the Kings of Bohemia had had for centuries. Charles ordered Czech translations made of Latin legends and meditations; at the Archbishop's residence (today just outside the entrance gate of Hradčany), a copyists' school produced copies of the Holy Scriptures for all convents in the country. The university—the first in Central Europe—was a Church institution. The Archbishop of Prague was also the university's Chancellor. The university would make sure that "the nation may find the fruits of learning set out on its own table." There were four faculties—theology, law, medicine, the arts. The *universitas* of magisters, baccalaurei and students elected the rector. The students were organized by national groups; members of the "Bohemian nation" were not only Czechs and Germans living in Bohemia, but also Hungarians. Famous law teachers were induced to come from Bologna, art professors from Paris. The professors lectured at home, priests in their convents. Soon the *studium generale* in Prague became renowned all over the Christian world. A few years after its foundation, the university had over a thousand students.

Prague was growing, and there were not enough churches for the faithful ones. Charles began to build churches and convents all over town: the Church of Our Lady of the Snow (kostel Panny Marie Sněžné) for the Carmelites; St. Ambrosius; St. Stephen's; St. Henry's, near today's Wenceslas Square; and he supervised the Gothic reconstruction of the old basilica in Vyšehrad. In the heart of the Old Town, near the university and the Old Town Square, the merchants and burghers built the Church of Our Lady of Týn that has remained to this day a sort of people's church in Prague. Jan Hus preached there, later followed by Ultraquist bishops, and Týn Church became *the* Hussite church.

Charles also built the great Monastery of Emmaus ("Na Slovanech") for the Slavonic Benedictines, as "a center of education and the arts." Emmaus later had a violent history, typical of Prague. In 1419, the Benedictines joined the Hussites. The monastery remained untouched during the Hussite wars. In 1445, it became the only Hussite monastery on earth. (Yet the Slavonic part of the Rheims Gospels, on which the Kings of France took the coronation oath until 1782, came from Emmaus.) During the Counter-Reformation, Spanish Benedictines came to Emmaus from Montserrat, the mystic mountain monastery near Barcelona, where Richard Wagner placed his Holy Grail in *Parsifal*. The Spanish monks restyled the Gothic monastery in Baroque, but the Beuron Benedictines who took the monastery over in 1880, after being banished from Germany, restored the building to its earlier Gothic appearance. In 1918, the monastery became Czech. In 1939, the Czech monks were driven out by the Nazis. A few weeks before the end of the war, the

The Mystical City

monastery was hit by "Anglo-American" bombs and burned out. In 1959, the monastery was restored and is now used as a secular building, housing several research institutes of the Czechoslovak Academy of Sciences.

Prague at the time of Charles IV was one large building site where Peter Parler installed an immense artistic workshop. Painters and sculptors were needed to decorate the new churches and palaces. Nikolaus Wurmser from Strasbourg became the Emperor's "court painter." The Italian tradition was represented by Tomaso Barisini from Modena. A local master, Theodoric, worked in Karlštejn. The nobility and the rich burghers also commissioned artists, who began to specialize. Some did only frescoes, while others created illuminated manuscripts, beautifully drawn and colored, showing both the Italian and French influence. The artists of Prague were organized in a *Zeche* (guild), one of Europe's earliest artists' academies. Their social status was so high that Peter Parler and his assistants dared place the portraits of the builders of St. Vitus Cathedral in the triforium, next to those of members of the ruling dynasty. Parler hardly could have done it without the Emperor's permission.

Cola di Rienzo came from Rome, an excommunicated fugitive with great ideas, and was an honored guest at Hradčany; but eventually Charles handed him over to the Archbishop, and two years later the great visionary, "God's tribune," wound up in Rome again, before the Papal judges. In 1356, Petrarch came to Prague, talked with the Emperor and after his return to Rome wrote excited letters to his new friends in Prague.

The following year, Peter Parler began to work on the most daring project of his life—the great bridge named after Charles that poets, painters, sculptors and a great many other people (not only in Prague) consider the most beautiful stone bridge on earth. It replaced an earlier, twelfth-century stone bridge that had been constructed by order of Judith, the wife of King Wladislaw I, and had been badly damaged by flood and ice. The remains of the old bridge had to be carried away with the help of primitive cranes; and sixteen pillars were sunk into the river next to the old foundations. (Some remains of the old pillars still remain on the Malá Strana bank.) Charles Bridge, the greatest among Prague's fourteen bridges, is half a kilometer long and ten meters wide. It is not straight but slightly curved against the flow of the river, for aesthetic and technical reasons, in order to deviate the pressure of the waves. Perhaps there was also a strategic reason: from the western bridgehead in Malá Strana the whole bridge could be easily protected. (During the Revolution in March, 1848, Prince Windischgraetz, the Austrian commander, occupied the western approaches of Charles Bridge and turned his guns against the Old Town.)

The unique beauty of Charles Bridge is due to the dramatic contrast of Romanesque elements (the heavy stones of the foundations) and the elegance of the Gothic arches and Gothic bridge towers on both sides, and the harmonious effect created by the statues of Baroque saints. The church tower on the eastern (Old Town) bank of the river is Europe's most beautiful medieval bridge tower. Peter Parler built it on the first pier of the bridge; and he created the magnificent sculptural decorations. Most people headed for Charles Bridge are so eager to see the famous bridge saints, with the magical silhouette of Malá Strana's Baroque cupolas and the Hradčany against the western sky in the rear that they pay scant attention to Parler's masterpiece. The sculptural decorations on the side facing the square have been preserved almost intact; the decorations on the side looking out on the bridge were destroyed during the Swedish siege of 1648. High up looking onto the square are sculptures of St. Adalbert and St. Sigismund and below them, on either side of a statue of St. Vitus, are the seated figures of Charles IV (who always had to be in the picture) and his son, Wenceslas IV. The face of St. Vitus is unforgettably moving. The lower part of the tower served as a prison for bankrupt debtors. The upper part was used by their guards, who enjoyed one of the finest views of Prague. On the Malá Strana side there are two towers as a counterpart to the tower on the Old Town side but they are much less beautiful.

The parapets of Charles Bridge are decorated with thirty statues and sculptural groups of saints, made of sandstone that has become black. They give the bridge a mystical beauty, especially at night, when the lights accentuate the deep shadows and bring the exultant Baroque saints to life. Most statues were set up at the turn of the seventeenth and eighteenth centuries when the bridge was already a few hundred years old, and some had to be replaced rather recently. St. Francis of Assisi was put up in 1855, donated by Count Kolovrat-Liebsteinský in memory of the attempted assassination of Emperor Franz Joseph I in Vienna (where the Votive Church is a reminder of it). The statue of Cyril and Method was put up in 1938, during the celebrations of the twentieth birthday of the Czechoslovak Republic.

Though the statues vary considerably in their artistic value, they form an aesthetic unity with the older bridge. The finest sculpture is the statue of St. Luitgarda, made in 1710 by the great Baroque sculptor Matthias Braun from Innsbruck; the most interesting is the gilded bronze cross with the Corpus Christi, and the Hebrew inscription; the most shocking, at least to the English-born wife of Frederick of Palatinate, the "Winter King," was the undressed figure of Christ on the Gothic cross; and the most popular, oldest statue on the bridge is St. John Nepomuk, with a bas-relief on the balustrade, showing the Saint's martyrdom. The statue, by Johann Brokoff and Matthias Rauchmiller, became the prototype of hundreds of similar statues all over Bohemia. Another interesting statue is Ferdinand Brokoff's St. Procopius, who is said to have "resurrected forty people from the dead and exorcized seventy devils." Such miracles are common knowledge in Prague, even today.

When Charles died in Prague in 1378 and was buried in the Royal Crypt of St. Vitus Cathedral, there were seventy-six churches and chapels in town, twenty-four convents and monasteries, and also twelve hundred priests who were exempt from taxes. Prague was a center of Church life in Europe, with all its pomp. But there had been a serious famine in the 1360s, and there was growing resentment against the moral debasement of the clergy. ("The bright aspects of Charles's reign throw its shadows into clear relief," writes Miloš Kratochvil, the present-day historian. "Wealth and prosperity were the prerogative of the royal court, the feudal lords, and the Church hierarchy. Charles was lavish in his support of the hierarchy because he considered it needful to keep in favor with his ally, the Pope. The rich burgher families too, and the traders and financiers prospered.")

That's what the children in Prague learn about Charles IV today. It is true but not the whole story. In his autobiographical writings, Charles IV expresses his fear of future dangers. He was not anti-social, he worried about hunger and poverty among his people, and he sensed the dark undercurrents that eventually led to the Reformation. He was suffering from a terrible guilt complex. Once Johann Milic of Kroměřiž, the fanatic Moravian preacher, who campaigned against loose life and "the wicked follies of fashion

The Mystical City

. . . the close-fitting men's clothes and low-cut women's dresses" had publicly called the Emperor "the anti-Christ," and Charles IV had done nothing about it. At the end of his life, the pious mystic was tortured by terrible doubts.

His son, Wenceslas IV, was too weak to carry on his father's inheritance. Appearances were deceiving in Prague. "I never saw such a rich city, so inundated with all kinds of things," wrote Uberto Decembrio, member of a delegation from Milan, in 1399. "When you go shopping, better think of old Cato, 'Beware, or you will come home with an empty purse.' The city has almost the appearance of the city of Romulus. Like Rome, Prague is adorned with hills and valleys, instead of the Tiber the Moldau is flowing through the town and across the river Charles built his glorious bridge . . ." The Milanese is highly critical of people's pleasures, the free life in the streets, and the university "which is more renowned in the arts and theology than in jurisprudence and medicine."

Uberto Decembrio didn't see underneath the glitter and luxury the growing social conflicts—between Wenceslas and the high nobility, between the high and the lesser nobility, between wealthy German burghers and the Czech working population, between the high Church hierarchy and the poor clergy. The Church owned almost half the cultivated land in the Czech kingdom through parishes and monasteries. There were similar tensions in France, Italy and England, but when they erupted in Bohemia, nineteen years after Wenceslas IV was deposed by the Electors in 1400, they shook "the heart of Europe" and later the entire continent. At last, there came the revolution Charles IV had been afraid of.

Twice the people of Prague reacted toward a political crisis (and made world history) by throwing their foes out of the window. Both Prague defenestrations started a chain reaction of events which no one could have foreseen. The first, in 1419, put into motion the Hussite revolutionary forces, which in turn led to the Reformation all over Europe. The second, in 1618, marked the beginning of the Thirty Years' War and "the Age of Darkness" in Bohemia's history. (And in 1948, Jan Masaryk, Czechoslovakia's Foreign Minister, died after a fall from a high window in the courtyard of Černín Palace, the Foreign Office. Perhaps he couldn't bear it that his world, and the world of his father, Tomáš G. Masaryk, was gone, and that the dark age of Stalinism had started. Or, perhaps future historians will once call his death the third Prague defenestration.)

The first defenestration occurred four years after Jan Hus had died as a heretic on the stake. Hus, a Catholic priest and Rector of Prague University, had preached from the pulpit of Bethlehem Chapel, which had been founded in 1391 by the merchants and burghers of the Old Town and thus was not under ecclesiastical authority. In today's Prague, Bethlehem Chapel is "one of the most hallowed places of the Czech nation," according to Alois Svoboda's *Prague* (1965):

Master John Hus preached here in Czech to the citizens of Prague. The fearless reformer of the Church and the founder of the revolutionary movement which shook the foundations all over Europe in the fifteenth century, was strongly influenced by the teachings of John Wycliffe of Oxford . . . Hus was followed in the pulpit of Bethlehem Chapel by other Hussite preachers. A hundred years later, Thomas Münzer preached here who tried to link up the tradition of the Hussite revolutionary movement with the growing revolutionary trends in Germany. After the victory of the Counter-Reformation, the Chapel was assigned to the Jesuits who destroyed every reminiscence of its revolutionary past: in 1786, it was demolished and the whole area built up with blocks of flats. In 1954, the Chapel was reconstructed, at great cost and effort, and the remains incorporated in the blocks of flats after old pictures, along with revolutionary inscriptions and Biblical texts which originally adorned the walls.

Bethlehem—that was Hus's life and struggle. In Bethlehem Chapel no high mass must be celebrated. According to a Church encyclical it remained forever a "chapel" though it could hold up to three thousand people, almost a tenth of the population of Prague at that time.

The restoration of "one of the most hallowed places" was a sacred obligation for the Communist regime, and created considerable problems. Shortly after the First World War, Alois Kubiček, a Prague architect, studied the old protocols of the Municipal Building Commission. One sentence attracted his attention: it said that for the new (post-1786) buildings in Bethelehem Square the old walls of the Chapel were retained "up to the second-floor level." Kubiček went to Bethlehem Square and traced the old walls of the Chapel in House No. 255 where a pork butcher made some delicious Prague sausages in his smoking chamber. The pork butcher was a patriot. Kubiček obtained permission to investigate. He broke down the walls and found a Gothic portal, the original entrance to the Chapel, and later he discovered three windows, a well and the foundations of several pillars. On the second floor, fragments of Hussite inscriptions were uncovered.

Kubiček reported his findings to the authorities but nothing happened. Not till the early 1950s did the Communist government order the reconstruction of Bethlehem Chapel. Property deeds, pictures, plans, were studied, samples of mortar were analyzed, part of the text from Hus's writings on the six heresies were uncovered on the Chapel walls. On the basis of all available information, Jaroslav Fragner, a noted architect, re-created the design for the Chapel. He was quite pleased *after* completion of the reconstructed Chapel, when an archivist in Mnichovo Hradiště found in an old book a plan of Bethlehem Chapel, dated 1786, after the demolition of the Chapel had been ordered. It turned out that the curbstone of the wall inside the Chapel, as Fragner had replaced it, differed from the plan of the original Chapel only by several centimeters in height. No effort nor expense were spared to recreate not only the Chapel but also its original atmosphere. Professors of the Academy of Arts projected on the walls of the Chapel color slides from old chronicles, and the contours were drawn into the damp plaster. The oak used for the door was sprayed under pressure with sand to give it the proper patina. Even experts would find it hard to guess that it was made from trees that had not yet been planted in the days of Jan Hus.

The Hussite movement was a genuine national revolution and the greatest moment in Czech history. Although it ended after an inglorious climax, its memory has sustained the identity of the Czech nation for five hundred years. It began as an intellectual movement. Hus was in close contact with the professors at the universities of Paris and Oxford. Other Czech writers also wrote clerical polemics, among them the Evangelist Petr Chelčický who called for a spiritual struggle of the people against their oppressors. At first, Hus only criticized the Church's "excessive love of gold," the priests' prebends, the indulgences guaranteeing salvation. Then he went further. He told the people that in the Lord's Prayer it does not say "*my* daily bread" but "*our* daily bread." It wasn't God's will that many starved while a few had too much. At the advice of Hus, King Wenceslas IV, by the Decree of Kutná Hora, modified the constitution of

Prague University and gave the Czechs and the Germans residing in Bohemia a majority of the votes. ("The national element in Hus's activities became obvious," wrote Oskar Schürer in *Prag*, published in 1935, and later considered the standard work during Hitler's occupation. "The Germans were infuriated. Over a thousand German professors emigrated to Erfurt and Leipzig . . .")

Hus reached the danger zone of "heresy" when he expressed doubts in the infallibility of the Pope and reserved absolute authority only to "the Word of God" (the Bible), which even the highest cleric must obey. John Wycliffe earlier confined his criticism to Latin tracts that were read mainly by theologians within the walls of universities. Hus addressed himself in Czech to the people of Prague, and they understood him. The Archbishop of Prague summoned Hus to renounce Wycliffe's doctrines. Hus refused to recant, left Prague in 1412 and began to preach in the countryside. There he also wrote grammatical works upholding the purity of the Czech language.

Eventually Hus became too much of a danger to the Church and was summoned to come to the Council of Constance and to defend his doctrine. The Holy German Emperor, Sigismund, the brother of the deposed Wenceslas IV, offered Hus an imperial promise of safe-conduct. But when Hus arrived in Constance, he was thrown into prison and charged with heresy. He was not allowed to defend himself. In vain he demanded that he should be "convinced and convicted" of his errors. He unconditionally refused to recant all that he had taught. On June 6, 1415, he was burned at the stake as an "incorrigible heretic."

Four years later, while unrest was mounting in Bohemia, Wenceslas IV, who had been deposed by the Electors in 1400, died. The Czechs refused to recognize Wenceslas' brother Sigismund as King of Bohemia. They said Sigismund had broken his word and handed over Hus to the Church. Riots started in Prague. At the Old Town Hall, seven of the King's envoys were thrown by the enraged Czechs through a large window into Old Town Square, where they landed on the pikes of the Hussite soldiers below. The Hussites set up their headquarters in the Bohemian town of Tábor (the fifth movement in Smetana's symphonic poem *My Country* is called "Tábor"), and called it "The Kingdom of God in Bohemia" (the title of a stirring play by the young Franz Werfel that was a great success at the Czech National Theater in Prague). Present-day historians consider Tábor "the first attempt to build a classless society ... The brave experiment was doomed to failure. Time was not ready yet for such a society."

The revolutionary Hussite movement broke up the old order. The Hussites claimed that not only bread but also wine must be received in the sacrament by every believer. The chalice as a religious symbol appeared on the Hussite banners. "Communion in both kinds" was one of the four principles demanded by the Hussites in the Prague Articles; the others were free preaching, removal of the worldly wealth of the priests, and punishment for mortal sins inflicted on all, whoever they were. The Hussite forces, mostly peasants and people from small towns armed with scythes, spiked flails, and spiked iron balls attached to chains, were led by the brilliant, one-eyed commander, John Žižka of Trocnov. (Prague's Vítkov Hill, where Žižka in 1420 won two victories, later became the district of "Žižkov.") The Hussites were badly outnumbered by the crusading knights and their mercenaries who wore heavy armor from head to foot. But the Hussites' fighting morale was stronger than armor, and they outfought their enemies by revolutionary tactics. Žižka would form a solid phalanx made of farm wagons manned by marksmen who repulsed powerful cavalry charges. The Hussites' indomitable spirit was feared by their adversaries. Once, at Domažlice, the crusaders fled from the battlefield when the Hussites advanced toward them, chanting their battle hymn "Ye Warriors of God."

After Žižka's death, Prokop Holý ("the Bald-Headed") took command of the Hussite forces. The Hussite forces reached beyond the frontiers of Bohemia, making "glorious raids" into Germany (where they reached the Baltic Sea in 1433), France, Belgium and Spain. Peter Payne, an English preacher and follower of Wycliffe, joined the Hussites in Bohemia. Latin manifestoes explained the Prague Article to people all over Europe. The response was strong in rural areas of Germany.

The Hussites were never defeated by their foes, but the movement broke up when the Emperor and the Pope opened secret negotiations in Basel with Hussite nobles, and concluded a secret treaty with them. The Basel *Compactata* were the result; the Church agreed to "Communion in both kinds," and Emperor Sigismund promised to recognize the confiscation of Church property. The Hussite nobles accepted the *Compactata* but the uncompromising field armies turned them down. At Lipany, in 1434, the two groups virtually exterminated each other in a fraticidal battle—another tragedy in Czech history, and a decisive date in Europe's history. In 1436, Sigismund at last ascended to the Czech throne. The Basel *Compactata* became the legal foundation of the Calixtine (Hussite) Church. The Hussites—and later their successors, the Utraquists—retained their own liturgy (Czech services, the chalice), and did not acknowledge papal authority. For the first time the absolutist power of Roman Catholicism had been broken.

A century later, Martin Luther called Jan Hus his predecessor. "In truth, I and all of us want to defend Jan Hus, and if all of Bohemia should reject him, which God forbid, he shall be ours!"

After an interregnum, during which the Hussite King George of Poděbrady and the dynasty of the Jagellons ruled in Bohemia, the Czech Estates in 1526 elected Ferdinand of Habsburg to be King of Bohemia. (Ferdinand's brother, Charles Quint, already controlled Spain, Flanders, Austria and Germany, and in 1521 he had divided his possessions with Ferdinand who had married Anna of Hungary and Bohemia, increasing the Habsburg possessions through another appropriate marriage, in accordance with the Habsburg House policy.) Ferdinand, the favorite grandson of King Ferdinand of Aragon, had been educated in Spain where the Inquisition had taught him how to deal with "heretics." After his brother's death he became Emperor Ferdinand I and and at once began the battle against the Protestant Estates in Vienna, then predominantly a Protestant town. He started out with ordinances and letters-patent, and continued with missionaries and executions. He crushed the mutiny of the Protestant Lower-Austrian Estates and had their leaders executed; he himself acted as presiding judge of the tribunal. In Prague, he crushed the "first revolt" of the Czech Estates, and had some of them tortured and executed. By 1551, he felt strong enough to call the Jesuits to Vienna and Prague; the Jesuit Canisius became his chief adviser.

At Hradčany Castle, Ferdinand introduced a style of ruling that was different from that of his predecessors, the Czech kings. Ferdinand saw himself as a Prince of the Renaissance. He didn't consider the Gothic Castle adequate for the luxuries of his court. Landscape compositions and formal gardens were laid out. There was not enough room in the Castle's inner area, and the architects created the Royal Garden at the farther side of Stag Moat, which is connected with the Castle by the Powder Bridge. In 1538, Paolo della Stella, an Italian architect, began work on the Belvedere, the new summer palace, a charming, elegant building with slender colonnades; later two other architects, Hans von Tirol and Boniface Wohlmuth of Constance, didn't improve its appearance by adding a top floor and a copper roof. New living apartments were built in the south wing of the Castle, and the former royal apartments at the Old Palace were converted into offices and archives—the Office of the Bohemian Nobiliary, the Bohemian Chancellery, the Imperial Chancellery.

After the terrible fire of 1541 in Malá Strana which spread all the way to the Castle and caused enormous damage, Hans von Tirol worked together with della Stella on many projects. Reconstruction and new building went on side by side. Wohlmuth created the Renaissance helm-shaped cupola that has puzzled many experts on the Czech-Gothic tower of St. Vitus Cathedral; he also built the Renaissance choir on the western side of the uncompleted Cathedral (which was transferred in 1925 to the northern part of the crossing). In the Old Diet, Wohlmuth constructed a new vault, imitating out of admiration the Late Gothic style of an earlier architectural genius, Benedikt Rejt of Pistov whose greatest work at the Castle is the present Vladislav Hall, one of the largest throne rooms in Europe. Built between 1487 and 1500, it combines the spirit of the Late Gothic (the vaulted ceiling with intersecting curved ribs) and the Early Renaissance (the windows). The great architects of the transitional periods were able to combine various styles into a harmonious whole. Rejt's famous doorway that opens into the Riders' Staircase is a mixture of Romanesque reminiscences with a successful blend of Late Gothic and Renaissance elements. In the northwest corner of the Diet, Wohlmuth built a Renaissance tribune. With an Italian architect, Oldřich Avostalis, he added a court for ball games. The Castle was beginning to look like a great Renaissance residence while Prague remained a Gothic city. Only the ruler was missing who would express the spirit of a complex, contrasting period in history, and he appeared in Prague in 1576, when Rudolph II of Habsburg decided to move his residence from Vienna to Hradčany Castle.

Rudolph's predecessor, the tolerant Maximilian II (who was said to have secret sympathies for the "heretic" Lutherans), had rarely been in Prague. Rudolph came there when he was twenty-four. He was the last of the great mystics at Hradčany, and he gave Prague her last Golden Age. He had been educated in Spain by fanatical priests in the strictest court ceremonial. When he came to Gothic Prague, he was immediately bewitched by the magic of the mystical city— the dark church towers and dim chapels, religious fanatics and strange superstitions, St. Vitus Cathedral and the Old Jewish Cemetery. This was the era of martyrs and saints, of the Cabala and the Golem. Like Charles IV, Rudolph was a fanatical collector, but unlike his great predecessor, he was no planner and organizer. He was a mystical dreamer; his world was the stars, by which he lived; he was not interested in architects but in astronomers. His pictures show a deeply tortured man, with a veil of insanity in the dark eyes. Among the politically astute Habsburgs who enlarged their empire by brilliant compromise and dynastic marriages, Rudolph— reticent, silent, melancholy, a lifelong bachelor though fond of pretty women—must have been something of an eccentric. He would have been impossible in gay, irresponsible Vienna. In Prague, the mystical city, they understood him.

In his earlier years, Rudolph tried to overcome his frequent depressions by escaping into festivities, splendor, make-believe. Hradčany Castle became a large stage where the Emperor's court artists performed for the European nobles. Rudolph had inherited his dynasty's love of music. His court orchestra was the best on earth. From the Habsburgs' Netherlands, then a center of great music, he summoned Jakob Regnard, Charles Luyton, Lambert de Savye, Philippe de Monte, Hans Lemmens. From Austria came Jacob Gallus, from Germany Hans Leo Hassler. Organists, singers, instrument makers settled in town. The nobles too had their own orchestras; one of them, Krystophe Harant of Polžice, was a noted composer. The Jewish Town had a famous dance orchestra. And the burghers later founded the *Collegium Musicum*. Music was opium for the Emperor. Even in his last years when his mind was dimmed, he found moments of peace in the works of the great composers.

Art historians call Rudolph a "fanatical" collector, owing to his passion for Albrecht Dürer and the Brueghels. He sent his emissaries to Nuremberg and Breslau and Wittenberg (where they purchased Dürer's "Anbetung der heiligen drei Könige"). Dürer's "Rosenkranzfest," which hung above the altar of San Bartolomeo in Venice, was bought and carried in 1601 by four strong men across the Alps, "hanging on poles, so it won't be damaged," all the way to the Castle in Prague. In Madrid, Rudolph's ambassador, Count Khevenhüller, offered 13,000 thalers for the collection left by Cardinal Granvelle—thirty-three paintings, among them Dürer's "Marter der Zehntausend." When the Emperor couldn't get a painting by Pieter Brueghel the Elder that he wanted very much, he told Pieter the Younger and Johann Brueghel to copy it. In 1604, Johann Brueghel was in Prague.

Rudolph was fascinated by the Italian Renaissance but the Gothic style was too deeply rooted in dark, mystic Prague, and Renaissance experiments usually ended in a compromise between Gothic and Renaissance ideas. The Belvedere, that masterpiece of pure Italian Renaissance, is the glorious exception; it has been called the most beautiful work of its kind north of the Alps. "It affects you as though it too had been carried from Italy across the Alps," writes Johanna Baroness Herzogenberg. It was planned by Paolo della Stella, during the reign of Ferdinand I, who wanted it for his wife. She didn't live to see it completed.

The era of Rudolph II is now remembered as the Golden Age of Czech literature. The two leading spiritual trends—European humanism and the Evangelical *Unitas Fratum*—spread the ideas of individual freedom and social justice. Czech writers, many of them still writing in Latin, were cosmopolitan-minded. The Králice Bible appeared—which for centuries set the highest literary standard in all Czech-speaking countries.

Rudolph summoned painters, sculptors and artisans from all over Europe. Italian architects designed ceremonial halls and galleries; Hradčany Castle became Europe's "art chamber," filled with paintings by Titian, Correggio (in addition to the many Dürers and Brueghels), sculptures, books, rare coins. In 1577, Jacopo Strada from Mantua, a famous numismatic scholar, became director of the Imperial collections. Unfortunately, worthless trinkets and monstrosities were placed among genuine art works. An inventory of the Prague Castle that is now kept at Vienna's National Library lists next to Italian masters, "all sorts of strange sea fish, a bat, a box with four thunderstones, two boxes with magnet stones, two iron nails, presumably from Noah's Ark, 'a stone that grows, a gift of Herr Rosenberg,' a crocodile, a monstrum with two heads. . . ."

Not surprisingly, the Prague Castle attracted artists and adventurers, honest dealers and sly crooks. The great Dutch artist, Adriaen de Vries, was named "court sculptor." His bronze horse, made in 1560, is now at the National Gallery in Sternberg Palace, and copies of his sculptures have remained in the gardens of the Waldstein (or Valdštejn) Palace, but the beautiful originals were taken away by the Swedes during the Thirty Years' War and are now in the park of the Royal Castle of Drottningholm. Rudolph installed a workshop for bronze-founding near the Romanesque Mihulka Tower. The fashion spread and many nobles in town ordered bronze fountains and bronze statues. Some of the biggest workshops at the Castle were turned into "kitchens" for Rudolph's favorite alchemists and charlatans who obtained a lot of genuine gold from him on the promise of producing a little. Two other Romanesque towers at the Castle, the White Tower and the Bishop's Tower (later called "Mathematical Tower"), were converted into astronomical and astrological observatories. Two of the world's great astronomers were in residence at the Castle, Tycho de Brahe and Johannes Kepler.

The court became a strange, remote world, full of mysteries and mysticism. Frightening rumors circulated in town about the Emperor and his advisers. It was said that Rudolph was interested mainly in mystical and allegorical *objets d'art*. The painters, sculptors, goldsmiths, instrument makers, who lived at the Castle, combined in their works the ideas of Late Renaissance Mannerism with mystical subject matter, elegance and subtlety. This was what the Emperor liked best. His court ceremonial, modeled on the Spanish Habsburg court, was gloomy, severe, formal. "Spanish" became the word for all that was grandiose. When a new ceremonial hall was built in 1598, it was called the "Spanish Hall." No one was exempted from the rigidity of the Spanish court ceremonial. The Emperor allowed no one to leave the table when he gave a ceremonial banquet. Tycho de Brahe, the Danish astronomer, is reported to have died at such a banquet of a burst bladder "because he had drunk too freely and didn't dare leave and relieve himself."

Rudolph was a lonely man. He loved the beautiful Katharina Strada, the daughter of his court antiquary Jacopo da Strada (whom Titian painted), and had six children by her, but couldn't think of marrying her. While he became more deeply immersed in his dream world, his Empire was falling apart. The Protestant Netherlands had seceded from Catholic Spain. In Hungary, the Protestants had demanded and obtained religious freedom. The religious schism grew everywhere—especially in Prague, "the heretical town," as they called it in Rome. In Malá Strana and in the Old Town the Catholics had the majority. In the New Town, the Czech Estates, many of them Utraquists (the successors of the Hussites) were getting strong and restive. Rudolph tried to avert the crisis by conceding to the Czech Estates equal status for the Catholic and Protestant faiths. No wonder the Habsburgs in Vienna and Madrid were shocked; the House was in serious trouble; Rudolph's brother, Matthias, demanded the replacement of "the eccentric and irresponsible celibate." Rudolph was forced to abdicate in favor of Matthias who was crowned in St. Vitus Cathedral in 1611.

Rudolph died the following year, a broken, bitter man, and perhaps demented, as many people said. The learned

Melchior Goldast who was permitted to see "the greatest head in Christendom" writes about the embalmed body, "the face was uncovered, and they'd put in glass eyes." The strangest Habsburg of all is buried in a modest coffin in St. Vitus Cathedral, in his beloved Prague. The crown that he had had made later became the crown of the Austrian Empire, after the end of the Holy Roman Empire of the German nation. The crown is now shown—not in Prague but at the Treasury in Vienna's Imperial Palace.

Matthias transferred his residence to Vienna but building continued at the Prague Castle where the Emperor was represented by two *Statthalter* (vice regents). The Italian builder Vincenzio Scamozzi (who created the great Baroque dome in Salzburg) designed the monumental Matthias Gateway in the second courtyard of Hradčany. The year was 1614: the Italian Baroque made its entrance in Prague.

Four years later, the religious and political tensions erupted. Riots broke out in Prague between the Protestant Estates that were allied with the Czech brethren, and the Catholics. The "second rising" of the Czech Estates was climaxed by the revolt of May 23, 1618. A large group of Czech nobles went to Hradčany and demanded an audience with the vice regents, Jaroslav Bořita of Martinice and Vilém Slavata of Chlum. They were received in the Bohemian Chancellery, and there were "sharp verbal exchanges." The vice regents were called "serfs of the Jesuits" and accused of being against religious freedom. Somebody shouted, "Throw them out of the window, *po staročesku!*" (as is the old Czech custom). Two aged nobles, Oberstburgrat von Sternberg and the Maltese Prior von Lobkowitz, were tactfully led out of the room "so they wouldn't be involved." Count Bořita fell to his knees and begged for mercy. When he asked to see a confessor, he was told "to turn to God Himself," because they wouldn't think of calling in "a roguish Jesuit." Thereupon, the Count was thrown, head forward, through the large window. According to the report of Count Slavata (whose turn was still to come),

Bořita of Martinice, while falling down, incessantly called out "Jesus, Maria!" and floated down so slowly on the ground as though he would sit down there, so that owing to the intercession of the Virgin Mary and God's protection the terrible fall didn't hurt his health though he was a heavy man. Certain pious and trustworthy people later claimed that while they crossed the bridge toward Malá Strana, they saw the Virgin Mary, while she carried Count Bořita in her robe . . . The Count himself didn't notice this but he realized it after his fall.

Count Slavata himself tried to put up some resistance which didn't help him. Out he went too, "making the sign of the Cross, saying with a contrite heart, '*Deus propitius esto mihi peccatori*,' May God be merciful to me, the sinner. His hat, trimmed with gold roses and diamonds, remained at the Chancellery."

Philippe Fabricius, the vice regents' secretary, told the Estates what he thought of them. Somebody wanted to stab him to death but Count Schlick said that "they must not desecrate the place with a murder." So they threw Fabricius after his masters "like a sheaf of corn."

The second Prague defenestration, which was followed by the Thirty Years' War and made a shambles out of Europe, ended on a note of low comedy. Though the three men fell fifty feet into the Castle moat, none of them was seriously hurt because the moat was filled with garbage. Bořita and Fabricius ran away; Fabricius went all the way to Vienna where he reported to His Majesty. Count Slavata was given first aid by Madame Polyxena, the attractive wife of Chancellor Lobkowitz. Funny songs were sung all over

The Mystical City

Prague about the defenestration which the chronicler Pavel Skála of Zhor called "an ancient Bohemian custom" that was also known "among the Romans and other famous people." But what came later, was not funny: the open revolt of the Czech Estates that led to the disastrous battle on the White Mountain. Today a streetcar (No. 1) will take you for one crown (3¢) from the former battlefield, past Hradčany (where the revolt began), almost to the Old Town Square (where the revolt ended with the execution of the leaders of the Estates).

There is much disagreement about the battle of the White Mountain among Czech historians, depending on where they stand. The present-day opinion is summed up by Alois Svoboda, "The common people could not see what the Czech gentry were fighting for, and would not take up arms; and so the fate of the struggle lay in the hands of mercenaries, badly paid and for the most part foreigners, adventurers interested only in booty."

November 8, 1620, most fateful day in Bohemia's history, was dark and gloomy, reflecting the low spirit of the army of the Bohemian Estates. Their troops were encamped along a two-mile stretch on Bílá Hora (White Mountain, now a pleasant residential suburb of Prague). The army consisted of Bohemians, Moravians, Germans, Hungarians, Austrian cavalrymen and various adventurers. There was also a regiment of English mercenaries. A few months earlier the Estates had elected Frederick of the Palatinate to be King of Bohemia. The "Winter King" (because he lasted just through the winter) was the son-in-law of King James I of England. The Estates hoped he would get help from England and the German Union, to which Frederick belonged. Their hope was not fulfilled.

Count Thurn, the Bohemian Minister of War, inspected his army and declared, "If we had fallen from heaven into formation, we couldn't have found a better spot." This turned out to be a somewhat over-optimistic appraisal of the situation. His commanders told him there were not enough spades available for digging trenches. Others complained about the morale of their troops. Thurn shrugged off their doubts. He said he was certain that the Imperial forces were "not yet ready for battle." (Some of the lower officers were not so certain. Chroniclers report that a great many officers of the Estates' army quietly slipped away into wine houses and brothels in nearby Malá Strana because they thought the battle was imminent, and they were not eager to be there when it started.)

The Bohemian Estates, whose intelligence was deplorable, had no idea that right then an Imperial council of war was being held, arguing whether to fight or not to fight. Colonel Spinelli of the Neapolitan infantry suggested an Austrian-style compromise: they would give the signal for "a major skirmish" but not for a real battle. The Imperial commanders agreed on the password "Sancta Maria" and put white ribbons—the battle emblem—on caps and sleeves. At about half past twelve, two companies of infantrymen started moving up the hill, beginning the "major skirmish." A Carmelite monk, Dominicus a Jesu, "inflamed the Imperial troops to destroy the heretics."

Thurn and the Bohemian commander, Christian Count of Anhalt, at once ordered their men to counter-attack. The Imperial troops were making progress, however, and Anhalt sent thirteen hundred men into the "skirmish" that was fast developing into a full-sized battle. There is confusion among the historians about what happened next, but most agree that the troops of the Estates didn't put up much of a fight.

The Mystical City

Some units were already seen in wild flight toward Prague. Then the young Count Anhalt, son of the Estates' commander, charged into the enemy's flank with a courageous cavalry attack (approximately where the Church of St. Mary now stands), causing confusion among the Imperial troops. The Austrian cavalrymen fighting with the Estates were ordered to make a charge but they stopped when they met the Imperial infantry, fired one volley, turned around and made off toward Prague; they had done their fighting for the day. Then the Polish Cossacks, fighting on the side of the Imperial army, charged the Hungarian cavalry of the Protestants. "Brandishing a sabre in each hand, holding the reins between their teeth, the Cossacks were a frightful sight," a chronicler reports. The Hungarians dismounted and fled through the vineyards.

Even the commanders were in flight now. When the Duke of Weimar asked the Hungarian Colonel Kornish to turn and face the enemy, the Hungarian pointed at the fleeing German cavalrymen and said. "*Germani currunt,*" the Germans are running. (The Estates' army commanders conversed in broken Latin.) Anhalt tried to argue with a group of cavalrymen "to turn and fight." They refused and ran away, and poor Anhalt had to join the retreat. He rode down to Prague, which was filled with confusion and fleeing soldiers, and went to see King Frederick who was sitting at the table, presiding at a lunch in honor of the English Ambassador. Anhalt told the King that the battle was going badly. The King "at once gave orders to pack."

But the battle wasn't over yet. The Czechs resisted stubbornly against the Imperial troops near the Star Hunting Lodge. There were eighteen hundred men of the reserves near the Lodge, but they were never ordered into battle. Joachim Andreas Count Schlick, a German Bohemian nobleman from Eger, tried a last-ditch defense, organizing his Moravian infantrymen in a semi-circle, but they were pushed into a deep hollow (which is still there, near the wall of the park). The five hundred Moravians fought bravely for a lost cause, and in the end most of them were killed, and when it was all over, "the dead were piled ten high by the wall." Among the mercenary officers of the Imperial army was a young adventurer named René Descartes who later became a French philosopher, physicist and mathematician.

All in all, the battle of the White Mountain had lasted "perhaps less than a hundred minutes," but it decided the fate of the Czech nation for the next three hundred years. The final act was the execution, on June 21, 1621, of twenty-seven leaders of the revolt—Czech and German noblemen and burghers of Prague and other Bohemian towns—in the Old Town Square. Contemporary pamphlets gave detailed descriptions of the gory event. The first man executed was Count Schlick (who had saved Fabricius from being killed because he didn't want the Chancellery to be "desecrated with murder"):

First Count Schlick, wearing a black silk coat and holding a prayer book in his hands stepped on the stage, quite confident and praying, unafraid and relaxed, as all the others who were about to be executed. His servant took the clothes off the upper part of his body, and the Count knelt down on the cloth and offered his head with great patience and truly invoking God. His decapitation was swiftly done, and then his right hand was also cut off, and head and hand were taken into custody ... After each execution a new cloth was spread out on the stage ...

A macabre Prague legend reports that twelve heads of the executed men were secretly buried ten years later at Týn Church "in the presence of sixty Protestant clergymen." At the nearby Škréta house that once belonged to Václav

Budovec of Budov, one of the executed men, a statue at the corner has "a stunted appearance . . . here the cutting edge of the executioner's sword and the shadow of the gallows are an almost physical emanation," writes Alois Svoboda.

Catholicism was proclaimed the only permitted religion although nine tenths of the population of Bohemia were then Protestants. Many members of the Czech nobility had their possessions confiscated by a commission headed by Prince Charles of Liechtenstein, Governor of Bohemia. (Liechtenstein himself kept several castles and much wooded land and founded his dynasty's enormous wealth much of which the Liechtensteins lost in 1945 when the Czechoslovak government expropriated the family's Czechoslovak possessions.) Another beneficiary was Generalissimo Albrecht von Wallenstein, the great adventurer, soldier, mystic.

Many Czech intellectuals emigrated. The most famous of them was John Amos Comenius, the last bishop of the Evangelical *Unitas Fratum* in Uherský Brod, Moravia—one of the great humanists that appear in irregular intervals in Czech history until Tomáš G. Masaryk. In 1957, UNESCO observed the three hundredth anniversary of the first publication of Comenius' *Opera Didactica Omnia*.

The rights of the Czech Estates were annulled. Only ecclesiastical and judicial institutions were permitted in Hradčany Castle. A Latin sign at the Office of the Nobiliary Quartos said, *Iuste indicate, filii hominum* (Judge justly, sons of men). Next to it a small Czech sign said, "Nobody will have anything read or written for him which has not first been paid in cash."

By the middle of the seventeenth century, Hradčany Castle had become a vast complex the size of a town—a town within the town of Prague. The jurisdiction of the Prague authorities ended at the ramparts of the Castle. Its territorial status attracted people who liked to be out of the reach of the Prague authorities—artisans, who had not been accepted into the guilds, tradesmen not eager to pay taxes and shady characters who liked to elude the law. Naturally, they couldn't live in the various palaces, and they began to install themselves in improvised huts and hovels between the buttresses of St. Vitus Cathedral, in the niches between the palaces, in the projections between the church buildings. The Castle was even then popular with tourists and sightseeing people. Tradesmen arranged their booths, and servants set up taprooms wherever there was space. (Not long ago, several wooden pegs were found under the floor of Vladislav Hall on which an innkeeper had marked his customers' debts for wine.)

Along the Romanesque and the Vladislav ramparts there ran a causeway which was supported by a succession of arches on pillars. Many "parasite" dwellings were haphazardly built under these arches, which were allotted as a special privilege to certain applicants. Rudolph II permitted his Castle gunners to live there. Later the gunners disappeared and more doubtful people settled in "Golden Lane," as it became known. There were no sanitary installations and people lived in crowded conditions. Prisoners at the nearby White Tower—mostly debtors who had failed to pay up—were permitted to receive visitors and to give parties, and some stored their own firewood in the Castle gangway connecting with Daliborka Tower, and kept their chickens there. The parasite dwellings were later demolished because they were a constant fire hazard. (In 1690, there was another terrible fire in Prague. In 1679, the Great Plague had killed "tens of thousands of people," though official figures don't exist.) Golden Lane remained there

The Mystical City

through the centuries, a breeding ground of legends about alchemists and tales about mystics.

When Lady Mary Wortley Montague, the wife of the British Ambassador in Vienna, visited Prague in 1716, she was not overwhelmed. "There are the remains of former splendor when Prague was one of the biggest cities in Germany," she wrote. "But the houses are old, hardly inhabited, poorly looking. People live in needy circumstances and can hardly be compared with those in Vienna." Lady Mary noticed that some people—she meant *her* kind of people—stayed here "for the music and the entertainment" and that there was an abundance of everything, "especially the best game I've ever eaten." Thanks to the good cooks of Prague, Lady Mary's journey was not a complete loss after all.

A guidebook for European travelers, published in 1736, calls it *"remarquable"* that "in the butcher shops of the Old Town no fly ever sits on the meat which, they say, must have been done by a magician." Another *remarquable* curiosity was the so-called English secular chapter house, founded in 1701 for the nobility; a Countess Berlepsch was the first abbess. But there were less *remarquable* aspects too. An Italian writer named Quarinoni complained that Prague was a wicked place. "The streets are full of small taverns and wine-houses crowded with drunks. One cannot lift one's eyes without seeing one of these scandalous inns."

After the Thirty Years' War, Prague was no longer one of the world's great cities and cultural centers, as it had been under Charles IV and Rudolph II. It was demoted to the status of a provincial capital. There were sieges, in 1741 and 1743, and in 1744 the Prussians occupied Prague, but history had bypassed it. In 1784, the four royal districts (Old Town, Malá Strana, New Town, Hradčany) were merged into the city of Prague. Still, Prague was not the seat of political power. The rulers came there from Vienna only for the coronation ceremony, if they cared enough to be crowned as Kings of Bohemia, or on state visits. Hradčany, the Castle of the Czech Kings, had become a noble monument of the past.

("Much worse, however, was that the old tradition of the Castle began to be misused in favor of Counter-Reformatory struggle, to promote the forcible re-Catholicization of Bohemia, and in support of monarchial absolutism," the authors of *The Prague Castle* write. "At St. Vitus Cathedral, close by the St. Wenceslas Chapel, the new patron saint, John Nepomuk, was buried in a magnificent sepulchral monument of silver.")

The struggle that had begun with the arrival of the Habsburgs in Bohemia in 1526 ended only in 1918. The Habsburgs ruled "by the Grace of God." They expected everybody in their lands to communicate with God in *their* fashion. Pressure started resistance. Resistance was met by force. The Thirty Years' War that began and ended in Prague is exemplified by the fascinating figure of Albrecht von Wallenstein, the mysterious Bohemian mystic of whom Friedrich Schiller, in his *Wallenstein* trilogy said, "His character fluctuates in history."

He was called a genius by some, a demon by others. No one understood him; perhaps he didn't understand himself. Wallenstein (also called Waldstein, or Valdštejn) was ambitious and ambiguous. Johannes Kepler, the great astronomer, had written Wallenstein's horoscope,

... Saturnus ascending creates melancholy thoughts, alchemism, black magic, intercommunion with ghosts, disregard for laws, customs, religions; suspicious toward God and people, as though

The Mystical City

it were only deceit . . . And because Mercurious is *in opposito* to Jovis, he will make people convinced of his dark powers and attract them, or lead a group of malcontents . . .

At the height of power, Wallenstein was Prague's "secret king." He received secret messengers from all courts in Europe. Just below Hradčany in Malá Strana, he built himself one of the most beautiful Baroque palaces. He didn't leave his dark cabinets for weeks, brooding over the counsels of his astrologers. He betrayed his Emperor and became turncoat again, fighting the Emperor's enemies. He drove the Swedes out of Prague but later got secretly in touch with them and was ready to betray the Emperor again. The Emperor was faster and had Wallenstein assassinated in Eger, in 1634. No one will ever know how many people Wallenstein had assassinated; once, in 1631, he ordered seventeen of his officers executed—in Prague's Old Town Square—for "cowardice in battle."

Always violence. The Counter-Reformation was more brutal in Bohemia, the country of Jan Hus, than elsewhere. The Church never forgot that it was in Prague, "the heretical city," where it had all started. Prague had a brief respite under the enlightened absolutism of Emperor Joseph II of Habsburg who disliked ecclesiastical pomp and in 1773 drove the Jesuits out of Prague. Ten years later, he dissolved the School of Painting and broke up the great "Kunstkammer" of Rudolph II.

Earlier, Joseph's grandfather, Charles VI, had ordered that some important paintings be brought from Prague to Vienna. When Joseph's mother, the Austrian Empress Maria Theresa, needed money to finance her wars against the Prussians, many paintings were sold to Saxony "through doubtful intermediaries." In 1749, sixty-nine paintings were sent to Dresden, among them Rubens' "Boar Hunt" and van Dyck's "Charles I with His Wife," for 50,000 thalers. Rudolph II had paid much less for them; the price of good paintings was already going up. Paintings by Correggio, Titian, Rembrandt and Velasquez were sold to St. Petersburg; they can now be admired in Leningrad's Hermitage. When Frederick of Prussia attacked Prague for the second time, in 1756, many valuable paintings, statues, porcelain, cameos and other art works were hurriedly taken down to subterranean vaults that had been hewn out of the rocks below Hradčany Castle. After the war, the art treasures were simply forgotten and left there. It is reported that in 1781 there were still paintings by van Dyck, Rubens, Paolo Veronese, Caravaggio and Tintoretto there. Then somebody "remembered," and Joseph II gave orders to take them to Vienna where they are now the glory of the Kunsthistorisches Museum.

The end of Rudolph's "art chamber" was as grotesque as some of its beginnings. In 1781, it was decided to turn part of the Prague Castle into artillery barracks. (The western part had just been reconstructed—after damages suffered during the Prussian sieges—in the style of classicist Baroque, under the Viennese architect Niccolo Pacassi, giving it more or less today's appearance.) The artillery would need ammunition, and the cellars were to become an ammunition magazine. A commission of artillery officers inspected the cellars and was "much amused" (as a chronicler reports) to find Rudolph's art treasures there, carelessly thrown together, half-broken statues, music instruments, armor, paintings; the place must have looked like a large antique store. The best things were sent to Vienna, and the rest was sold, during a memorable auction, in May, 1782. Semi-precious stones were inventoried "in bulk according to color." Old, Imperial letters were sold as "parchment" and "used paper."

Heintz's copy of Correggio's "Leda" was offered as "naked woman, bitten by angry goose." Masterpieces were practically given away, provided the buyer would carry away the "junk" *(Gerümpel)* at once.

Smart connoisseurs founded their collection that day. The great statue of Iloneus that Hans von Aachen had bought two hundred years earlier for 34,000 guilders, and which had lost its head and arms, was offered for 50 kreutzer (half a thaler). "Everybody laughed," reports an anonymous chronicler. An antique dealer named Helfer offered 51 kreutzer and walked away with the torso. He later sold it to a stonemason named Malinsky for 4 guilders, at a 1000 per cent profit. (When Helfer later discovered the head of the statue, he sent it to Malinsky, free of charge.) There the Viennese collector Barth found the statue and took it to Vienna for an undisclosed price. During the Congress of Vienna, the Crown Prince of Bavaria saw it at Barth's and bought it immediately for 6000 ducats. The Iloneus torso is now one of the priceless treasures of the Munich Glyptothek.

"A Poem Written in Stone"

SIGHTSEEING BUSES now "make" the city of Prague in a couple of hours, including time for refreshments and writing picture postcards, but that's the wrong way of seeing the sights. To catch the magic and mystique of Prague, one has to walk—alone or in congenial company—slowly and deliberately, prying into the secrets of old houses and the interiors of mysterious courtyards, especially in the Malá Strana district. "There is not one stone here that is not in harmony with the whims of history," writes Jacques Guenne. "In Prague, during a short walk, we see real poems," Jan Neruda wrote in 1890. When he said "Prague" he meant "Malá Strana," where he'd been born and lived all his life. He wrote about houses and inns with strange names ("To the Three Ostriches," "At the Green Crab," or "At the Two Suns"—Neruda's own house) and about the small shopkeepers and artisans, the seamstresses and old women living there. When Detlev von Liliencron (who called Prague "a golden net of poems") walked with a friend to Malá Strana, he stopped in the middle of Charles Bridge and stared down into the dark river. "Do you think the water is deep enough here?" he asked. The friend didn't ask, "Deep enough for what?" He understood. Charles Bridge and Malá Strana do this to people.

L. N. Zvěřina, a Czech writer, calls Malá Strana "a poem written in stone," and the spiritual home of poets. Neruda, Arbes, Vrchlický, Hašek lived here. Zeyer, Sládek, Sova came for inspiration. They understood the stone poetry and got drunk on it . . . Each palace here is a capital letter, the beginning of a line of poetry." This was the Prague of Rilke and Meyrink and the older generation of poets, and later of Kafka and Werfel and Brod who rarely talked about Prague because they wanted to be more "realistic" about their city than the older "mystics." "But our thoughts were full of Prague," Brod admits, "and of Malá Strana where we walked and which was a different world, far more important than the modern Prague."

Malá Strana is a symphony in High Baroque, a timeless

fairy-tale world of churches, monasteries and palaces (most of the palaces are now ministries or embassies), of hidden squares with unusual names ("Square of the Five Churches"), of towers and cupolas and chapels and street-corner saints that were placed there to lead the heretic citizens to the True Faith and to remind the poor sinners of Heaven and Hell, mostly Hell. There are dark corners where time seems to have stopped. Any moment Charles IV will emerge from one of the secret underground passages; they haven't been discovered yet but everybody claims they are there, and the Emperor used them when he wanted to spend a few hours away from the court ceremonial and have some incognito fun in town; he was fond of wine and women and had valuable collections of both. Malá Strana is a large alfresco museum, and walking there is like turning the pages of petrified history. The façades are not merely historical decorations but curtains shielding a strange, secret life. In Malá Strana, I always feel that Prague has two faces: today's face and, behind it, the invisible, eternal face that one must search for with love. Prague gives herself only to those who court her for a long time.

Nowadays some people in Prague say that one must fight off "that mystical feeling you get in Malá Strana." They say it isn't "realistic" or that it's "politically unwise." At the end of the twentieth century one must not believe "in these things." I know a young, successful architect who supports the regime though he is not a member of the Communist Party; he even admits that many mistakes are made but he is optimistic about the future of socialism. He has no patience with what he calls "the mystical nonsense of Prague." Yet once in a while he walks—alone—in Malá Strana. He loves Our Lady of Loretto Church with Giovanni Battista Orsi's beautiful copy of the Santa Casa in Loretto, near Ravenna, revered as the supposed dwelling of the Virgin and Jesus in Nazareth. Loretto was the first Baroque church built in Prague, six years after the battle at the White Mountain. It was a pilgrimage church and the clerical authorities kept beautifying it for half a century. Having learned his socialist history, the young architect knows that Loretto, like the canonization, a hundred years later, of St. John Nepomuk, was intended to make the Czech people forget their national "saint," Jan Hus. Loretto became an attraction by offering the services of four much-needed saints. St. Sebastian would guarantee protection against the plague that killed off almost one third of the population of Bohemia during the Thirty Years' War. St. Florian gave protection against fire, and St. Anthony against both plague *and* fire. And for those suffering from a toothache there was St. Apollonia. Arne Novák, a modern writer who perceived the spirit of the Baroque, calls Loretto "a meeting place of love." There is love on the ceiling of the Casa Santa, showing the Virgin surounded by saints, or around St. Appollonia and the angels love everywhere.

The young architect, strictly a non-believer, knows all this, but he goes there "because it is so beautiful." The façade of Loretto is one of the most beautiful works of Kilian Ignatius Dientzenhofer, who was the greatest architect of the Baroque Prague. Inside, there is an early Baroque courtyard with cloistered arcades and fountains. Every hour the twenty-seven bells of the carillon in the dome-covered bell tower play a sweet melody which doesn't sound kitschy at all as one listens in the courtyard. Upstairs is the great Loretto Treasure, a collection of inestimable monstrances, among them the Diamond Monstrance, made by a Viennese goldsmith in 1699 who used 6222 diamonds. Benvenuto Cellini would have loved it. The Loretto monstrances dis-

The Mystical City

appeared during the last war, and it was assumed that they had been stolen by a prominent Nazi art lover. But one day in 1961, workmen tearing down a wall found several parcels wrapped in newspapers that had been hidden under stones and were covered with pieces of mortar. What made the parcels interesting were the newspapers in which they had been wrapped: they were dated 1941, when the Nazi terror had been very bad in Prague. The parcels contained the monstrances, chalices and other relics that had disappeared. Someone must have been in an awful hurry as he wrapped the parcels and hastily put up the wall; whoever it was may have been warned that the Gestapo was about to enter Loretto. Efforts to find the mysterious savior of the Loretto Treasure remained unsuccessful although in 1961 he would have been certain of the nation's gratitude. It is assumed that he or she is dead. Another unsolved mystery of Prague.

Prague's Baroque began a few years prior to the battle of the White Mountain, penetrated Malá Strana during the Thirty Years' War and developed to its greatest beauty during the saddest period in the city's history. ("It underlines the contention of historians that periods of unusual development in the arts do not necessarily coincide with the forward movement of society as a whole," writes Václav Pelišek in 1966.) The Hussite era, the most glorious epoch in Czech history, from 1400 to 1526, produced little art in Prague. Not a single church was built in Prague, since the Hussites opposed all religious building. Iconoclast "crusaders" broke up many valuable statues, and Vyšehrad Castle was razed.

While Comenius in his *Labyrinth of the World* wrote about the "vanity of palaces, churches, cupolas, towers" and called their construction "a sensuous pleasure," the Jesuits systematically transformed the Gothic town where the Renaissance had become hardly noticeable into Europe's most beautiful Baroque town. Not a single religious building remained in Prague that wasn't remodeled during the seventeenth or eighteenth centuries. At Hradčany Castle, the influence of the Baroque is hardly evident—except in St. Vitus Cathedral where the Baroque artist F. M. Kanka built a small chapel consecrated to St. John Nepomuk whose canonization had been announced in 1721 by Pope Benedict XIII. The younger Fischer von Erlach in Vienna was commissioned to design a Baroque tomb, "made of thirty-seven hundredweights of silver," that gives the impression that "the Saint is dancing in his grave." An enormous Baroque scaffold was set up for the celebration; and the canonization, in 1729, lasted a whole week.

Not only the Church was building in Malá Strana. After the victory at the White Mountain, the Emperor had distributed the property of executed or exiled Bohemian nobles among his loyal generals, and the great condottieri built themselves magnificent showplaces of secular Baroque. The greatest and least loyal of the condottieri, Albrecht von Waldstein, Duke of Friedland, the Emperor's generalissimus, had an immense district razed where an army of Italian workmen under Andrea Spezza built a truly imperial residence. It was noted that from his windows he could see the slopes of Hradčany, with the Imperial residence. There he lived in imperial style. Friedrich Lebzelter, a Saxonian agent, wrote in 1631, "The Duke of Friedland has a large court, including several counts and knights, and fifty servants, keeping four dining rooms and 160 horses. They pay their servants every quarter of the year. But otherwise the Duke is quite parsimonious . . ."

Waldstein believed in astrology. For several years he had Johannes Kepler in his house. After Kepler's death in 1630, the astrologer Seni had great influence at the palace. Some historians consider Seni a paid stool pigeon of the Viennese court where people worried about the ambitious generalissimus who was later killed in Eger, by order of the Emperor, for "treason."

His palace remains a masterpiece of the secular Baroque, with its fantastic marble hall, galleries and vestibules, a beautiful *sala terrena* (now the scene of lovely summer evening concerts) with fountains, grottos, statues (some made by Adriaen de Vries), an ornamental lake, stalactites and a great burial place for the horse that had been killed under Wallenstein in the Battle of Luetzen—truly a pre-Wagnerian idea.

The Gothic Prague of Charles IV had been created by artists from France (Matthias of Arras) and Germany (Peter Parler and his disciples). The few Renaissance buildings were done by Italians. The Baroque of Prague that now dominates the appearance of the city was also mostly the work of foreign artists. The Dientzenhofers came from Bavaria, the Luragos from Italy, the Brokoffs from Hungary. Matthias Braun, the great sculptor, came from Tyrol, and so did Johann Georg Bendel. But no matter where they came from, they fell under the spell of Prague, and their Baroque is quite distinct from the Baroque in Italy, in Austria, in Dresden. Obviously the *genius loci* of Prague was so strong that it made the great artists there create something that could only be in Prague. The city never originated a new style but modified the great styles by its atmosphere.

In Italy, the Baroque had emerged as a reaction against the Renaissance that was devoted to the ideals of Greek and Roman art, not exactly a "Christian" style spiritually. The Baroque developed as a "religious" style after the middle of the sixteenth century when the Church suffered many disasters. It was not "ordered" by the Popes and "executed" by the Jesuits as some fashionable art historians now claim in Prague. But after the victory of the Counter-Reformation was a certainty, the Church considered the Baroque an efficient means of architectural propaganda. Not surprisingly, the main "campaign" was directed against "heretical" Prague, which was surrounded by a cloud of sulphur ever since Jan Hus had preached in Bethlehem Chapel. From the Church's point of view, the appearance of Prague had to be changed.

The great Baroque artists were more interested in decorative effect than in architectural creation. They sensed that their style was able to animate lifeless material. They turned cold stone into living matter. The great Renaissance artists preserved discipline and dignity even when their heroes—as Michelangelo's—are agonized with suffering. The heroes of the Baroque have no such inhibitions. They smile at the onlooker and stretch out their hands. They unmistakably communicate their exultation or their grief. The statue of St. John Nepomuk on Charles Bridge, made by Johann Brokoff, which was later imitated hundreds of times, is a true Baroque work of art. With an indescribably melancholy face the saint gazes toward Heaven, embracing Christ in his hands.

The Baroque didn't want to be austere as the Gothic or serene as the Renaissance; the Baroque artists probably sensed that their work was not always in impeccable taste. But it fulfilled a purpose. The Baroque cupolas polarized the vertical towers of the Gothic town. Even today the Baroque of Prague's Malá Strana keeps many spectators spellbound. One doesn't have to be a believer to get excited in St. Nicholas Church, the masterpiece of Christopher and Kilian Ignatius Dientzenhofer, with its fantastic cupola, its strangely luxurious interior, its mystical dimness, its violent rhythm swinging among the big pillars. Everywhere there is a confusion of frescoes, stucco, marble, gold, triumphant saints, altars and more gold. The various components have been criticized on aesthetic grounds, but the overall impression is overwhelming. No other Baroque church on earth compares with it, not even Vienna's flamboyant Charles Church. It is not exactly a church for the performance of Bach's *St. Matthew Passion* but rather for Verdi's *Requiem*. (I would love to hear his "Dies Irae" there. I wouldn't be surprised if the exultant saints would suddenly come to life.)

"The art of the Baroque found perhaps its happiest expression in Prague, more than in Vienna, in Bavaria or in Italy," writes Paul Claudel. "Here it achieved the difficult moment, the balance between sincerity and lyrical transfiguration." In Prague's Baroque, there is none of the elegant splendor of Vienna's Belvedere or the airy charm of Dresden's Zwinger. Prague is located halfway between Vienna and Dresden but she remains withdrawn and mysterious, the somber, suffering city under a dark sky. The Prague Baroque is the most powerful of all because it is an architectural expression of mysticism. In Italy and Vienna, the Baroque often covers up former styles and creates harmony—in Italy, visual harmony, and in Vienna, musical harmony. In Prague, there is never harmony—always drama and contrast.

Except in Prague's great Baroque gardens. I've never seen anything similar elsewhere. The gardens are the result of a problem that has always bothered the great Baroque architects in Prague: lack of space. Magnificent buildings—

St. Nicholas Church in Malá Strana, St. John on the Rock, and the immense Černín Palace, a seventeenth-century skyscraper, had to be built on limited sites. Černín Palace, across from Our Lady of Loretto, was built by Francesco Caratti for Jan Humprecht Černín of Chudenitz, a former ambassador at Venice. Its 450-foot-long, four-story façade is cut by thirty demi-columns between the windows, and the cornice of the roof forms a long, horizontal bar. It looks like a Florentine palace magically transposed to Prague. During the War of the Austrian Succession, the French occupiers in 1742 decided to demolish the palace but refrained from doing so when the Austrians threatened to destroy the Elector's residence in Munich which *they* kept occupied; the deterrent was already a means of practical diplomacy. The Baroque artists F. M. Kanka and Anselmo Lurago later restored Černín Palace, showing how much beauty could be concentrated in a very small space.

These architects considered the Baroque gardens alfresco extensions of the palaces to which they belonged. Putting sculptures, terraces, loggias, fountains, into these gardens, they merged them completely with the buildings, achieving yet another effect: the palaces, in turn, became part of the Baroque landscape.

You will have to do some walking up to enjoy the full beauty of the gardens in Malá Strana. Most of them are artistically laid out on narrow, steep slopes behind the buildings. Since there was so little horizontal space, the garden architects of the Baroque simply built up and up. My favorite Baroque garden (neither the largest nor the most famous) is the intimate, lovely paradise behind the Vrtba Palace. The Vrtbas were Bohemian nobles living in rather modest circumstances by the exalted standards of Baroque Prague where it was not unusual to build one's own theater

The Mystical City

for the guests (as Count Sporck did) or to lose a fortune during a night of gambling (as Wallenstein did), whereupon one went to confession.

The Late-Renaissance Vrtba Palace (now housing the Czechoslovak Foreign Institute) is no match for the magnificent Malá Strana residences of other nobles and generals —Wallenstein, Schönborn, Palffy, Golz, Gallas, Nostic, Piccolomini, Sporck, Kolovrat, Fürstenberg, Morzin, Thun and others. All the Vrtbas could afford was a portal ornamented with sculptures, but they had them done by the best Baroque sculptor in Prague, Matthias Braun, who also did the sculptures and vases for their garden. They must have had a firstrate garden architect. He created a magical atmosphere on very limited space behind the house. On a gently terraced slope, one walks up between statues that make you forget how steep the slope is. Gradually a magnificent panorama unfolds, as one reaches the top of the garden—a small platform between rosebushes and Baroque sculptures.

Looking from left to right, one sees the "Prague of The Hundred Towers"—Hradčany with Parler's tall bell-tower of St. Vitus, St. Nicholas in Malá Strana with Dientzenhofer's greenish cupola and Lurago's belfry tower, the violet spire of St. Thomas with the famous "black beer" brewery of the Augustinians (in Prague the monks were always the best beer brewers), Parler's tower on Charles Bridge, the unsymmetric towers of Týn Church, the Clementinum, and at the extreme right, the Renaissance façade of St. Savior. The guests of the Vrtbas must have been delighted with the view, and a garden party was a success before it even began.

In a small house below the slope, Mikoláš Aleš, the famous and now fashionable Czech painter, had his study. There is nothing Baroque about the robust, realistic characters in Aleš' paintings but he loved the intimate atmosphere of this garden. The intimacy of the gardens of Prague sets them apart from the more grandiose gardens in Rome, Paris, Vienna. Even the large ones—Wallenstein, Ledebour, Fürstenberg—have an air of elegant seclusion about them. At the Fürstenberg Garden, there is a small Baroque pavilion that was sometimes used as a bathtub by the Countess. "The purpose was perhaps not only a cleansing bath," writes an anonymous chronicler. At the Palffy Gardens, there are hidden corridors, loggias, tritons and fountains. At the nearby Ledebour Gardens there is a *sala terrena*, where Shakespeare comedies are now performed in summertime in a charming setting. Looking up one sees Rajská Zahrada (the Paradise Garden) with its summer houses and fountains; it deserves its name.

Nothing in Malá Strana adds a wrong, disturbing note. In certain parts—Na Tržiště, Nerudova, Valdštejn Square—no houses were put up after the Baroque era, and the spell of the past remains unbroken. Little restoration has been done in the past thirty years and the paint begins to peel off some façades. Heavy trucks and cars rumbling by over the cobblestone pavement have done heavy damage to the palaces and churches, which were not built to withstand the shocks of motorized traffic. They now talk of keeping certain streets and squares closed to all traffic to keep them alive a little longer.

Many Czechs—sober, rational people—have an instinctive distrust of the Baroque. The feeling is especially strong among Protestants, Utraquists, members of the Bohemian Brethren, and lately among atheists. Few people try to get close to the spirit of the Baroque as did Arne Novák, who belonged to T. G. Masaryk's circle and wrote in 1911, "The Prague Baroque represents a new love for the hierarchy of a new society . . . directed against those loyal to the state. It announces the blood-soaked glory of the aristocracy and Church imperialism. The face of a humiliated people was built into the foundations of the magnificent Prague Baroque." (A Communist writer, Dr. Josef Janáček, assesses the Baroque from the viewpoint of social realism. "Baroque ... became the outer symbol of the citizenry's economic and political impotence. This state expressed itself in the frightening power of the nobility and the Church over ordinary burghers. Palaces, monasteries, and churches swallowed up whole blocks of burghers' houses. . . . The depression lasted up to the middle of the eighteenth century.")

The Baroque had no sense of social justice; one sympathizes with the impoverished slum dwellers in Malá Strana who were chased out of their crowded, unsanitary homes (God knows where they went) because Wallenstein just wanted to have an enormous palace there, with a tomb for a dead horse. But the "depression" also made Prague one of the most beautiful cities on earth. The Baroque was no style for ordinary mortals; only princes and cardinals could afford it. By contrast, on Castle Hill overlooking Budapest, the Baroque architects didn't build "palaces, monasteries and churches" but simply fixed up the burghers' older houses, which had been damaged during the Turkish domination. This bourgeois "provincial" Baroque compares poorly with the noble Baroque in Prague. When the Hungarian nobles, the Palffys or Eszterhazys, wanted a great, Baroque palace, they had it built in Vienna or Prague.

Malá Strana may need a new coat of paint now but its aristocratic beauty has survived for three hundred years. Will this be said one day of the architectural achievements of the present regime—the depressing rows of faceless apartment houses, the functional structures of a soulless era, that are always proudly shown to visiting delegations? Prague's largest Communist monument—the enormous Stalin statue—was less outstanding for style and taste than for size and servility. Its religious appeal lasted a much shorter time than the tombs of St. Wenceslas and St. John Nepomuk.

Toward the end of the past century, Czech artists, writers and architects became concerned about the beauty of Prague. Could the old city be saved from an inevitable deterioration? As early as 1873, Vítězslav Hálek wrote about the smoke problem in Prague, "the city not only of a hundred churches but of a hundred chimneys." The experts agreed that the harmonious lines of Prague's beautiful panorama must be preserved." In 1899, Vilém Mrštík wrote, "The fight for Prague is the first big test of our cultural life."

Many thought that Prague was losing the fight. Ignát Hermann wrote, "Old houses collapse and are replaced by buildings without character . . . picturesque districts disappear or are turning into building sites." Everybody agreed that the Municipal House, next to the beautiful fifteenth-century Prašná Brána (Powder Tower, because it was once used as a gunpowder magazine), was "the most monumental artistic disgrace of our time." A Czech art historian, Dr. Gustav Pazourek, asked St. John Nepomuk "to arrange for a locally limited earthquake." Emile Bourdet, the sculptor, took one horrified look at the atrocious Secession-style façade and exclaimed, *"Fi donc!"* He was told that at one time the authorities wanted to tear down the beautiful Powder Tower.

In 1900, J. Heran bitterly complained that during the preceding century over five hundred valuable old statues had been wilfully destroyed and "terrible things were done under the guise of regulation, canalization, navigation . . ." The Czech writer, Ladislav Procházka, in 1924 asked people to

The Mystical City

pray for each old house. "The young generation talks about unhealthy districts. But the old parts of our city are the most beautiful; let's admit that what was built in the past hundred years isn't worth much. When they say that Prague is beautiful, they don't mean the new Prague. The old Prague that is in our hearts is not only the property of our nation but of the whole world." Another Czech writer, Zdeněk Wirth, who admitted that the great building epoch of Prague had ended with the Baroque, in 1921 evoked "the spirit of a modern Charles IV" to create a new Prague "that would be Prague *and* European in its character, just as the Prague Gothic and the Prague Baroque were."

No one knows how to save for eternity the Old Jewish Cemetery whose oldest tombstone, of the poet Avigdor Karo, bears the date: April 25, 1439. Though it was enlarged several times, the Cemetery became too small as the Jewish population increased. There was no more horizontal space to enlarge it. The only solution remained to cover the existing graves with fresh soil and put the new coffins in. After a few more centuries, there were twelve different layers of graves, one on top of the other, and now the agglomeration of tombstones gives a picture of the conditions in the former Prague ghetto. The twelve thousand stones are only one sixth of all the people buried at the Cemetery. No more funerals took place after 1787 when Emperor Joseph II prohibited burials amidst the residential parts of the town. The Old Jewish Cemetery remained a cultural and historical relic.

In 1903, some parts of the Old Jewish Cemetery had to be liquidated to make space for the construction of roads and the new Industrial Art Museum. The tombstones from the liquidated area were brought to the remaining parts and placed in less densely occupied corners or in the surrounding walls. The sandstones—gray, reddish, dark, black—wear off slowly and inexorably. In winter, the cold bites into them, and all year long, there are exhaust fumes from the street and the mist from the nearby river. The tombstones that have no space lean against each other and sometimes fall on top of each other, like drunks. The Talmud says they must not be moved, but even the Talmud cannot prevent them from sinking lower into the earth as the years go by. Every century, the tombstones disappear another ten centimeters; of some, only the tops remain visible; and one day, there will be none, and only the catalogued tombstone inscriptions will remain of twelve superimposed layers of graves.

The Hebrew inscriptions are mostly simple: the date of death, the name of the deceased, sometimes a short eulogy, indicating the deceased's profession and social status, or a simple image, derived from the name: a lion, a deer, a bear, a dove. A lance for a surgeon, a pair of scissors for a tailor. Often the letters have disappeared and the image is all that remains.

During the Nazi occupation, the Old Jewish Cemetery was the only place assigned to the Jews of Prague for their walks and to their children as a playground; all other parks and playgrounds were forbidden to them. Walking between the tombstones, the people could prepare themselves for their eventual fate (though they didn't know then that most of them would never have a tombstone). Occasionally, an old Jewish scholar, Dr. Tobias Jakobovic, was escorted to the Cemetery by S. S. guards to blow the *shofar* (ram's horn) amidst the tombstones for the entertainment of visiting Nazi and S. S. bosses. Jakobovic knew well of course that the Talmud forbids the *shofar* to be blown except on the Jewish New Year, but he had strictest orders from Hans Günther, head of the S. S. Central Office for Jewish Affairs (read: extinction) in Bohemia and Moravia.

Günther also issued instructions that all objects found in synagogues and in the homes of Jews who were sent away for liquidation would have to be delivered in Prague; he even postponed executions for Jewish scholars who could decipher old Hebrew texts. At the Klaus and Pinkas Synagogues, Günther set up a Jewish Museum that would one day show "the culture of an extinct race." Today the Pinkas Synagogue is a Memorial, its walls showing the names of seventy-seven thousand and two hundred and ninety people—Jewish men, women and children from Bohemia and Moravia who were made "extinct" by the Nazis.

In the 1920s, Karel Čapek wrote, "The fight for Old Prague is already lost if it isn't tied up with the building of modern Prague. And with the lost battle, modern Prague loses much that she should keep as a family jewel," and he called, "the Castle, the Old Town Square and the National Theater the three symbols of Prague." He complained that every new "landlord" at the Castle had "torn down, ruined, rebuilt, moved things around, enlarged and torn down again." Before 1918, the Castle had been badly kept. Grass blades grew between the stones of the pavement.

In Prague, a political city, architecture was always a political art. The Counter-Reformation had shown that a political and religious idea was strong enough to change the appearance of whole city districts. The art historians of the present regime are critical of the work done at the Castle during the "bourgeois" Republic. ("The former nimbus of a royal residence was replaced by a bourgeois republican nimbus . . . Republican present often clashed sharply with feudal past, inscribed inerasably in the stone book of the

Castle.") A Slovene architect, Josip Plečnik of Ljublana, designed plans for the reconstruction of the Third Courtyard (where excavations had uncovered remains of old fortifications). He created reception rooms in the southern wing, and designed plans for the bastion garden, the Paradise Garden, and the garden on the ramparts.

Present planners claim that "the romantic approach to architectural alterations is dead" but admit that Plečnik had an imposing breadth of conception." When he began work at the Castle, the Third Courtyard gravitated down toward the Old Palace. Plečnik created a monumental level square south of St. Vitus Cathedral, and a small square in front of the western façade. Between the two new level spaces he placed a monolith, and in the center of the panorama he put a Gothic sculpture of St. George on a modern pedestal.

Today restoration continues at the Castle—under a different aspect. The official guidebook says, "Hradčany continues to be the seat of the President of the Czechoslovak Socialist Republic. . . . Mainly, however, the Castle is an art-historical and cultural monument designed to call up in the mind of the visitor the past and present of the Czechoslovak people." The building program is directed by the Ideological Council of Hradčany; the President of the Republic is its chairman. (Actually, President Antonín Novotný had his offices in Hradčany but lived in a small, comfortable villa in the garden near Belvedere Palace. So does President Ludvík Svoboda.) At the Castle, important Communist Party sessions are held, and acts of state take place.

The Castle Riding School was converted into an exhibition hall. The covered Ball Court (Mičovna) in the royal gardens was restored. Between the Second and Third Courtyard an Information Center for visitors, with refreshment rooms and an exchange office, was installed. The Renaissance building of the Old Burgrave's House has become the House of Czechoslovak Children. Ceiling and wall paintings in the St. Wenceslas Chapel were restored. An investigation of the Institute of the Theory and History of Art confirmed the existence of some great paintings (Rubens, Tintoretto, Paolo Veronese, Pordenone and others) among the old pictures in the Castle depositories, survivals of the collections of the Habsburg emperors.

Future plans of projects in and around Hradčany are discussed by architects, urban planners, historians and sociologists. "The possibilities of structural alterations are being studied from the ideological viewpoint," an architect tells me. The ideological architects survey the surroundings of the Castle. A new bridge may be built over Stag Moat (Jelení příkop), and the northern approaches of the Castle in the vicinity of the Riding School are studied. The Castle is a national monument and more paths are needed around it to give the increasing number of visitors a chance of looking at it from various approaches. The present thinking is summed up by Václav Formánek:

Our modern scientific age is far removed from the dark and complicated symbolism of the St. Wenceslas cult and its view of the false halo surrounding feudal and bourgeois fetishes. . . . Prague Castle nevertheless always will have a firm place in the life of the Czechoslovak people as a monument of its own history, a memorial in stone brought to life by a collective vision of its past and its future.

A Great Place for Music

"Music is part of the life of the Czechs," Bedřich Smetana said in 1868, when the cornerstone was laid for the National Theater in Prague. Music was always a vital component of the Czech national character. Dr. Charles Burney, the English eighteenth-century musicologist, called Bohemia "Europe's Conservatory." ("Not only in every large town but in every village there is a reading and writing school, the children are taught music.") Actually, the first conservatory in Central Europe was founded in 1810 in Prague, in the Dominican monastery near St. Giles Church. Long before the emergence of a Czech national music, the *České muzikanti* (Czech musicians) were as famous in Europe as Czech humanists and Czech heretics, Czech tailors and Czech artisans.

One thousand years ago, St. Vojtěch is said to have composed the first Czech hymn, "Hospodine, pomiluj ny" (Oh God, Have Mercy on Us). And the old song about the death of King Wenceslas has become a sort of popular national prayer (which doesn't much please the present regime). The Bohemian countryside was always filled with music—folk melodies, village dances, drinking songs. Jaromir Erben published a collection of folk songs and polka dances but he didn't do the thorough job that Béla Bartók and Zoltan Kodály did when they traveled for years through Hungary's

The Mystical City

backwoods villages to save the country's folk songs from oblivion. A great many old Czech songs have disappeared because they were never written down.

King John, the father of Charles IV, brought Guillaume de Machaut, poet, scholar and creator of the French *ars nova*, to Hradčany Castle, and some Franco-Flemish musicians came to the court of Prague. During the Hussite era, music for the first time reached the soul of the people. Two great battle hymns of the Hussites have been preserved, stirring songs that terrified their enemies: "Povstan, povstan, veliké město Pražské!" (Rise Up, Great City of Prague), and "Ktož jsu boži bojovníci" (Ye Warriors of God) which Smetana artfully used in the last two movements of *My Country*. In 1875, Smetana wrote, "On the basis of this Hussite melody, the rebirth of the Czech people will be worked out, their future happiness and glory." He was already totally deaf (his sickness, worse than Beethoven's, later led to insanity), but he could still see the future. Other old Hussite "fighting and mocking songs" from the fifteenth century have been preserved in the *Jistebnice Cantional*. Some were written by Jan Hus, an able composer himself (just as Martin Luther was a century later). In fact, Luther's hymns have the rousing spirit and the rugged strength that one finds earlier in the songs of Jan Hus. Throughout the whole fight between Catholicism and Reformation, music played an important part.

The music-filled era came to an end with the battle of the White Mountain in 1620, which was followed by the Thirty Years' War. For a long time, the only sounds heard in Prague were the distant thunder of artillery and the ominous rolls of drums, the somber background of executions. Then the militant leaders of the Counter-Reformation began to realize the importance of music. Using the old melodies, the

Jesuits wrote new lyrics for the education of the "heretics" in Bohemia. Many Czech musicians emigrated. Johann V. Stamitz (1717–1757) joined the remarkable group of musicians known as "the Mannheim school" that Duke Carl Theodor, Elector Palatine, assembled at his court in Mannheim. Stamitz is now admired as the precursor of the classical symphony. "The Scherzo in Beethoven's Fifth Symphony was indeed modeled after the Finale of Stamitz' modest trio sonata, opus IV, No. 3," writes Paul Henry Lang. Other Bohemian musicians, who couldn't make a living at home, emigrated to Vienna: Bohuslav Černohorsky, Johann Dismas Zelenka, Franz Tůma, Johann Zach, Josef Mysliveček, Anton Jiránek. Later Zelenka and Jiránek went to Dresden, Mysliveček to Rome, Georg Benda to Berlin, Franz Benda to Gotha. In Vienna, Leopold Anton Koželuh wrote pre-classical symphonies. Jan Stefani from Prague went to Warsaw and founded Poland's national opera there. Antonin Rejha taught composition at the Paris Conservatory (among his pupils were Berlioz, Liszt, Franck, Gounod). Hundreds of Czech orchestra musicians worked all over Europe. Today's cultural ideologists resent the expression *České muzikanti*, which seems to give them an inferiority complex. ("It implies that the Czechs were a nation of *muzikanti*.") Things could be worse; the British are known as a "nation of shopkeepers," the Swiss a "nation of innkeepers." The music-makers of Bohemia made a historical contribution to the glory of "Europe's Conservatory."

Italian opera was performed by Italian companies at Hradčany Castle in the eighteenth century. In 1723, the opera *Costanza e Fortezza* by the Austrian composer Johann Josef Fux was produced for four thousand listeners during the coronation festivities for Charles VI. Later, opera was given

The Mystical City

for ordinary citizens in other theaters in town, always by Italian managers.

But Prague's greatest contribution to the art of music is an indirect one: Prague made the short, unhappy life of the world's greatest musical genius a little happier. Mozart was twice in Prague and he loved every moment of it.

On January 13, 1787, the *Prager Oberpostamtszeitung* reported, "Last night our great and beloved composer, Hr. Mozard [*sic*], arrived here from Vienna. We expect that in his honor Hr. Bondini will schedule performances of 'The Marriage of Figaro,' this popular work of his musical genius ... We also wish to hear Hr. Mozart play the piano."

The following day Mozart wrote to Gottfried von Jacquin, his friend in Vienna, about "the so-called Bretfeld Ball" (in Malá Strana's Neruda Street) and the beautiful women of Prague who were there:

That would have been something for you, my friend. I mean, I can see you run—well, maybe rather hobble—after all these beautiful girls and women. I didn't dance and I didn't eat anything: the first because I was too tired and the last out of my congenital stupidity [*Blöde*]. I looked on with sheer delight as all the people merrily flew about to the music of my Figaro, arranged for Counter Dances and German Dances. Here they talk nothing but Figaro. Nothing is played, sung or whistled but Figaro. No opera is drawing like Figaro. Certainly a great honor for me.

Mozart, in a happy, exuberant mood, goes on with the names which he and his party invented for themselves on their journey to Prague. "I am Punktititi. My wife is Schabla Pumfa ... My dog is Schamanuzky ..." Franz Xaver Niemetschek, the Mozart biographer, remembers in 1808, that

Mozart was cheered at the theater and later played the piano there in a "Big Musical Academy." Niemetschek beautifully conveys the impression of Mozart's genius:

> We didn't know what to admire more, the extraordinary composition or the extraordinary performance; both created a total impression on our souls akin to a sweet enchantment. At the end of the Academy, Mozart improvised alone on the piano-forte for half an hour and heightened our fascination to the highest degree, and there were overflowing ovations. In fact, his improvisations surpassed everything that one could imagine about piano playing . . . Certainly, as this Academy was unique for the people of Prague, Mozart counted this day to be the best in his life . . .

A few weeks earlier, Mozart had finished in Vienna his D Major Symphony (K.504), known as the "Prague" Symphony, or "Symphony without Minuet," which was performed there in January, 1787, and, according to Niemetschek, "remained a favorite piece of Prague audiences though it must have been heard a hundred times . . . Mozart loved to be in Prague."

The most important result of the trip was Mozart's decision to follow up his comic masterpiece *Le Nozze di Figaro* with one of the greatest dramatic masterpieces of all times, *Don Giovanni*. Pasquale Bondini, manager of the Italian opera company, wanted to cash in on Mozart's local popularity, and gave him a contract. The opera would also be performed at the Nostitz Theater. Built by Count F. A. Nostitz, from 1781 to 1783, it was, and still is, one of Europe's most charming Baroque theaters, with its beautiful frescoes, its tiers of richly decorated boxes, its low corridors with uneven floors; only the ladies and gentlemen with their powdered wigs from the days of Mozart are missing. In 1798, the theater became the property of the Estates for 60,000 guilders, and was renamed Estates Theater until 1945, when it was called Tyl Theater, after Josef Kajetan Tyl.

Mozart returned to Vienna in the spring of 1787, and at once began to discuss with Lorenzo da Ponte the libretto of the Don Juan theme that had interested him for some time. Da Ponte wrote *Il Dissoluto Punito Ossia Il Don Giovanni*. It was a time of great sorrow for Mozart. His friend, the physician Barisani, died, and then he lost his beloved father. In these dark days, he conceived the unfathomably beautiful music of *Don Giovanni*.

In the summer, he went back to his beloved Prague to finish the score, which he dedicated to the people of Prague. The singers and the technical apparatus of Bondini's theater were not quite up to Mozart's exalted standards. The premiere had been scheduled for the wedding trip of Prince Anton of Saxony and Maria Theresa, the sister of Emperor Joseph II, but it had to be postponed, and instead, *Figaro* was given as a gala performance. On October 29, 1787, Mozart conducted the world premiere of *Don Giovanni*. He had feverishly worked during the last days and nights preceding the premiere at the nearby house in No. 420 Rytířská, a charming building erected on low arcades. Here, according to a much-cherished Prague legend, he finished the magnificent overture just in time for the performance, and the musicians had to sight-read it "from the pages still wet." If there is some truth in it, as in so many Prague legends, the musicians must have been very good. But Mozart once said, "My orchestra is in Prague." Perhaps the legend is true after all.

On November 3, the *Oberpostamtszeitung*, which by now had learned to correctly spell the composer's name, reported:

Connoisseurs and composers agree that such a work has never been given in Prague. Hr. Mozart conducted himself, and when he stepped into the orchestra pit, he received three ovations, and this happened again when he left. The opera is very hard to execute and everybody admires the good performance after a short rehearsal time.

Apparently, the paper's music critic stuck to the essentials of the performance, cautiously reserving critical judgment on the artistic merits of Mozart's masterpiece. Maybe he didn't really understand it; he wasn't the only one. *Don Giovanni* was a terrific success. Domenico Guardasoni, the stage manager, told Mozart and da Ponte that "as long as they lived there would never be any more bad seasons." *Don Giovanni* was performed 532 times in Prague in the hundred years following the premiere. Casanova was in the audience; he may have contributed some substitutions to the text. He might have watched *Don Giovanni* with mixed feelings. The great seducer fails lamentably in his last efforts. The Don is turned down by Donna Anna; he gets in trouble with his former fiancée, Donna Elvira; he can't even seduce Zerlina, the pretty peasant girl; and then he gets comeuppance from the icy hand of the stony Commendatore. The supreme irony of *Don Giovanni*, which Mozart appreciated, is that it could have been called "The Last, Unhappy Days of Don Giovanni." Mozart later wrote to Jacquin of the enormous applause at the first performance and all that followed. "I wished that my good friends were here for one night to take part in my happiness." And he asked, worried, "Will my opera be given in Vienna? I wish for it."

He had worked hard with his Italian artists. Luigi Bassi from Pesaro, the birthplace of Rossini, was an attractive Don. Teresa Saporiti was a beautiful Donna Anna. Caterina Bondini, the wife of the manager, sang the part of Zerlina. When she didn't utter a convincing cry for help at the end of the first act, Mozart is said to have pinched her backstage to get a realistic effect.

These were the last happy days of his life. ("A tender public and true friends carried him so-to-speak on hands," writes Niemetschek.) His antagonists, the composers Antonio Salieri and Leopold Koželuh, had come to Prague to intrigue against Mozart. Mozart had done another opera, during the journey to Prague and the preparations for *Don Giovanni*. This was *La Clemenza di Tito*, which he also conducted in Prague, with no success. He was already sick when he went back to Vienna. There, news of the Prague premiere of *Don Giovanni* had reached the ears of the Emperor. After the customary intrigues and delays, it was performed there at the Burgtheater, on May 7, 1788, with no success. The Viennese considered it "confused and dissonant." The only man who appreciated *Don Giovanni* was Joseph Haydn.

The people of Prague have lovingly catalogued all the places that Mozart frequented. At first he stayed with Count Thun at the palace that is now the seat of the British Ambassador. He played the organ in the chapel of Strahov Monastery. The wine cellar in Temple Street and the "New Inn" in Celetná no longer exist. There Mozart listened to Josef Haisler who could read no music and knew nothing about counterpoint but played the harp with such virtuosity that Mozart invited him up to his room and played a theme on his spinet which he thereupon presented as a gift to Haisler. The harp virtuoso immediately began to play his own variations on Mozart's theme.

Mozart was often seen at Steinitz' coffeehouse near the Malá Strana bridgetower. The Villa Bertramka where he stayed with his friends, the composer Franz Dušek and his wife Josephine, a noted singer, is now a Mozart Museum, with electric chandeliers and central heating. It is a charming pink-and-white rococo house surrounded by a lovely garden. It was public knowledge that the house had been built by Count Clam as a "Tusculum" for Madame Dušek. Egon Erwin Kisch reports that from the garden one could see Malvazinka Cemetery. "In this gallant atmosphere each gentleman was a Don Giovanni who was after his Donna Anna and whose Donna Elvira was thinking of vengeance." In Mozart's days, the Villa Bertramka was on the outskirts of the town. Today it is surrounded by factories and apartment houses.

On December 31, 1791, the *Musikalisches Wochenblatt* in Berlin wrote:

Mozart is dead.—He returned from Prague, very ill. He died in Vienna, at the end of last week. His body was badly swollen and it is believed that he was poisoned. One of his last works is said to be a Requiem Mass. Now that he is dead, the Viennese will realize what they lost in him. Neither his "Figaro" nor his "Don Juan" were successful there, but the more in Prague. Peace to his ashes!

On December 14, nine days after Mozart's body had been dumped unceremoniously into a mass grave in Vienna Hundsturm Cemetery, four thousand people came to St. Nicholas Church in Prague's Malá Strana where his *Requiem Mass* was performed. Josephine Dušek sang the soprano solo. On January 13, 1792, an "Academy" was given at the National Theater in honor of the dead composer.

Mozart's success in Prague proves how intimately the musical Prague was connected with Vienna's musical classicism. In a way, Mozart repaid to Prague the debt which Vienna owed the Czechs for taking away and assimilating so many excellent Bohemian musicians. (After a visit to Prague, Beethoven wrote to his brother, "My art is gaining me both friends and respect—what more could I ask?")

There was no Czech national music until the early nineteenth century, and no Czech opera. Opera needs the help of the language, and the Czech language, which for centuries had been considered "only a peasant's language," was then slowly being resurrected by Josef Jungmann who created the first Czech-German Dictionary, by the historian František Palacký, and the biologist Jan Evangelista Purkyně. ("The former Czech serfs were going to work in manufacture," writes the contemporary historian Miloš Kratochvil. "A new intelligentsia was coming forward imbued with patriotism and enlightened ideals.")

In 1806, Mozart's *The Abduction from the Seraglio* was given for the first time in a Czech translation. In 1825, the Theater of the Estates gave the first performance of a Czech opera, *Drátenik* (The Tinker), by František Škroup, a simple, comic work that is still in the repertory of many Czech companies. Škroup later became immortal as the composer of "Kde Domov Můj?" (Where Is My Home?), the melancholy, beautiful Czech national anthem—the only one on earth that begins with a question. Perhaps the Czechs were not yet sure where their home was, but Škroup gave them the answer: in the woods and by the rivers and on the meadows, there is my home. Škroup himself had to leave his home; he couldn't make a living in Prague and emigrated to Holland, and there he died in exile. No other Czech opera was successful until Smetana came along—the right genius at the right moment. The time had come for Czech national music, and Smetana was the man to write it.

Born in 1824 in the small Bohemian town of Litomyšl, Smetana was a gifted composer and a Czech patriot. He had firm convictions about his artistic *and* national mission. He considered music an important expression of human emotions; ideas should be expressed in music, in a broad human sense. Smetana instinctively turned toward the musical drama, which seemed to offer the best possibilities. He has been called "the father of Czech music," and for once the popular epithet is justified. Instead of imitating his Italian and German predecessors, Smetana went back to the sources of folk music, the lore of his country. The national and historical elements in his music are not "exotic color" but the very spirit of this music. He owes much to Beethoven, Schumann, Chopin and Wagner but he was too talented to be overwhelmed by others. His best music sounds like Smetana's and no one else's—the music of Bohemia, often haunting and sad in its harmonies, then again merry with Slav rhythms and dance tunes. His best melodies have the innocence and simplicity of genuine folk melodies.

After several years in Gøteborg, Sweden, where he'd gone to make some money, he returned to Prague in 1861, determined to say in music what other Czechs were beginning to say in political speeches. He is a romantic composer. His romanticism doesn't come from nature but from his nation's history; there are epic, heroic undertones in his music, which is always national music. Smetana understood Gluck's operatic reforms, and though he couldn't quite shake off Richard Wagner's influence—no one could, at that time—he didn't share the Bayreuth superman's pseudo-philosophy and strange aesthetic theories. Smetana had to learn to compose for the Czech language, which is not exactly singable, with many words consisting only of consonants. (The classic example is the sentence, "Strč prst skrz krk," which means, "Put the finger down the throat.")

Smetana's *The Bartered Bride* is considered in Prague

"the direct and worthy descendant of Mozart's 'Figaro,'" says Pavel Eckstein. Such comparisons are always problematical; but *The Bartered Bride* is a masterpiece, with a wide range of human emotions, a great comic opera from the scintillating overture to the happy end. Smetana never repeated its success. *The Bartered Bride*, the Czech's national opera, has been performed almost three thousand times in Prague alone; the people there never get tired of it, as the Viennese never get tired of *The Magic Flute*, the Parisians of *Faust*, the Russians of *Boris Godunov*, the Poles of *Halka*. Ironically, *The Bartered Bride* was no success in Prague when it was first performed there. Only after its triumph in Vienna, in a German translation, did it become a hit in Prague. The Viennese have reciprocated for what the people of Prague did earlier for Mozart's *Figaro*.

The tradition of Smetana was continued by Antonín Dvořák, not really an operatic composer though he said toward the end of his life, "People think of me only as a composer of symphonic music but for many years I've expressed my deep affection for opera." Dvořák's earlier works have imagination, temperament and great beauty; everybody liked them except Dvořák, who later wrote "program music." He is not considered *persona gratissima* by the *kultura* bureaucrats of today's regime; perhaps they feel there are "cosmopolitan" sounds in Dvořák's beautiful music, in the "New World" Symphony and the "American" String Quartet, the result of a trip to the United States where he was always homesick for Bohemia. But the bureaucrats and the experts have often been wrong in Prague. Leoš Janáček from Moravia was sixty-two when his masterpiece, *Jenufa*, written twelve years earlier, was at last given in Prague, in 1916; until then, the Prague music critics considered him "a nobody from the provinces." The militant leader of the anti-

Janáček forces was Zdeněk Nejedlý, musicologist and university professor who dismissed the composer because of the folklore elements in his music. Nejedlý later became the powerful Minister of Culture of the Communist government under Klement Gottwald and completely reversed his earlier opinions on Janáček, when folklore became the big thing officially, but that was long after Janáček's death. Incredibly, *Jenufa*, now considered a masterpiece, had been performed for twelve years in Brno, the capital of Moravia, but apparently no one from Prague ever bothered to hear it. Elsewhere Janáček was completely unknown until Max Brod, at Janáček's urgent request, translated *Jeji Pastorkyně* into *Jenufa*.

Even then it was still a long way toward success. *Jenufa* was accepted by the Vienna Court Opera, allegedly at the personal wish of Emperor Charles, the last Habsburg (he was the nephew of Franz Joseph I), who wanted to show his conciliatory attitude toward the Czechs. It was too little and too late; *Jenufa* was given in February, 1918, eight months before the collapse of the Habsburg Monarchy. Maria Jeritza sang the title role. The critics panned the work, which disappeared from the program after ten performances. (It did better though than the original *Figaro*, with only nine performances.) Only the Berlin performance of *Jenufa*, conducted by Erich Kleiber in 1926, started its belated worldwide triumph.

Two years later, Janáček died. His own nation recognized his greatness only after his death—just as the Hungarians realized the genius of Béla Bartók only after he had died in 1945. Both Janáček and Bartók used folklore as the source of their own music; each of them created his own, modern, musical language that is timeless and great. Today Janáček

The Mystical City

is very much honored in Prague. Each line he wrote is researched, analyzed, interpreted, approved and officially sanctioned. The soft-spoken, modest genius from the Moravian village of Kukvaldy would be rather amused.

Prague, known as a musical city the world over, never was a musically creative city, such as Vienna where the streets and squares and hills vibrated with music and radiated music. Gluck, Haydn, Mozart, Beethoven found inspiration in the houses of Vienna; Schubert went out to the Heuriger inns in the suburbs; Brahms and Johann Strauss walked in the Vienna Woods; Schönberg, Berg and Webern created a new musical language in Vienna, which no one there understood. The classical, the romantic and the modern epoch in Western music began in the city of Vienna.

By contrast, Czech and Moravian music is bucolic, not urban, in character. Czech and Moravian composers were inspired by the music-filled countryside—the sounds of the woods, the dances in the villages.

One hears these sounds in Smetana's *The Bartered Bride*, in Dvořák's *Rusálka*, in Janáček's *The Cunning Little Vixen*. The best-known movement in Smetana's *My Country* is the "Moldau," but its very heart is the fourth movement, "From Bohemia's Woods and Fields." The opening movement is "Vyšehrad," but Smetana is less concerned with the old castle in the vicinity of Prague than with the legend of Princess Libuše and the beginnings of Czech history. (The arpeggio of the seeress' harp at the beginning of the movement is the musical signature of Radio Prague.)

Even the "Moldau," where Smetana traces its course, by his own explanation, "from listening to its two springs, the warm and the cold Vltava . . . until it flows into the Elbe," does not reflect on the story of Prague, the stone bridge with its dark, ecstatic saints. Smetana did not write a tone poem about Hradčany. He dedicated the score of *My Country* "to the Royal Capital of Prague," which, in turn dedicated the Smetana Museum to his memory. (The "Prague Spring" Festival, one of Europe's finest, always opens with a performance of *My Country* in Prague's Smetana Hall. Mozart is performed in the Garden of the Knights of Malta, Beethoven in the Garden of the Valdštejn Palace. Prague is more than a mere stage—it becomes part of the music and reason for it.)

The finest music of Antonín Dvořák does not refer to the city of Prague. Its melodies and harmonies suggest the haunting melancholy, the eternal beauty and sometimes the earthly gaiety of the countryside. Janáček, who may one day be considered the greatest musical genius his country produced, creates a new musical idiom out of the impressionistic sounds of his Moravian meadows and woods, with their mystery and magic, sad people and dark secrets. His beautiful opera *The Cunning Vixen*, a moving poem dedicated to love and nature and eternity, begins and ends in the forests. It is Janáček's own *Midsummer Night's Dream*.

Prague never inspired its greatest composers—but the people of Prague always appreciated great music. "My Prager understand me," said Mozart. Berlioz, who conducted concerts here in 1845, and performed *Roméo et Juliette* in the presence of Liszt, called the Prague chorus "outstanding and magnificent," and later wrote, "I haven't said yet what a tender yearning I feel for Prague and its people . . . *O, Praga! Quando te aspiciam*?" (When shall I see you again?) Berlioz reports that Liszt, who was to give a concert at noon the next day, drank champagne all night long and was still asleep at half past eleven. "But he arrived at the

The Mystical City

concert hall in time and he played as he'd never played in his life... There must be a God of the pianists!"

Tchaikovsky gave a concert at the National Theater on February 21, 1888. Afterward he wrote a short sentence in his diary which he underlined with trembling fingers: "One minute of absolute bliss." Many composers, conductors and great performers have since felt one minute of absolute bliss when they performed in Prague where the people love music.

The year 1888 was remembered by the Germans in Prague for the opening of the German Theater. The theater was built out of private contributions and had a national and often polemical mission, as everything else in Prague. Its first director, Angelo Neumann, was a baptized Jew from Vienna, and one of the earliest, most ardent followers of Richard Wagner. Neumann produced in 1885—only nine years after the first Bayreuth Festival!—a complete *Ring des Nibelungen* in Prague. Two years later, he arranged a complete Mozart cycle. Long before Hugo von Hofmannsthal and Max Reinhardt discussed their ideas for a Salzburg Festival, Neumann set up a May Festival at his theater, during which he presented modern works and dramatic masterpieces from all over the world. He was a theatrical genius who made the German Theater in Prague a famous "springboard" for artists who spent their early years there before they became world-famous. Among its conductors were Gustav Mahler (before he became director of the Vienna Court Opera), Leo Blech, Arthur Bodansky, Otto Klemperer, Alexander von Zemlinsky (Schönberg's teacher and brother-in-law) and George Szell. During the short, happy years of the Masaryk Republic there was a mutually rewarding exchange of works between the German Theater and the (Czech) National Theater in Prague. The German

Theater performed Karel Čapek and Leoš Janáček, and the National Theater gave Goethe and Wagner.

The cornerstone for the National Theater (Národní Divadlo) was laid on May 18, 1868, a significant date in the life of the Czech nation. It was to be more than a theater: the symbol of Czech hope for eventual liberation. Ever since 1848 and the Pan-Slav Congress in Prague, a strong patriotic movement had been alive, under Palacký, Karel Havlíček, František Rieger. Around the magazine *Lumír*, a generation of young Czech scientists gathered—the historian Jaroslav Goll, the aesthete Otakar Hostinský, the cultural historian Miloslav Tyrš, the poet Jaroslav Vrchlický, and later Jan Gebauer, an innovator of the Czech language, and Tomáš Masaryk, the realistic philosopher who continued the ideas of the Hussites and of the great educator and humanist John Amos Comenius.

("The Middle Class National Party split into the Old Czechs and the Young Czechs," writes Communist historian Miloš Kratochvil. "The former, with the support of the aristocratic landowners and businessmen, wanted a Czech provincial government within the Austrian Monarchy. The Young Czechs represented the interests of the peasants, craftsmen and professional workers . . . The teachings of Karl Marx and Friedrich Engels found many adherents for they gave a clear aim to the elementary struggle of the workers for economic and political rights.")

"There exist few buildings in Europe whose tones convey so much sentiment and love," wrote the Prague art historian M. Štech about the National Theater. It was built entirely out of contributions of the Czech people; for years collections were made in obscure villages and small towns; the motto on the façade, "Národ Sobě" (From the Nation to Itself), appeared justified.

Smetana wrote his opera *Libuše* for the opening on June 15, 1881. Two months later, on August 12, owing to an incautious worker, the theater burned down. It was a national tragedy but the forces set in motion were too strong to be stopped. Again collections were made—this time even the Emperor and the Germans in Prague contributed—and the National Theater was rebuilt and re-opened, with *Libuše*. It has been a national shrine ever since—a fortress of the best in Czech culture in bad and good days. It was built on one of the finest sites of Prague, overlooking the Moldau with its quays and flocks of wild white ducks flowing over the dark water. Behind, there are the towers and palaces of Malá Strana, and farther in the rear, the majestic contours of Hradčany Castle.

The Czechs consider the National Theater the finest work of Czech nineteenth-century art. Perhaps a national shrine must not be judged by purely aesthetic considerations. Josef Zítek designed the building in the style of the late North-Italian Renaissance. Václav Myslbek did the sculptures at the portal showing the statues of "Opera" and "Drama"; Mikuláš Aleš painted the lunettes "Homeland" in the foyer; Vojtěch Hynais painted the curtain, eulogizing the nation's self-sacrifice; František Ženíšek did the frescoes on the ceiling of the auditorium. There is a mood of affection, warmth and grandeur inside that affects many people.

The National Theater has remained Prague's unofficial "court theater" and has first call on any work—opera, drama, ballet—it seems worthy to perform. (Works not given there may be performed at one of Prague's other twenty-four theaters.) The National Theater has two full orchestras, two independent choruses, a large ballet company, some seventy soloists and eight conductors. The company is required to give fifteen operatic performances a week in three houses—the National Theater, the Smetana Theater (the former German Theater until 1945) and the Týl (Nostitz or Estates) Theater, where Mozart's works are performed. Of about sixty operas in the repertory of the National Theater, half are works by Czech and Moravian composers, including contemporary works. Clearly, the company is a *national* theater, built on native talent, in the spirit of the ensemble and repertory theater that is only a memory in the great houses of New York, Milan, Vienna and London, with their fast-traveling singing stars. It is not unusual to choose between performances of Mozart, Verdi and Janáček on what the opera lovers of Prague call "a typical night." Prague is a great place for music.

Josef Švejk and Josef K.

JAROSLAV HAŠEK's *The Adventures of the Good Soldier Švejk* ("Švejk" begins with "sh" and rhymes with "break") is now compared to the satirical masterpieces of Rabelais, Cervantes, Swift, but Hašek is still widely unknown abroad. The current *Encyclopaedia Britannica* does not list his name. Even in his native Prague, more legends than facts are remembered about him. Until ten years ago, Hašek was blacklisted by the Communist regime. Cautious people didn't mention his name, or Kafka's. "The Prague Czech popular writer, Jaroslav Hašek, achieved what hundreds of authors try in vain during their lifetime: to create a character that is a human being as well as a prototype," wrote Kafka's friend Max Brod, one of the very few people who early recognized Hašek's greatness. ("I thank you for the lovely review of my book," Hašek humbly wrote to Brod.) Brod and Hans Reimann later created a German dramatic version of *Švejk* for Erwin Piscator in Berlin that made Hašek posthumously world-famous.

The character that Hašek created and named "Švejk" (his first name was Josef) has always existed in Prague. Hašek had the insight and the genius to express in words what other people had instinctively long felt. When "The Good Soldier Švejk" made his appearance in the Czech lands, a great many people recognized him, as though they had intimately known him, and greeted him like a dear, old friend who has been away for a long, long time. Plays about Švejk (by various playwrights, including Brecht) have been performed in many countries. But it is a curious fact that only Czech actors are able to perfectly portray the character of the Good Soldier; the performance by Josef Noll remains unsurpassed, even by the great German comedian, Max Pallenberg, who misunderstood the character and played it for effect. Švejk is a subtle fellow, seemingly an idiot, who is much smarter than many so-called smart people.

Today Švejk is no longer a Czech type. He is a universal species—a good-natured, kind-hearted, naive-but-cunning little man who confounds confusion by following verbatim the letter of the law, reducing bureaucrats, politicians and militarists to absurdity by taking them absurdly seriously. He wants to do everything right and always does everything wrong. He is forever in trouble but nothing perturbs his philosophical state of mind. Deep down in his heart he knows he is a good citizen who really does the right thing though others may not agree. After being drafted by the Austrian army, he tells the arbitration board,

I shall serve His Majesty to my last breath. Now that I am here, I'm going to stay here. I am now a soldier. I must serve His Majesty. No one can expel me from the army, even if the general would kick me in the behind and throw me out of the barracks. I would come right back and say, "I obediently report, general, Sir, that I must serve His Majesty to my last breath, and that I shall return to my company." And if they don't want to have me there, I shall join the navy, so I can at least serve His Majesty on board ship. And if they don't want me even there and the admiral would kick me in the behind, I am going to serve His Majesty in the air.

Nowadays, Švejk is often associated with the Czech national character. There may be something "of the Švejk" in the actions and reactions of many Czechs today but the current overestimation of Hašek's fictitious character results from the apathy of the Czech literary critics in Hašek's early years. He was unable to find a publisher for his book, and it was finally printed in installments on cheap newsprint in "colportage" booklets, each costing a crown. The author himself would peddle the installments from house to house, to janitors, cooks, servant girls. He was often intoxicated, and there were arguments when he asked for advance payment. For educated Czechs, Jaroslav Hašek, the author of "cheap colportage," did not exist. In his defense of the great writer, Brod attacked the Czech literary establishment as he had earlier attacked the country's musical establishment when he defended Leoš Janáček.

No one except a few faithful drinking companions took notice of Hašek's death in 1923. And while the critics ignored him, the people reading the installments were beginning to identify themselves with Švejk. Wasn't that the little guy down at the *výčep* (the beer joint) down the street who thoughtfully sipped his beer and philosophized about mankind and the world? Like Don Quixote, Švejk began as a caricature and ended up as a symbol—though, actually, he is closer to Sancho Panza than to Don Quixote.

Always a loyal Austrian patriot (this was Hašek's supreme joke, much appreciated by the Czechs in those days), Švejk regrets the Archduke's assassination in Sarajewo, but what interests him most is the construction of the murder weapon. And as a soldier in the k. & k. (Imperial & Royal) Army,

> Švejk was smiling, delightful in his manners, and perhaps for this reason nearly always in jail. And when he came back from jail, he would smilingly answer all questions, and with complete composure went to jail again, and soon all officers of the garrison became afraid of him. Not of his toughness, but of his kindness, his obedient answers, his brotherly smile, that was a nightmare for them.

Švejk is "just an ordinary man," who has a deep, almost religious belief in order and authority, and thus nothing ever surprises him. When he is arrested for high treason, he accepts this as an inevitable fate of the loyal citizen. Asked to sign the protocol accusing him of *lèse-majesté*, he doesn't hesitate because he doesn't want "to create complications." As a good citizen he knows there must be order—a subtle *reductio ad absurdum* of the idiotic German saying, *Ordnung ist die erste Bürgerpflicht* (to keep order is the citizen's first duty). Švejk who always says "yes" is the antithesis of

Heinrich von Kleist's Michael Kohlhaas who always says "no," banging his head against the wall. Unlike Kohlhaas who breaks his head, Švejk gloriously proves that his head is stronger than the wall.

By explicitly executing the silliest orders, he gets his superiors into terrible predicaments. When he stands guard in front of the powder magazine and a fire breaks out, Švejk keeps away the fire brigade who don't know the code word, for according to his orders, "No one must approach without knowing the code word." When asked why he didn't think, Švejk says politely, "I obediently report that I do not think because a soldier is not permitted to think. His officers think for him. When a soldier begins to think, he is no longer a soldier but a nuisance, a damned civilian." (This may sound ludicrous, but it was exactly the philosophy of my infantry company commander when I served in the Czechoslovak Army a few years after the death of Jaroslav Hašek. We were not permitted to read *Švejk*, and read it secretly.)

The fortunes of Hašek's masterpiece in Prague fluctuated with the vicissitudes of the political situations. After a brief spell of glory during the Masaryk Republic, Hašek became unpopular among the Czech intellectuals, who claimed that he conveyed the wrong image of the nation. They said it was bad enough for the Czechs to be known abroad as a nation of *muzikanti*, and now they would be known as a nation of Švejks. During the Second World War, Švejk became the nation's secret hero and the idol of the resistance fighters who drove the Germans to despair by explicitly executing stupid military orders and practicing the subtle art of passive resistance. Shipments of arms and ammunition would get mysteriously detoured, trains unaccountably wound up on sidings, reams of official files were filled with inane double-talk. It was pure *Švejkovina*, the Švejkian state of mind.

During the short democratic postwar interlude, 1945-48, Švejk was a great fellow; but the Communist regime put Hašek's works on the index. The ideologists were exasperated about Švejk, an able-bodied citizen who had never joined the Party, was neither a worker nor a peasant, but lived off the sale of mongrel dogs and spent his nights at the tavern "U Kalicha" (At the Chalice). Only when a different political wind began to blow after the Twentieth Party Congress in Moscow (with Khrushchev's nine-hour denunciation of Stalin that ended the personality cult) was Hašek "rediscovered," this time as a sort of early Communist primitive. By higher orders, Hašek's favorite tavern, U Kalicha, was rebuilt, decorated in the style of Josef Lada's book illustrations, and has been a tourist attraction ever since. The famous life-size painting of Emperor Franz Josef I (that creates the initial complications in the book) is hanging there. The window niches are adorned with quotations from Hašek's book, in German, English and Russian. (Not in Czech, but the people of Prague rarely go to U Kalicha nowadays.) Neither would Švejk, if he saw the place now. He wouldn't tell Sapper Vodička, "When the war's over, drop in to see me—you'll find me at the Chalice every evening after six."

Švejk has brought new fame to the Chalice and that unique Prague institution, the beer parlor. Unlike Vienna and Budapest, Prague was never a city of coffeehouses. In the 1830s, when Vienna had over a hundred coffeehouses, there were only two in Prague, "At the Golden Tiger," in Dominikánská, and Pastor's Kavárna. (*Kavárna* means café.) People went there to drink "coffee in the Turkish manner," to have their pipes filled with Turkish tobacco and to read the newspapers; originally, the news had been written on a blackboard. The Baroque artists—Dientzenhofer, Brandl, Steinfels, Reiner and Canevalli all went to Pastor's Kavárna, and so did Mozart, since it was located in Ovocný Trh (Fruit Market) near the Nostitz Theater.

Around the turn of the century, the Czech intelligentsia, and the Germans and Jews, began to frequent "their" coffeehouses but the common man in Prague had his beer parlor, or *pivnice*. It was his club, retreat, debating society and political forum. It was a local invention in the capital of Bohemia, where some of the world's earliest and best beer had been brewed six hundred years ago. Prague's beer houses range from the small, anonymous *výčep*, a sort of neighborhood pub, to large establishments with a great history and a strange name ("At the Three Ostriches," "At the Red Chestnut," "At the King of Brabant"). Prague's oldest brewery, "U Sv. Tomáše" (At St. Thomas), is named after the nearby church. The Augustinian monks there had a special recipe for their famous "black" beer since 1352. At the nearby "U Schnellů" the beer was said to have such a heavy foam that customers would test it by placing a five-crown coin on top of the foam. The coin never dropped through the foam.

Another famous Prague beer house, "U Fleků," is first mentioned in a document dated 1499, when one Vitus Skřemenec bought the already established brewery and the adjoining warehouse. The present name dates from 1762, when Jakob and Dorothea Flek bought the place. The letters of the name form the dial on the clock above the entrance; Prague, the city of beer taverns, is also the city of strange, archaic clocks. Generations have gone to "Flek's Inn" for the famous "brown" beer, and business was so good that the competing monks at St. Thomas claimed that the brown beer, unlike their black one, was "an invention of the devil." Flek's beer is known as "13," because of its 13 per cent alcoholic content. Other beers in Prague contain from 7 to 18 per cent alcohol. Only at U Fleků do they make "13," right in the kitchen; nothing else is sold there.

U Fleků has vault-like rooms, wood panels, bas-reliefs enormous tables, heavy oak chairs. The rooms have various names—"Hopyard," "Academy," "Knights' Room," the long-stretched "Sausage," the "Trunk" with its low ceiling, and one called after St. Wenceslas. The geography is dearly familiar to the habitués, who would never go to the "wrong" room. They are artists, students, writers, painters, bums, philosophers, clerks, workers—everybody. Political secrets were conceived and betrayed here, revolutions were plotted or at least hoped for, dreams spoken into the air. Many habitués left melancholy impressions on the walls, such as

> Dearest beer, if you would die,
> Many orphans here would cry . . .

or,

> I drank my beer and paid the band,
> And off I went to Happy Land.

Food is not important in the beer taverns of Prague. One goes there for the beer, and above all for the companionship, the togetherness, the gripes, the exchange of political opinions or simply for escape. (One of the bas-reliefs at U Fleků shows a woman who drags off her husband after too many glasses of "13.") At the beginning of *The Good Soldier Švejk*, the Austrian police stool pigeon Bretschneider arrests Švejk at the Chalice, and later also takes Palivec, the owner of the tavern, to the police. Long before and ever since, local stool pigeons have frequented the beer taverns of Prague where people, after too many glasses, betray their most intimate secrets.

In 1957, the Czech critic, Rudolf Toman, wrote in a foreword to the East German edition of Jaroslav Hašek's *Confession* that "Švejk personifies the soldier who fights against the imperialistic wars." This may surprise some readers but it wouldn't surprise Švejk who once said. "Everybody may make a mistake, and the more he thinks about something, the more mistakes he makes."

Jaroslav Hašek came from a bourgeois family in Prague. He was thrown out of school for taking part in an anti-Habsburg demonstration around the turn of the century. After working as an apprentice in a drugstore, he was fired and began to wander all over Slovakia in the company of gypsies and other interesting people, became a bank clerk, was fired again and joined the anarchists. (Kafka who knew Hašek slightly told Janouch that anarchists were "sweet, amusing people.") Somehow, Hašek was named editor of the magazine *Svět Zvířat* (The World of the Animals). He lost his job when he wrote and published learned articles about animals which were extremely interesting though the animals didn't exist. This caused irritation among some humorless subscribers—natural-science teachers and frustrated zoologists. Next, Hašek began to buy and sell dogs (just as Švejk does) and set up a "Kynological Institute." (Kynology was described by Hašek as "the art and science of training dogs.")

He also invented improbable stories which he sold as strange facts to starved local reporters for a glass of beer. Egon Erwin Kisch reports several Hašek "scoops" in his

The Mystical City

book, *Prager Sensationen*. Once Hašek claimed to have seen a man-eating shark in the Moldau, near the Pathological Institute. Another time he had seen two employees of a noted funeral establishment who, being refused by two girls at a dance, "danced with the dead body of a lady that they were about to take to the cemetery." Another news item concerned a five-year-old boy who bit off his playmate's nose and swallowed it, whereupon the injured boy's father was "looking all over Prague for his son's nose."

During the national election of 1911 for the Austrian Parliament, Hašek founded his "Party of Moderate Reactionaries Within The Limits of The Law." Among other things, the Party demanded "the nationalization of the janitors," and protested against "too many earthquakes in Mexico." Hašek —whom Brod describes as a pale man with a round face and a pointed-up nose, not unlike Josef Lada's famous drawings of Švejk—promised every voter a pocket aquarium as a gift. His election rallies took place in cheap beer gardens and dim, dubious cabarets. During his speeches Hašek, who wore a Cossack's hat, was often interrupted by Homeric laughter. He would have been a refreshing figure in the political arena but unfortunately he couldn't get elected because it turned out that he'd forgotten to register as a candidate.

According to the current, official and humorless version, Hašek began to write as a soldier during the First World War, "with Maxim Gorki as his model." He deserted the Austrian Army on the Russian front and joined the Czechoslovak Legion in Russia. Later he returned to Prague and became a member of the Communist Party. "He was no longer the Prague bohemian but became active as an army and Party functionary," writes critic Toman. This doesn't tally with the reminiscences of Max Brod who (unlike

Toman) saw Hašek during the writer's last years. According to Brod, Hašek returned from Russia with a new wife, "a Duchess Lwowska," though he hadn't bothered to get a divorce from his first wife, Jarmila, who lived in Prague with their child. Perhaps he was still the Prague bohemian. He sold the dramatic rights to *Švejk* to a manager "for a glass of Pilsen beer." Toman reports that Hašek wrote for the Communist Party paper *Rudé Pravo*. "His humor is directed against the Church, petit-bourgeois degeneration, the nobility, against bureaucracy, against all weakness of history and society." Hašek certainly was a Czech patriot. In his *Švejk* he writes:

First Lieutenant Lukaš was the type of the professional officer of the Austrian Monarchy who had become a somewhat amphibious character in officers' school. When he was with other people he spoke German and he wrote fluent German, but he read only Czech books, and when he instructed a group of one-year voluntaries, all of them Czechs, he said, rather confidentially, "Let's be Czechs, but no one must know about it. I am also Czech." He considered the Czech nationality a sort of secret organization that one should rather avoid.

Brod reports that in 1921 Hašek was sent by his doctor to Lipnice, a small village on the Sazava River, because he had been drinking too much. It was hoped he might stop drinking in the tranquil, rustic environment. This was a vain hope, for Hašek was bored in Lipnice and never left the local tavern. Brod published a postcard dated December 12, 1921, signed by Hašek and his friend, the actor A. E. Longen. Hašek writes, "We are rehearsing the big scenes from 'Švejk,' especially the one about the army chaplain getting dead-drunk with Švejk." Two years later he was dead.

Hašek supplied his biographers with valuable documents.

In 1912, he published a short autobiography titled *Jaroslav Hašek, the Greatest Czech Writer:*

People will have to learn to appreciate me, not only as an enormous literary talent but also for my incomparably decent character. Why do I sing my own praise, you may ask? Because I know myself better than anyone else . . . I shall say it quite simply. In the history of mankind there is only one completely developed human being: I. In my writing, each sentence has its deeper meaning. Each word is in the right place. Everything is true. My Czech is better than that of the Králice Bible. It is a great delight to read every week one single sentence in my writings. If you do it, a sense of enchantment will fill your soul, and you'll smile blissfully. In fact, you won't be able to put the book away. I read each of my printed works to my wife Jarmila, the most charming, most intelligent woman on earth. I can never suppress the thought, "What a wonderful mind must this Jaroslav Hašek have!" I am living proof that our critics lie when they write we Czechs have no authors of world stature. A man who writes as beautifully as I must have a beautiful soul. At the next election the electorate will be ashamed should they overlook the most noble-minded man in the whole Monarchy . . .

A year later, in 1913, Toman reports that "the police tried in vain to locate Hašek." In order to further confuse his critics, "the most noble-minded man in the whole Monarchy" wrote in 1921, two years before his death, a document called *My Confession:*

I admit that I am not only a terrible rascal and a rotter but also an awful libertine. My birth created severe troubles for my dear mother who afterwards couldn't sleep for several days and nights. At the age of three months I bit my wet-nurse to death. When I was six years old, I ate my older brother, and I stole from his coffin the pictures of some saints that I concealed in the bed of our cook. She was sent to prison for ten years for robbing a coffin. Her fiancé hung himself, leaving six illegitimate children. Some of them became hotel thieves. One became the Abbot of the Premonstrant Convent in Strahov. At the age of three, I was the most debauched boy in Prague, and had an affair with the wife of a very high-ranking personage. At five, I broke into St. Thomas Church and stole a golden chalice which I sold, spending the money in a house of ill fame. Then I went to Vienna where I robbed a bank and was forced to strangle four bank clerks, one after another. At last I returned to Prague. During the railroad journey I lured an old lady out on the platform, took away her handbag, and pushed her out, telling the people that she'd got off at the last station. Unfortunately I didn't find my dear parents alive. My father had killed himself in a fit of despondency. My mother jumped from Charles Bridge into the Moldau, and when they tried to rescue her, she overturned the boat with her rescuers, and they too drowned. I grew up all by myself because I had poisoned my last uncle, stole his savings books and falsified the figure . . . My pen refuses to go on. To end my Confession before the Czech nation, I ask to be accepted by the Radical-Socialist Party. Please tell me where and when I should pay my first membership dues. For the time being, *Na shledanou* [See you again] . . .

For the world-at-large Hašek remains a one-book author, but his *Two Dozens Stories*, the result of his wandering years, are bitter, brilliant tales about Carpathian robbers, Rumanian thieves, beautiful gypsy girls. He left many short essays, among them "The Complete Etiquette." Samples: "If you manage to get into the leading lady's dressing room at the theatre, you should quietly hide below the table so you won't frighten her when she gets undressed." Or, "At a ball game, it is unfair to kill the umpire with a rusty blade."

In a remarkable essay, written in 1921, "What I Would Advise the Communists if I Were Editor-in-Chief of The Official Paper, *Československá Republika*," Hašek suggested, "The Communists should not try to deal with politics and the solution of social problems. Instead of holding meetings they should arrange games in the park . . ."

The Pražan

GREAT CITIES shape their inhabitants; some shape them more than others. "Local patriotism," a provincial attitude, has existed since the Athenians considered themselves far superior to the citizens of Sparta. (A famous Prague soccer club of the 1930s was called "Sparta"; the Communists now have "Spartakiades," tough physical-education contests.) The Florentines have looked down upon the Romans for a thousand years, and today both the people of Rome and Florence dislike (and secretly admire) the successful Milanese for their business-minded aggressiveness. The distinctions between Bostonians and New Yorkers, or between Angelenos and San Franciscans may be largely superficial yet they exist. But is there a prototype among the inhabitants of a certain city? The unkempt concierge or the cigarette-chewing habitué of the neighborhood bistro are "typical" Parisians, but so are the left-bank intellectual and the midinette from the Faubourg St. Honoré.

It is easy to define the difference between a Viennese and a *Pražan* (the sound "z" is a softly pronounced "sh," somewhat as the "j" in "jazz"), but difficult to define *the* citizen of Prague. Until the Second World War, a *Pražan* was the lower-class, ordinary, little fellow, Prague's common man whom the comic Vlasta Burian addressed, for want of a more impressive title, "*pane kolemvedoucí*," Mr. Passer-by. There was also the educated middle-class Czech who was "from Prague," but not a *Pražan*. A more obvious distinction existed between the "Prague Czechs," the "Prague Germans" and the "Prague Jews." The "Prague Jews," in turn, were either Czech-speaking or German-speaking Prague Jews, and between the two groups there was surprisingly little contact.

Today the problem no longer exists. Prague is a Czech city. (Many middle-aged people speak German and some speak French, and many young people speak English, "the language of the Western world." They also speak Russian, the language of the Eastern world, which they learned in school. In the 1930s, when Prague had half a million Czech inhabitants, we were told that the largest Czech-speaking city on earth was Chicago, Illinois. Now Prague has a million people, less than half of them natives of Prague. It is a young city—the average age of the people is thirty-five years. And for 1000 men there are now 1135 women.

There are still, or rather, again, class distinctions. Prague used to be a middle-class city. The First Republic had dispossessed the aristocrats, whose estates were expropriated and divided by the land reform. The working-class population was concentrated in the factory suburbs. Now the former upper-middle class (many of them German and Jewish bankers, industrialists, big businessmen) has disappeared. The middle class has been submerged with the lower-middle class into faceless "people." A small, new super-class of Party bosses, top bureaucrats, technological managers and successful artists has emerged, leading their own lives, more or less separated from the rest of the population. Since many members of the new super-class were once merely "people," they are trying hard to establish their new status by specifically Western-style symbols (a Mercedes or Peugeot, not a Škoda or Wartburg; a passport valid for a whole year, not just for one trip to the West; a house or apartment next to the residence of an "important" ambassador, not just His Excellency from Mali or Mauritania).

Yet the curious thing is that after twenty years of communism with all its revolutions (political, national, social, financial, cultural and so on) the "typical" *Pražan* is not basically different from the *Pražan* during the Masaryk Republic or, for that matter, from the *Pražan* around the turn of the century. He speaks the same slang, and is the same petit bourgeois he used to be. Political education has not turned him into a revolutionary fighter. Of course, he marches in the First-of-May parade—because he has to; otherwise there may be trouble at the factory or office where he works. But he doesn't like it, and at night he will say so while he has his glass of beer in the little *pivnice* (beer house) or the shabby *výčep* (dive) among congenial fellow beer-drinkers. Griping is the *Pražan*'s favorite pastime—griping about the "system," the shortages, the latest changes (there are always some changes, for no apparent reason), the high cost of living, low salaries, and "those fellows up there," the new rulers at the Castle.

The *Pražan* is fed up with politics, and no wonder, for he is a burned child. But he cannot afford to ignore national politics; he must know what goes on, out of a sense of self-preservation, because politics may concern his very life and his family—the tiny plot of privacy he has staked out for himself, his job, his future. He is always on the defensive waiting for something to happen that might further complicate life, which is already complicated enough. Look at the new economic reform; Heaven knows what it's going to do to him. He loves to gossip. In 1891, Jan Neruda wrote, "What

Paris is for civilization and Birmingham for industry, Prague is for *klep* (scandal-mongering)."

Prague—or rather the small neighborhood district where he lives—is his world. Once in a while he may walk across Charles Bridge to Malá Strana, and up to Hradčany, which gives him the feeling of being a tourist in his own city. Sometimes he goes *na Václavák*, to Wenceslas Square to see a movie, or to the theater. He loves the movies and the theater. But for the rest of the year he sticks to his dearly familiar neighborhood, with its small corners, quiet nooks, St. John Nepomuk statues and the small *výčep* where he hears all the dope.

His tastes in food, drink, girls, are healthy and robust. A pork roast with dumplings and sauerkraut. A glass of cold beer—he prefers beer, the national beverage, to wine. There are endless arguments about which beer is the best. Smíchov? Pilsen? Budějovice? And a girl that "has everything." Today the girls of Prague reflect their predilection for dumplings and sweets; the ethereal type is not too popular. Such a girl is all right to look at in a movie but what would you do with her on a Sunday afternoon? The girls of Prague were once among the prettiest in Europe, if you liked the type—high cheekbones, knowing eyes, husky voices. "The eyes of the women of Prague, no matter what color, show their deep soul," wrote Rudolf Gerlein in 1838. "I saw eyes of sky-blue and of deep black that showed the same expression, sweet and romantic and mysterious." In 1902, Auguste Rodin said that "the aristocratic beauty of the women of Prague, their exclusive gait, their attractive, elegant dresses reminded me of Dante's Paradise."

The average *Pražan* comes from peasant stock. The grandparents probably still lived *na vesnici*, out there in the village. He has a peasant's realistic attitude toward life, and is always watching out for disaster as a peasant is always worried about bad weather. Temperamentally, the Czechs are the most sober among the Slavs, quite different from the imaginative Slovaks, the romantic Poles, the often melancholy Russians. The *Pražan* likes to live and let live. He hated the Nazis less for their racist nonsense than for their rigorous attitudes, their brutality, their mania for orderliness. One of the underlying reasons of his dislike for today's regime is that it has no understanding for live and let live. But having gone through so much, the *Pražan* is mainly concerned with survival. He has learned not to take life too seriously.

His peasant's shrewdness makes him a first cousin of Švejk, that lovable character whom nothing shakes out of his composure. Instead of fighting his problems, the Švejk in the *Pražan* has a way of getting around them. He has a sense of joke rather than a sense of humor. Even the most humorless, most disgraceful situation is turned into a joke, often a painful one. The popularity of a politician can be assessed by the jokes told about him. If he is no longer the butt of popular, though not always printable jokes, he may be in trouble. The *Pražan*'s cunning smile, his pretense not to understand what it's all about though he knows damn well, his virtuosity at playing dumb when he is attacked, upsets the bureaucratic *apparatchiks* of the hammer-and-sickle regime as much as Švejk upset the bureaucrats and generals of k. & k. (Imperial & Royal) Austria.

But now there is something else in the *Pražan* that wasn't there before. Like Kafka's Joseph K., he now feels helpless and frustrated by the ubiquitous bureaucrats; he is a mere number, an unperson, and there is nothing he can do about it. Josef Švejk and Joseph K. have become the two antipoles in the soul of the citizen of Prague. It can be no accident that Jaroslav Hašek who wrote *Švejk* was born in Prague on

April 30, 1883, exactly sixty-four days before Kafka, the creator of Joseph K., was born there, on July 3. Their early photographs show boyish faces that soon matured, through sickness. Both had to do things they disliked, in order to write, the only thing they loved to do. Both were ignored as "dilettantes" by their contemporaries, when they were great masters of the art of the grotesque. Both died within the same year, at the age of forty-one. The Joseph K. complex of today's *Pražan* is getting stronger because the "system" is getting stronger. "The farther an inundation reaches, the shallower and dirtier the water is getting," Kafka is quoted as saying in Janouch's *Conversations*. "The revolution evaporates, and only the mud of a new bureaucracy remains. The handcuffs of a tortured mankind are made of red tape."

In a remarkable Czech film, *Concerning the Feast and the Guests*, by Jan Němec, there is a mysterious unseen power that threatens the guests at a feast in the forest—separating men from women, forbidding them to speak, accusing them of crimes they don't remember having committed; Kafka's terror, and they are helpless against it. The sensitive artists who make the fine, modern Czech films are well aware of the nationwide Švejk-and-Joseph K. complex, man's growing isolation in a dark, hostile world, the terrifying sense of unreality, man's hopeless search for his own existence—and also his Švejkian, grotesque ways of trying to obstruct the unseen, ubiquitous forces. The gifted, courageous writers and artists of Czechoslovakia (a unique phenomenon in the Communist world) are concerned about, and often critical of, the regime. This haunting feeling that never seems to leave them is stronger among educated people than among the simple fellows who don't think too much, letting others do their thinking, but it's there just the same. People feel they are no longer masters of their own fate, suspended like puppets from millions of invisible threads. Kafka's horrifying predictions have come true.

Two years ago, a friend of mine came from a country in Western Europe to Prague to work there for his firm. He hadn't been in town for over a week when he was approached by people drifting out of the darkness who came to whisper in his ears that what he saw and heard wasn't real—whereupon they proceeded to tell him "how it really was." His own sense of unreality increased when he discovered that on the same corridor of his apartment house there lived: (1) a retired lion tamer with a colored woman and a child that wasn't theirs; (2) a young man with his mother who kept a picture of Lenin decorated with fresh flowers; (3) a gypsy musician with his family, ranging from five to fifteen members, some of whom had no key and entered their apartment through a small window in the corridor on a ladder which they borrowed from my friend. The gypsy's wife, very pretty, often used the ladder when she came home late and was afraid of being beaten up by her jealous husband.

Prior to the Second World War, people in Prague used to say that when life in the big city became too difficult, one could always move out and live *no venkově*, in the countryside, or *na vesnici*, in the village, where one had relatives and in-laws. Now many relatives and in-laws have become statefarm or co-operative workers—Kafka's anonymous serfs, laboring under an unseen, cruel Master. No one from Prague wants to go there today.

I've heard it said in Prague that "every fifth person in town is an informer." I hope it's an exaggeration. But one doesn't have to be there very long to sense that a great many people are always a little worried about being spied on. There seems to be an invisible network of informers everywhere. These days one isn't taken to Pankrác Prison for making "dangerous" statements. Drunks loudly curse the government, and nothing happens. In a *výčep* I heard a man shout, "Damn fool that I was, I voted for the Communists in '48." Everybody nodded silently, and the man who ran the (State-owned) pub gave the fellow a glass of beer, on the house; nothing happened. Another time a man in a long, silent, suffering queue suddenly exploded: "This is what we've come to after twenty years!" Again nothing happened to the man, though I could feel how the people froze up inside. Still—today a man may open his mouth but who knows what's going to happen tomorrow? You've heard about those writers who dared open their mouths. Brave men, and everybody secretly admires them. But now the writers are waiting for the tomorrow, and God knows whether they can sleep quietly. Some people are said to inform for money, and others out of "patriotism" or "social discipline." And some have to do it because they are blackmailed. The police have something on them.

Feeling surrounded by an invisible network, the people seem to stick to each other instinctively. "In bad times the people of Prague are always nicer to each other," an elderly man says who has seen many bad times and a few good times here. Everybody is trying to be a little more helpful, to carry the neighbor's load. (The opposite is true in the prosperous society of other countries where people never had it so good.) So many old women are working—as streetcar conductors, in stores, as charwomen. Doesn't the socialist state take care of its old people? It does, but not always sufficiently. Some people's pension is too small to keep body and soul together; they have to work. When the streetcar is empty, in the late evening hours, the old woman conductor furtively sits down, which is forbidden to her. People pretend not to notice; it's exhausting to be up on one's feet so many hours since "the earthless, weeping dream light of the early day." Yes, if Franz Werfel were around, he could write another strophe about "the old Czech women."

There is a deep malaise among the young people that often leads to long spells of depression. The number of suicides among younger people has gone up to such an extent that it worries the government. No statistical figures are available but doctors and social workers believe Prague to be the city with Europe's largest numbers of suicides, worse even than Berlin, the record holder after the city's split. The experts agree on nothing except the cause: the young people (they say) see the future realistically and are unable to cope with it. They can't find another way out. Some drift into a sort of existentialist nihilism. Others try to find consolation in religion, in "the mystical St. Wenceslas cult."

I think of the N.s, a young couple that got married a few years ago. Economically, they are doing well. Both are employed. They live in a modern, co-operative apartment in a suburb, about an hour's streetcar ride from their respective working place. They have a small car which they use only on weekends. They can't really afford it, and know it, and it goes against their very way of life; but "everybody" in the building has a car, you would be a "nobody" without the car. They save where it hurts to be able to buy a new gadget for the car. Mrs. N. begs the mothers of other children in their house for worn clothes for her child, since she can't afford to buy them. They wanted a second child but decided against it; "there was no money for that."

"Perhaps the worst is that no one here considers it strange to beg for children's clothes and then buy new seat covers for the car," a friend says, with a meaningful shrug.

When the N.s come home from work—the child has spent

the day in a State kindergarten—they have a hurried, cold supper. All of them had an inexpensive, hot lunch—the parents at their working place canteens, the child in kindergarten. After the child has been brought to bed, the N.s sit down in front of the *televisor*, today's opium for the people. You don't have to talk or think; you just look. Thinking or talking will inevitably lead to depression. Better look and drug yourself.

But sometimes one can't help thinking, and then one remembers that one was twenty years old in 1945, full of youthful enthusiasm and hope; and now one is forty-five, and the only hope that remains is that the Old-Guard Communists will die out and that modern, young, more pragmatic Communists will take over. After twenty-two years of the system that began in 1948, life is almost as gray as at the end of the last war. Everybody wears the same dark-blue raincoat, eats the same canteen meal. If you want to buy a jar of skin cream, good stockings, a bottle of Scotch, a piece of Swiss chocolate, a pack of American cigarettes, you must shop at the State-run Tuzex stores, where only hard currencies or Tuzex bonds are taken for payment; if you don't have friends or relatives in the West (or take a chance and buy Tuzex bonds in the black market, which is a criminal offense), you are just out of luck.

In front of a bakery in Wenceslas Square people always queue up; a fine smell drifts out of the shop; the bakery is known for the quality of its bread, rolls and poppy-seed croissants. Across from the bakery people queue up in front of a handcart on which a man has some oranges or grapes. Twenty-two years after "they" took over this former country of milk-and-honey!

There are more bookstores than before the war, and books are commendably cheap. But often it is strange that one cannot buy the books one wants. I tried to find a Czech-English dictionary, but there was none for sale in all Prague; a sudden shortage, no doubt. Would I want to take a Czech-Portuguese dictionary instead? Or a Czech-Russian dictionary of technical terms? A West-German newspaper, an American magazine thrown into the wastebasket in a hotel room, are carefully retrieved and start a secret, new life, being read by many people until the pages are torn. The baggage porter expecting the "Vindobona" Express from Vienna asks the passengers, "Haven't you got any newspapers?" People who feel themselves closely tied to the West, are starved for unbiased news from the West.

Today, over two decades after the Communist regime took over, promising the people a glorious, new life, the citizens of this highly industrialized country are able to buy only "second-quality" goods because all "first-quality" goods are marked for export. "After all these years you're getting tired —tired of shoddy products, of unfulfilled promises, of being told to wait and be patient. Many educated Czechs today know that Prague, where the Germans first drove out the Jews and the Czechs later drove out the Germans, and where many Czechs were driven out by other Czechs, has lost much of its inner tension and intellectual stimulation."

Years ago, Johannes Urzidil wrote, "The common destiny created not only a history of struggle and contention but also fruitful competition and mutual impregnation." The fruitful competition no longer exists. Prague has become a one-color city, intellectually and culturally. The polychromy of languages, ideas, cultures, is gone that quickened its pulse beat and was felt over Europe. The members of the family are among each other at last—and they are bored to death with one another. They feel (and sometimes admit it, reluctantly) that Prague lost something which was very important—the mutual reactions and cross-reactions between the various national and cultural groups that created the peculiarly tense, cultural atmosphere of Prague which was always a give-and-take, a crossroads where people from various cultures met, talked, argued, fought and even made up occasionally.

A young Czech writer who knows his history spoke to me about the terrible emotional vacuum in which so many people now live. The "little man," whose parents were peasants somewhere in Bohemia, a first-generation *Pražan*, who feels "one hundred and ten per cent" Prague, doesn't feel it so much. His intellectual horizon is limited. But people who have learned more and know more are bothered by spells of melancholy:

One tries to fight it but one feels caught in a current of sorrow. Alexej Kusak, the Marxist interpreter of Kafka, calls it "the prototyping of a feeling of absurdity about the human condition." Some of us read the new atheistic literature but this is no way out either. It only destroys old values without building new values on the site of destruction. I honestly believe that our nation is in greater despair now than in the dark age of the seventeenth century when the Jesuit Counter-Reformation during the Germanizing Habsburg regime was trying to systematically destroy people's will to live.

There is growing apathy—people are no longer interested in anything but the dreadful routine of going on and on. Some live in a mystical dream world that becomes more real to them than the real world. Others resort to the tried-and-proven methods of Švejk. I heard the story of the little fellow in Prague who rides on the platform of a streetcar. A big, strong man gets on and ruthlessly steps on the little fellow's toe. Everybody notices it but no one dares to open his mouth; the big man is too strong. He keeps his heavy foot there until he gets off.

Then another passenger says to the little fellow, "Goodness, how could you stand it? You didn't even ask him to take his foot off your toe."

The little fellow keeps massaging his toe that hurts him so much but he smiles. "No, I didn't. But I quietly burned a big hole in his new jacket with my cigarette."

Too Many Wrongs

THE HISTORY OF Prague, from its beginning a thousand years ago to this day, repeats the truism that wrong always begets wrong. Assassinations among the early Přemyslid rulers were followed by much bloodshed under the Luxemburgers when social conflicts erupted between rulers and the Estates, between the Estates and the burghers, between wealthy German and impoverished Czech people, between rich and poor clerics. In 1464, George of Poděbrady, the Hussite noble who became King of Bohemia, submitted his proposals for a community of free nations that should renounce the settlement of conflicts by force of arms, render mutual aid against the Turkish aggressors and submit disputes to an international court. It read like a fifteenth-century United Nations Charter but was never accepted.

The nineteenth century in Prague was one long chain reaction of political, social, national, conflict. The first part of the century is called by Czech historians "the national revival." After the battle of the White Mountain, the country had been radically Germanized by the Habsburgs, and Czech was spoken only among the peasantry. In 1817, the Czechs demanded, and obtained, a professorship of Czech language at the Prague University; in Prague, "language" has always been synonymous with "nationality." The mathematician Stanislav Vryda and the encyclopedist Josef Dobrovský were among the first lecturers. (Czech historians now call Dobrovský "the founder of modern Czech grammar," while German nationalists, such as Schürer, have tried to prove that "Dobrovský felt he belonged to the German cultural circle," *Kulturkreis*. It isn't only Wallenstein's image that "fluctuates in History.")

The Czech bourgeoisie remained rather indifferent to the national awakening but the students were always close to the people. There was great curiosity in Czech language and literature. Joseph Jungmann recorded the vocabulary of ancient and modern Czech in his Czech-German dictionary. František Palacký, the greatest Czech historian and author of *History of the Czech Nation in Bohemia and Moravia*, became the intellectual leader of the Czech Renaissance. A Moravian Protestant, he continued the humanist traditions that began with Comenius and—so far—have ended with Tomáš G. Masaryk. (Curiously, all great Czech humanists come from Moravia.) Palacký once said, "With all my holy love for my nation I consider the interests of humanity and science more important than nationality." And it took courage to say, "If the Austrian Monarchy didn't exist, one would have to create it in the interest of Europe and humanity." (Today, there is subdued but persistent talk in Prague, Belgrade, Bucharest and Vienna—yes, Vienna—of a future "Danube Federation" that strangely resembles the broken-up Habsburg Monarchy.) The idea of humanity dominated the Czech Renaissance for a long time, until humanity capitulated under the impact of chauvinism. In 1786, the poet Herder, a great German humanist, had praised the Slavs in his *Ideas Concerning the Philosophy and History of Humanity*, calling the language "their true homeland." But 1786 was also the year when the Bethlehem Chapel in Prague, where Hus had preached in Czech, was destroyed by order of the Jesuits.

The idea of humanity dominated the first Slav Congress, held in Prague in early June, 1848, which was attended by representatives of all Slav nations. The Congress did not oppose Austria's sovereignty but demanded liberty, equality and fraternity of all peoples in Europe, as the Polish Prince Lubomirski stated it. Palacký said the Slavs wanted to acknowledge membership of their great family. But the motto of the Congress, and of the entire national Renaissance movement, was expressed by the Slovak Protestant, J. J. Šafařik, "Either we shall realize that we can say proudly, 'I am a Slav,' or we stop being Slavs."

The spirit of humanity ended abruptly a few days later, at Whitsuntide, when the Austrian general, Alfred Prince Windischgraetz ("his iron slogan was 'Alles für Österreich,' Everything for Austria," writes Schürer) was named supreme commander of the Prague garrison. Immediately, riots started in Prague, barricades went up all over town, and after a while the riots escalated into revolt, and the revolt into revolution; Windischgraetz occupied Charles Bridge and used its strategic position to turn his guns from the western bridgehead against the Old Town. That was too much, even for the hawks in Vienna: Windischgraetz was suddenly replaced by General Count Mensdorff, a more moderate military man. But the fighting continued for days, and once again the pavement of Prague "drank blood." In the end, the revolutionaries were beaten, and a state of siege was declared in Prague. (Three months later, in October, 1848, the Revolution broke out in Vienna, and was crushed by Windischgraetz. The Czech liberals opposed the Viennese revolutionaries, which today's Communist historians consider a terrible mistake. "The treachery of the Czech liberal bourgeoisie brought them no reward," writes Miloš Kratochvil.)

Emperor Ferdinand V, "the Good One," abdicated in favor of his eighteen-year-old nephew, Franz Joseph I, and came to Prague where he spent the last years of his life in Hradčany Castle as an Imperial pensioner. He was often seen walking in Ferdinand Street, named after him (today Národní Třída), or driving his carriage "to collect in person the rents of houses which belonged to the Crown." Bedřich Smetana was named his Court Director of Music, and was occasionally summoned to the Castle to play for the ex-Kaiser his favorite military marches on the piano. Franz Joseph I was never crowned in Prague as King of Bohemia. In the early 1860s, there was some talk of a coronation and the Spanish Hall and the Rudolphian Gallery at the Castle were given new pseudo-Baroque stucco decorations. Then the workers moved over to St. Vitus Cathedral to continue their never-ending job there.

The forces of nationalism which eventually led to the collapse of the Habsburg Monarchy could no longer be stopped. The second half of the nineteenth century is a continuous struggle between Czechs and Germans in Prague. The Jews were no longer able to play the traditional role of mediators. The Czech revival created German chauvinism, which in turn created Czech chauvinism. After the Austro-Hungarian "dual" Monarchy was established in 1867, the Czechs wanted their independence too, but were opposed by the

German and Hungarian members of the Reichsrat (Diet) in Vienna. The first Czech political parties were founded: the Social Democrats, in 1878; the nationalist Young Czechs and the National-Socialists, in 1897; and the Agrarian Party and Masaryk's ("Realist") Party in 1900. The first ugly racist sounds were heard among the "Sudetan Germans" in Bohemia, Moravia and Silesia when Georg Ritter von Schönerer expounded his theories of "the German master race."

Tomáš Garrigue Masaryk (he took the middle name from his mother, an American woman from Brooklyn) won the fight for self-determination and political independence of his nation, but he couldn't win the bigger fight to make the Republic of Czechoslovakia a sort of Central-European Switzerland where Czechs, Slovaks, Germans, Jews, Hungarians and other minorities would live together in peace. Looking back, one cannot fail to see the short interlude between the world wars in Czechoslovakia as a time of Western-style democracy and Western-style prosperity, at least up to the economic world crisis after 1929. In those years, "Made in Czechoslovakia" became an internationally respected trademark of quality, and the Czechoslovaks were called "the Americans of Europe." This is not, however the view now taken by contemporary historians in Prague. As Miloš Kratochvil writes:

> Independence brought Czech capital right to the top in the industrial and financial world. Czech banks sought financial support abroad for big industrial enterprises. As they grew more prosperous, the capitalists became politically influential and won positions in the government. Although they enacted some progressive measures such as the eight-hour day, the socialist parties did not nationalize the key industries. . . . The economic boom of 1923 to 1929 strengthened big business. About 25 con-

cerns controlled 80 per cent of the capital, with three big banks dominating industry. Unemployment declined, pension insurance for workers was introduced together with other reforms, but the full benefits of economic recovery were not felt by workers and employees.

Still, the country's President was a great philosopher and humanist—a luxury few countries ever permitted themselves in history. While social inequities existed, nearly everybody had work and enough to eat. There was freedom of speech and of the press, religious and political freedom. At one time there were seventeen different political parties represented at the Czechoslovak Parliament in Prague. It may have been a "bourgeois" republic, as it is now (officially) called, but it is also (unofficially) remembered as a lost paradise by the majority of the inhabitants of the present Socialist People's Republic—by all the people who are old enough to remember.

Masaryk's Republic didn't last. When the Sudeten-German Party got two thirds of all German votes in Czechoslovakia in 1935, the handwriting was on the wall. The Sudeten-German Führer, Konrad Henlein, took his orders (and considerable secret subsidies) from Hitler in neighboring Germany. He was told to ask always for more than the Czechoslovak Government could possibly give him. On May 28, 1938, Hitler told his Wehrmacht generals, "It is my unshakable will to extinguish Czechoslovakia from the map of Europe." The Czechs mobilized their armed forces but did not fight, which turned out to be a tragic mistake. Instead, they relied on their great friends, the Western powers. The so-called Munich agreement of September 29 prepared the opening for the German invasion. On March 15, 1939—the blackest day in the country's history since King Přemysl Otakar's defeat on the Marchfeld, the suicidal Hussite battle of Lipany and the battle of the White Mountain—the German tanks rumbled into Prague. Hitler promised the Czech nation "an autonomous development of its national life."

This was "the autonomous development": at least 300,000 men and women, out of a population of thirteen million, were killed by Nazi executioners. Executions took place nearly every day in all cities. "In the Moravian capital of Brno, the House for University Students was turned into a prison by the Gestapo," writes Traugott Krischke, a German writer:

There 1300 Czechoslovaks, men and women, were hung, shot or tortured to death between September 28, 1941, and April 18, 1945. The Nazis in Brno were permitted to watch the executions as interested spectators; the price of a ticket was three Reichsmark. The Pankrác Prison in Prague was the scene of an uninterrupted chain of executions, and so were the rifle ranges of Ruzyně (near today's Prague Airport) and Kobylisy. Half a million Czech workers were deported to Germany as forced-laborers. After the assassination of Reinhard Heydrich, on May 27, 1942, the village of Lidice was "erased" because the Gestapo claimed—falsely—that the assassins had been hiding there. Mass murder also occurred in Ležáky, near Pardubice; in the village of Moravka, near the Slovak border, and in nearby Plostina; in the Bohemian villages of Leskovice and Sedlec. . . . In the first week following the death of Heydrich, 1800 "political prisoners" were executed. It cannot be ascertained whether this figure includes 1300 Jews who were murdered in Prague after the assassination. Of the Jewish pre-war population of 315,000, only 60,000 were still alive after the departure of the Nazis. . . . The losses of human lives can only be estimated. The exact number will never be known, and neither will be the cause of death. . . .

Wrong always begets wrong. "On May 5, the people of Prague rose in arms against the Germans," writes Kratochvil. "The rising was led by the Czech National Council co-ordinating all resistance groups. Over 30,000 fought in

Prague where 2,000 street barricades were hastily put up. For four days Prague, cut off from the outside world, held out against German tanks, artillery and planes. On May 9, 1945, a Soviet tank rolled up to the foremost barricade . . ."

I can still see that tank—it has now become a national monument—and I can almost hear the hysterical shouts of the people who greeted it. Everybody was crying. I happened to be there that day. I had come with two American fellow-soldiers from nearby Pilsen, where our troops had had orders to remain. We drove in a jeep and we'd put an American flag on top of the windshield. It gave many people the hope that "the Americans were coming," whom they wanted to see much more than the Russians. But the Americans were not coming, and the Stars and Stripes flying from our jeep was the only American flag in Prague during the Liberation.

"The number of people who died shortly before or during the Liberation will never be known," writes Krischke. "Tens of thousands of people who were murdered, killed, hit by bullets, burned to death—men, women, children. It was the outbreak of a volcano, and the volcano was Prague. For six interminable years the people of Prague had silently endured evil, torture and murder. This does not excuse the massacre—but it may help to explain it."

Afterward, there was never any doubt in Prague: the Sudeten Germans would have to leave. Forever. Three million of them were expelled—though many of them, no doubt, had never done anything wrong, not actively anyway. Maybe they knew what had been going on during the six terrible years; and maybe they didn't know. Now they had to leave, *all* of them. "Evaluating the historical sins of the Czechs one must never forget how much persistent wrong was done to them," writes Johannes Urzidil, the German writer from Prague:

The Mystical City

Most of their violent actions are the desperate reaction of a nation that was driven into extremes by the idiocy of despotism. All who participated in the history of the Bohemian lands have a mutually incriminating conscience: the Czechs are on the conscience of their German neighbors, and the neighbors on the conscience of the Czechs. The tyranny during the time of the "Protectorate" will always remain a guilt complex on the conscience of the Germans. And the indiscriminate expulsion of the Sudeten-Germans from the land where they had lived nine hundred years will forever remain a heavy guilt on the conscience of the Czechs.

Nowadays, many Sudeten-Germans, traveling to Prague on an Austrian or West-German passport, come back there for a visit, prosperous-looking and well-dressed, in shiny new cars. They enjoy being catered to in the best hotels, where the Czech employees—speaking German—beg them for a German newspaper or a few American cigarettes. Who would have thought twenty-five years ago that history would play such a cruel joke? Some of the visitors feel that it isn't quite right—but, then, nothing was ever quite right in Golden Prague, the guilty, violent city.

The "Prague Spring"

No one in Prague who lived through the "Prague Spring," the brief, exhilarating interlude of freedom, will ever forget it. On January 5, 1968, Alexander Dubček replaced the hated Antonín Novotný as First Secretary of the Communist

Party. After twenty-five years of terror, first under the Nazi protectorate and then under the Stalinist protectorate, the people tasted the sweet taste of liberty that the younger generation had never known—and they got drunk on it. Unlike earlier revolutions, the "Prague Spring" wasn't set in motion by anarchists, workers, juntas or soldiers but by writers, scientists, artists and students. They preached nonviolence and tolerance, not the guillotine and revenge. Paradoxically, the breakup of the Stalinist Novotný regime occurred at the very center of power, in the highest councils of the Party. The reformers were Communist intellectuals who believed in communism. They didn't want to overthrow, but to liberalize, giving communism a "human face."

In June, 1968, the day after the National Assembly had abolished censorship, *Literární Listy*, the great weekly published by the Writers' Union, printed one of the all-time great documents of political freedom. "Two Thousand Words" was "inspired by the scientists," written by Ludvík Vaculík, and directed "against selfish, domineering people with a bad conscience":

Let us request the departure of people who misused their power, damaged public property, behaved dishonestly or cruelly. We have to find means of forcing them to resign, by public criticism, resolutions, demonstrations, strikes and boycott of their doors . . .

No one had ever used such language in the Communist world and gotten away with it. Officially, the Party didn't go along with the proclamation but all public media supported it. Once again, the city of Jan Hus had become a city of heretics. Moscow's *Pravda* spoke ominously of "counter-revolutionary elements" in Prague. Cautious people saw the handwriting on the wall when the Soviets and their allies sent their "Warsaw Letter" to the "dear comrades" in

Prague who were summoned to Warsaw to stand up and be counted. Dubček and his fellow reformers replied—not in the ambiguous Party jargon but in lucid, clear language—that they were always ready for bilateral talks but would not appear in Warsaw as defendants.

They had nothing to hide. To Waldeck-Rochet, the French Communist leader, who came from Moscow through Prague to warn the "dear comrades," Dubček said: "In the question of socialism, our friendship with the Soviet Union, the Warsaw Pact, there are no differences between us. . . . There is no counter-revolution here." But that wasn't the way Walter Ulbricht saw it when he went to talk to his neighbor, Dubček, in Karlsbad (Karlovy Vary). He immediately noticed the symptoms of freedom, tolerance, liberalism; and he was terrified they might spread across the borders of East Germany; he knew what had happened there in 1953, when he had been saved only by the intervention of the Soviet tanks. Ulbricht went to Moscow to warn his protectors. It is highly probable that he triggered off their decision to invade the "heretic" country.

Looking back now, people in Prague agree on the inexorability of the events that followed, as in a Greek tragedy. The invasion of the Warsaw Pact troops, in the morning hours of August 21, 1968, was the beginning of the end. People in Prague will discuss for many years to come whether the Czechoslovak army should have resisted the invasion. But most knew right then that "the beautiful dream of freedom from which we never want to wake up," as A. J. Liehm, the noted Communist writer, had called it, was already a sad memory.

During one last, glorious week of spiritual and moral—but not physical—resistance, while Soviet tanks were rolling through Prague, almost the entire nation was united as never before. (A few traitors were hiding.) No one ran away. The exodus started only on August 27, when Dubček, just back from his ordeal in Moscow, twice fainted during his speech to the nation. It was all over. In the last uncensored issue of *Listy*, Ivan Bystřina wrote,

> In the consciousness of our nation, defeats and capitulations, perfidy and treachery always played a bigger part than victories. . . . Our victories were always moral victories rather than victories of brute force. . . . The historical and geographical location of our country creates the tragedies which pose the old dilemma between courage and capitulation.

Moscow-trained Communists know more about the strategy of terror than about the mystery of freedom. Too late, Dubček learned that the explosion of liberty is harder to control than the spread of police methods. Today many people say that there was "too much freedom too fast," that Moscow might have been more patient if the reformers hadn't attacked the sacred cows of communism—the planned economy, censorship, the secret police. In January, 1969, the immolation of Jan Palach, a philosophy student at Prague's Charles University, in front of the St. Wenceslas monument, as a protest against the Soviet occupation, once more briefly rallied the nation. It was the last gasp of solidarity. The night of April 18, when Dubček was removed and Gustav Husák became First Party Secretary, the Soviets took over Ruzyně Airport, clearing all runways—just in case Russian planes might have to bring in more tanks and troops. There were no more demonstrations though. After more than a year, the "Prague Spring" had come to an end.

All countries are nominally sovereign but some countries in the Eastern Bloc are more sovereign than others. In Prague, they now say bitterly that Czechoslovakia is sovereign in name only. After the demise of Novotný, "the bad people"—the police agents, the informers, the torturers, the commissars of the Stalinist terror machine—had disappeared from sight but the machine was never smashed; it was only stopped. The bad guys are back. They were never cut off completely from the sources of power, remaining in touch with each other, and with their friends in the Soviet Embassy. The Czechs say that the rats have re-entered the sinking ship. Some say bitterly that Dubček should have got rid of them when he was in charge. But how could he, without discrediting the very idea of "communism with a human face"?

Ever since, "perfidy and treachery" have played a big part in Prague. Dubček was gradually deprived of all functions though his only "crimes" were his human dignity and political ineptness. Finally, he was expelled from the Communist Party which tried hard to obliterate his image. The Party people didn't succeed. The people of Czechoslovakia secretly admire Dubček's decency and courage. He could have defected to the West when he was Ambassador to Turkey. Nothing could have pleased the present leadership more. Instead he went back to Prague to face his inquisitors, as Jan Hus had done in Constance. And like Hus, Alexander Dubček did not recant. He seems already a somewhat distant figure in his country's tormented history, almost a legend. "The problem of a small country is somewhat like the problem of a little man," wrote T. G. Masaryk. "His human dignity must be respected without regard to the material difference in bigness."

Three years after the end of the "Prague Spring," the elusive, mystical beauty of Prague emerges more powerfully than in a long, long time. After decades of neglect, the government has launched a large-scale restoration program to save the Gothic structures of the Old Town and the Baroque palaces of Malá Strana. On Charles Bridge, the black sandstone statues of the suffering saints are getting a thorough cleansing. The taverns near the bridge are crowded with young people, talking, drinking beer, listening to music. They look proud and defiant. It's the only way in which they may show their protest; they cannot talk openly now. The students are no longer active politically. In Old Town Square, small children play on the sidewalk where twenty-seven white crosses mark the spot of the executions of the Bohemian nobles in 1621. Elderly people sit on yellow benches that were placed around the monument of Jan Hus so the people couldn't get too close to it and place flowers. The monument of St. Wenceslas too has been made less accessible. All seems peaceful, almost idyllic. But Prague never was, and isn't today, a peaceful city.

Once again, people speak softly, and some say nothing at all. Fear is everywhere, invisible and omnipresent. First, one hears only vague rumors of arrests, beatings, persecutions. After a while, the rumors condense into facts. The man on the third floor—yes, Pan So-and-so—lost his job because he was seen placing some wildflowers on the grave of Jan Palach. Somebody else was taken away by the secret police and hasn't come back. Most worried of all are the Communists. The day of reckoning has come. Every member of the Party has to account for what he did, or omitted to do, during the past two years. Everybody had to turn in his Party membership card. Many were given a new one only after a satisfactory "interview" before the Party's "control-and-auditing" commission. Everybody was considered guilty until proven innocent. Everybody became a Josef K. in Kafka's "The Trial."

Loss of the Party membership also means loss of job, apartment, future, all hope. The children may be barred from secondary schools and the university. Thousands of honest Communists who supported Alexander Dubček— writers, scientists, officials, artists—have suddenly become third-class citizens. Some were sent to work in the fields, on building sites, in the coal mines; and some are in prison. The writers no longer write, the scientists no longer teach, the artists no longer perform. (Some writers write "for the drawer," knowing they won't get published now.) The country's judiciary is purged, and the stage was set for more purges even. People who love their country are deeply shocked; this time it's not Czechs and Slovaks against the foreign invaders but against each other. The nation is tragically split, as it was after the Hussite wars.

Nobody feels like working hard. "What's the sense of working for the Russians?" they say. During the Dubček regime, they took pride in their country; they knew they were working for *themselves*. Today there is no incentive. They cannot travel to the West, they won't be able to buy first-rate goods. They have no hope.

On August 21, 1969, the anniversary of the invasion, eleven prominent Communists addressed an open letter to the Party and the government that became known as "Ten Points." Vaculík, who had written "Two Thousand Words," is one of the signers of the bold, courageous document:

We reject censorship which sets us back a hundred years. . . . We do not acknowledge the Communist Party as a power organization having a superior position above the state organs. . . . We reject in advance the customary accusations and abuses which we anticipate.

Several of the signers of "Ten Points" were sent to jail. Czechoslovakia's Olympic champion, Emil Zátopek, an army colonel, was dismissed from the army, and later fired from his lowly job as a garbage truck collector, when people recognized him and wanted to help him with his work. "Many people are persecuted," it said in "Ten Points." And more will be.

"*Dieses Mütterchen hat Krallen*," Kafka wrote in 1902. Prague, the little mother, has claws. After a thousand years of violence, Prague will surely survive the present phase of fear and terror. But for the time being, the beautiful, mystical city is once again "pain-filled and polemical."

Index

Aachen, Hans von, 141
Adalbert, Saint, 100, 105
Adler, Friedrich, 20, 54
Aleš, Mikoláš, 96, 151–52, 177
Anhalt, Christian, Count of, 132–33
Anna of Hungary and Bohemia, 122, 126
Anthony, Saint, 144
Anton, Prince of Saxony, 165
Apollinaire, Guillaume, 15, 51, 61–62
Apollonia, Saint, 144
Arabes, Jakub, 55–56, 142
Aretino, Pietro, 19
Arnošt, Archbishop of Pardubice, 104
Avostalis, Oldřich, 124
Austrian-Prussian War, 2

Bach, Johann Sebastian, 149
Bachmann, Erich, 91
Bakri, Abu Obaid al, 93
Barea, Ilsa, 105
Barisani, Dr., 165
Barisini, Tomaso, 111
Bartók, Béla, 160, 172
Bassi, Luigi, 166
Batelli, Guido, 4

Baum, Oscar, 6, 53
Bednář, Jaroslav, 63
Beethoven, Ludwig van, 169, 173
Benda, Franz, 162
Benda, Georg, 162
Bendel, Johann Georg, 147
Bendict XIII, Pope, 146
Beneš, Eduard, 79
Berg, Alban, 173
Bergmann, Hugo, 69
Berlioz, Hector, 162, 174
Bethlehem Chapel, 116–18
Bezruč, Petr, 20
Biebel, Konstantin, 63
Blech, Leo, 175
Blei, Franz, 19
Bodansky, Arthur, 175
Boleslav I, King of Bohemia, 97
Bondini, Caterina, 166–67
Bondini, Pasquale, 163–65
Bořita, Jaroslav, 129–30
Bořivoj, Prince of Bohemia, 97
Bourdet, Emile, 154
Brahe, Tycho de, 18, 37, 47, 127, 128
Brahms, Johannes, 173
Brand, Karl, 76

Brandl (artist), 184
Braun, Matthias, 113, 147, 151
Brecht, Bertolt, 54, 179
Brentano, Clemens, 37
Březina, Otakar, 20, 82
Brod, Max, 19–20, 68, 77, 89
  descriptions of Prague by, 12, 19, 85–86
  early publication of, 53
  family of, 54
  on Hašek, 12, 179, 180, 187–88
  Janáček and, 12, 172, 180
  Jewish culture and, 52
  Kafka and, 12, 68, 70, 73, 74, 78, 83–84
  on Langner, 48–49
  on Meyrink, 40–43
  translation of *Jenufa* by, 172
Brody, Heinrich, 51
Brokoff, Johann, 114, 147, 148
Brueghel, Johann, 126
Brueghel, Pieter the Elder, 125–26
Brueghel, Pieter the Younger, 126
Budovec, Václav, 134–35
Burian, Vlasta, 192
Burney, Charles, 160
Bystřina, Ivan, 214

Canevalli (artist), 184
Canisius, Saint Peter, 122
Čapek, Karel, 20, 63–65, 157, 176
  grave of, 96
Caretti, Francesco, 150
Carl Theodor, Elector Palatine, 162
Caruso, Enrico, 18
Casanova de Seingalt, Giovanni Giacomo, 166
Čech, Svatopluk, 1, 21
Černin, Jan Humprecht, 150
Chajim, Abraham, 38
Charles, Prince of Liechtenstein, 135
Charles Bridge, 90–92, 101, 111–14, 205, 216
Charles Franz Joseph, 8
Charles I, Emperor of Austria, 172
Charles IV, Holy Roman Emperor, King of Bohemia, 7, 17–18, 72, 99–105, 107–15, 143, 147
  death of, 114
  founding of New Town by, 7, 108–109
  founding of Prague University by, 109–10
Charles V (Charles Quint), of Hapsburg, Holy Roman Emperor, 122
Charles VI, Holy Roman Emperor, 139, 162
Chateaubriand, François-René de, 4
Chelčický, Peter, 118
Chevadam, André, 15
Clam, Count, 168
Claudel, Paul, 35
Clemens VI, Pope (Pierre Roger), 100, 109
Cohen-Portheim, Paul, 53
Comenius, John Amos (Komenský), 11, 135, 145–46, 176, 204
Constantine (Cyril) (monk), 95
Czech language, 12–16, 25–26, 169, 204
Czech National Theater, 175–78

Dalibor, 21
Dante Alighieri, 98
Da Ponte, Lorenzo, 165
David-Rhonfeld, Valerie, 21
Decembrio, Uberto, 115
Dee, John, 59
Demetz, Paul, 12, 20, 76
  on language of Kafka, 24–25
  on Leppin, 45
Denis, Ernest, 3–4
Descartes, René, 134
Dientzenhofer, Christopher, 147, 149, 184
Dientzenhofer, Kilian Ignatius, 144, 147, 184
Dobranský, Dr., 61
Dobrovský, Josef, 14, 204
Dominicus a Jesu, 132
Dubček, Alexander, 32, 81, 211–15, 217
Duhamel, Georges, 64
Dürer, Albrecht, 125
Dušek, Franz, 167
Dušek, Josephine, 167–68
Dvořák, Antonín, 20, 96, 171, 173, 174
Dymeš, Ladislav, 63

Ebert, Karl Egon, 24
Eckstein, Pavel, 171

Edison, Thomas, 75
Ehrenfeld, Nathan, 51
Eisner, Pavel, 20, 82
Eisnerova, Dagmar, 76
Elekta, Maria, 56
Elizabeth I, Queen of England, 59
Elizabeth of Pommern, 101
Emmaus, Monastery of, 110–11
Engels, Friedrich, 176
Erben, Jaromir, 160

Fabricus, Philippe, 130, 134
Ferdinand, King of Aragon, 122
Ferdinand I, of Habsburg, Holy Roman Emperor, King of Bohemia, 122–23, 126
Ferdinand III, King of Bohemia, 106
Ferdinand V (the Good One), Emperor of Austria, 105–106, 206
Fiala, Wenzel, 40
Fischer, Ernest, 83
Fischer von Erlach, Johann Bernard, 102
Fischer von Erlach, Joseph Emmanuel, 107, 146
Flaubert, Gustave, 70
Fleischmann, Ivo, 3
Flek, Dorothea, 184
Flek, Jakob, 184
Florian, Saint, 144
Foch, Ferdinand, 9
Formánek, Vaclav, 103, 159
Fragner, Jaroslav, 118
Franck, César, 162
Franz Joseph I, Emperor of Austria-Hungary, 17, 106, 206
Frederick, King of Prussia, 140
Frederick Barbarossa, 97
Frederick of the Palatinate, 66, 131, 133
Fuchs, Rudolf, 20, 77
Fučík, Julius, 64–65
Fux, Johann Josef, 162

Gallus, Jacob, 125
Gans, David, 37
Gebauer, Jan, 176
George of Poděbrady, King of Bohemia, 58, 66, 122
Gerlein, Rudolf, 194

German population of Prague, 7, 11, 177
  achievements of, 17, 175
  conflict of with Czechs, 6, 15–20, 23
  language of, 24–25
  size of, 16
Gersonide family, 51
Gide, André, 3
Gluck, Christoph Willibald, 170, 173
Goethe, Johann Wolfgang von, 2–3, 13, 70, 176
Goldast, Melchior, 129
Goldstücker, Eduard, 80–81
Golem legend, 28, 35–40, 45, 64, 85
Goll, Jaroslav, 176
Gorki, Maxim, 187
Gottwald, Klement, 79, 172
Gounod, Charles, 162
Graf, Max, 15
Grillparzer, Franz, 4, 36, 98
Grimm, Jakob, 13
Guardasoni, Domenico, 166
Guenne, Jacques, 7, 88, 102, 142
Guillaune de Machaut, 161
Günther, Hans, 156–57

Hass, Willy, 20, 23, 27, 50, 52, 54–55
  family of, 54
  on Kafka, 70–71
Habsburg regime
  establishment of, 98, 122
  resistance against, 2, 22, 98–99, 138
  rulers of
    Charles Franz Joseph, 8
    Charles V, 122
    Charles VI, 139, 162
    Ferdinand I, 122–23, 126
    Ferdinand III, 106
    Ferdinand V, 105–106, 206
    Franz Joseph I, 17, 106, 206
    Joseph II, 51, 139, 140, 155, 165
    Leopold II, 106
    Maria Theresa, 139
    Maximilian II, 124
    Rudolph II, 36, 45–47, 57–60, 90, 98, 124–29, 139–41
Haisler, Josef, 167
Hájek, Jiří, 83
Hájek, Thaddeus, 59
Hálek, Vitězslav, 154
Hakam II, Al, 93

Hanka, Václav, 13-14
Harant, Krystophe, 125
Harlas, F. X., 2
Hašek, Jarmila, 188, 189
Hašek, Jaroslav, 12, 50, 82, 142, 178-83, 186-91, 195-96
    character of, 186-91
    Communist attitude toward, 178-79, 183
    early life of, 186-87
Hasenberg, Johann von, 58
Hassler, Hans Leo, 125
Hausenstein, Wilhelm, 108
Havlíček, Karel, 176
Haydn, Joseph, 167, 173
Hebbel, Friedrich, 15, 26
Heine, Heinrich, 46-47
Henlein, Konrad, 208
Henry I, King of Germany, 97
Heran, J., 154
Herben, Jan, 26
Herder, Johann Gottfried von, 205
Hermann, Ignát, 154
Herzogenberg, Johanna Baroness, 126
Heydrich, Reinhard, 106, 209
Hilsner, Leopold, 14
Hirsch, Marcus, 51
Hitler, Adolph, 23, 208
Hladik, Karel, 66
Hofmannsthal, Hugo von, 48, 175
Holý, Prokop, 121
Hoover, Herbert, 8
Hora, Josef, 63, 96
Hostinský, Otakar, 176
Hradčany Castle, 30, 68, 98-100, 106, 135-38, 157
    building of, 95-96
    descriptions of, 21-22, 47, 53
    devastation of, 57, 102, 123
    enlargement of, 122-24
    restoration of, 158-59
Hugo, Victor, 38
Hus, Jan, 110, 116-22, 144, 215
    as composer, 161
    heresy of, 119
    as subject of poem, 21
    use of Czech language by, 12-13
    Vyšehrad and, 47
Husák, Gustav, 214
Hussite revolution, 116, 118-22
Hynais, Vojtech, 177

Ibn Jacub, Ibrahim, 92-93

Jacquin, Gottfried von, 163, 166
Jagellon dynasty, 122
Jakobovic, Tobias, 156
James I, King of England, 131
Janáček, Josef, 153
Janáček, Leoš, 12, 20, 89, 171-74, 176
Janouch, Gustav, 5, 6, 71, 75-76, 78, 186, 196
Jeritza, Maria, 172
Jerome, Jerome K., 15
Jesenká, Milena, 23-24
Jewish population of Prague, 7, 27-53
    anti-Semitism, 23
    Battle of Prague, 52
    early history of, 96
    exclusion of, 50-51, 108
    myths of, 27-29, 35-46, 50
    during Nazi occupation, 29, 156-57
    size of, 16
    writers, 20
Jiránek, Anton, 162
Jirásek, Alois, 57
John of Luxemburg, King of Bohemia, 88, 99, 161
Joseph II, Emperor of Austria-Hungary, 51, 139, 140, 155, 165
Judith, Queen of Bohemia, 112
Jungmann, Josef, 9, 13, 169

Kafka, Franz, 26, 55, 66-85, 88, 195, 218
    on anarchists, 186
    birth of, 66, 196
    burial of, 68
    Communist attitude toward, 80-83, 179
    comparisons of with Čapek, 64-65
    contrasted with Leppin and Perutz, 45
    early publication of, 53
    family of, 54
    influence of, 27
    influence of Meissner on, 47
    influence of Old Prague on, 54
    Jewish culture and, 49, 52
    language of, 24-25
    love letters of, 23-24
    Meyrink and, 45, 71

The Mystical City

supposed play by, 49–50
teacher of, 49
Kafka, Ottla, 75
Kahler, Eugen von, 53
Kandinsky, Vassily, 53
Kanka, F. M., 146, 150
Kaper von Kaperstein, Johann, 59
Karásek ze Lvovic, Jiří, 62
Karl, Weissenstein, 50
Karo, Abigdor, 92, 155
Kautman, František, 82
Kelley, Edward, 57, 59–60
Kepler, Johannes, 18, 127, 138
   Wallenstein and, 147
Khevenhüller, Count, 125
Khrushchev, Nikita, 81, 183
Kisch, Egon Erwin, 5, 9, 24, 168, 186–87
   on German-speaking proletariat, 16–17
   Golem legend and, 39
   official regard for, 17
Klee, Paul, 53
Kleist, Heinrich von, 70, 182
Klemperer, Otto, 175
Kodály, Zoltan, 160
Kohen, Isak, 37
Kokoschka, Oskar, 75
Kolovrat-Liebsteinský, Count, 113
Kornish, Colonel, 133
Koželuh, Leopold, 162, 167
Kralovy Dvur manuscripts, 13–14
Kratochvil, Miloš, 79, 98, 114, 169, 176, 206
   on Czech economy, 207–208
   on Czech independence, 207–208
   on resistance to occupation, 209–10
Krischke, Traugott, 6, 209, 210
Kubelik, Jan, 96
Kubiček, Alois, 117
Küchelbecker, Johann Basilius, 33
Kühne, Ferdinand Gustav, 95
Kusak, Alexej, 202

Lada, Josef, 183
La Motte-Fouquet, Frederick Freiherr de, 4, 13
Landau, Ezekiel, 51
Lang, Paul Henry, 162
Langer, František, 20, 48–49

225

Langer, George (Jiří Mordechai), 48–50, 78
Langer, Jaroslav, 49–50
Laquedem, Isaak, 62
Lažanský, Prokap, 3
Lebzelter, Friedrich, 146
Lemmens, Hans, 125
Leopold II, of Habsburg, King of Bohemia, 106
Leppin, Paul, 43–46, 49
   contrasted with Kafka, 45
Liehm, A. J., 213
Liliencron, Detlev von, 2, 25, 142
Lipany, Battle of, 121
Liszt, Franz, 162, 174–75
Lobkowitz, Polyxena, 130
Lobkowitz, Prior von, 129
Loew, Rabbi, 28, 35–40, 45–47
   essay on, 49
   tomb of, 107
Longen, A. E., 188
Loretto Treasure, 144–45
Löw von Löwenstein, Nikolaus, 59
Lubomirski, Prince, 205
Ludmila, Princess of Bohemia, 97
Ludmilla, Saint, relics of, 105
Lurago, Anselmo, 104, 150
Luther, Martin, 122, 161
Luyton, Charles, 125

Mácha, Karel Hynek, 20, 62, 96
Machaut, Guillaume de, see Guillaume de Machaut
Mahler, Gustav, 175
Maisel, Esther, 45–46
Maisel, Jacob, 46
Maisel, Mordechai, 45–46
Majerová, Marie, 81
Mánes, Josef, 67
Mann, Thomas, 5, 69
Marchfeld, Battle of, 98
Marcus Aurelius, Emperor, 95
Maria Theresa, Empress of Austria, 139
Maria Theresa, Princess of Saxony, 165
Marx, Karl, 16, 81, 176
Masaryk, Jan, 116
Masaryk, Tomáš Garrique, 64, 135, 176, 204, 207–208, 215
   defense of Hilsner by, 14–75

motto of, 15
official disregard of, 80
on Prague, 11
Zelena Hora manuscripts and, 14
Mašek, Jiří, 62
Matthias, Emperor of Germany, 129
Matthias of Arras, 102–104, 147
Matuška, Alexander, 64, 65
Maximilian II, King of Bohemia, 124
Meissner, Alfred, 46–47
Mensdorff, Count, 205
Method (Methodious) (monk), 95
Meyer, Maria, 40
Meyrink (Meyer), Gustav, 40–44, 58, 85
  first publication of, 53
  Kafka and, 45, 71
Michael III, Emperor of Byzantium, 95
Milic, Johann, 114–15
Mithard, Jindřich, 109
Mladota, Ferdinand Antonín, 57
Montague, Lady Mary Wortley, 137
Monte, Philippe de, 125
Mozart, Leopold, 74
Mozart, Wolfgang Amadeus, 9–10, 70, 74, 163–68, 173, 174, 184
  The Abduction from the Seraglio, 169
  Don Giovanni, 164–67
  The Marriage of Figaro, 163–65, 171
Mrštík, Vilém, 154
Mrva, Rudolf, 22
Munich Pact, 4
Münsterberg, Ignaz von, 58
Münzer, Thomas, 116
Myslbek, Jan, 96, 177
Myslivecček, Josef, 162

Nazis, occupation of Prague by, 8, 29, 106, 110–11, 156–57, 208–11
Nejedlý, Zdeněk, 172
Němcová, Božena, 20, 96
Němec, Jan, 196
Nepomuk, Saint John (Johannes de Pomuk), 32–34, 55, 86–87
  canonization of, 144, 146
  relics of, 105
  tomb of, 107, 138
Neruda, Jan, 10, 20, 26, 194

  grave of, 96
  on Malá Strana, 56–57, 142
Neumann, Angelo, 175
Nezval, Vitezslav, 63, 96
Niemetschek, Franz Xavier, 163–64, 167
Noll, Josef, 179
Nostitz, Franz Anton Reichsgraf von, 8, 164
Novák, Arne, 31, 144, 152–53
Novotný, Antonín, 56, 81, 158, 211–12

Obolensky, L. E., 4
Old Jewish Cemetary, 155–56
Ondříček, František, 10
Opavský, Wenceslas, 57
Oppenheim, David, 51
Orlik, Emil, 22–23
Orsi, Giovanni Battista, 143
Otakar II, King of Bohemia, 98
Otto I, Emperor of Germany, 93

Pacassi, Niccolo, 140
Palach, Jan, 32, 214
Palacký, František, 11, 14, 169, 176, 204, 205
Palko, F. X., 56
Pallenberg, Max, 179
Parler, Peter, 91, 102–104, 111, 147, 151
  building of Charles Bridge by, 111–12
Patin, Charles, 34
Payne, Peter, 121
Pazourek, Gustav, 154
Pedrazzi, Orazio, 12
Pekář, Josef, 13
Pelišek, Václav, 145
Perutz, Otto, 45–47
  contrasted with Kafka, 45
Petrarch, 111
Piccolomini, Aeneas Silvius, 13
Pick, Otto, 20
Piscator, Erwin, 179
Plečnik, Josip, 158
Politzer, Heinz, 50
Pomuk, Johannes de (Saint John Nepomuk), 32–34, 55, 86–87
  canonization of, 144, 146
  relics of, 105
  tomb of, 107, 138

The Mystical City

Prague
  early history of, 66, 92–99
  effect of Thirty Years' War on, 137
  German population of, 7, 11, 177
    achievements of, 17, 175
    conflict of with Czechs, 6, 15–20, 23
    language of, 24–25
    size of, 16
  Jewish population of, 7, 27–53
    anti-Semitism, 23
    Battle of Prague, 52
    early history, 96
    exclusion of, 50–51, 108
    myths of, 27–29, 35–46, 50
    during Nazi occupation, 29, 156–57
    size of, 16
  Malá Strana district of, 7, 21–22, 55–57, 78–79, 123, 142–46, 152–54
    founding of, 98
    restoration of, 216
  modern life in, 191–203
  Nazi occupation of, 8, 29, 106, 110–11, 156–57, 208–11
  New Town district of, 7, 108
  Old Town district of, 7, 46, 67–69, 88, 137, 216
  Russian invasions of, 31–32, 67–69, 211–14, 217
  topography of, 7
Prague, Battle of, 52
Prague defenestrations, 66, 115–16, 120, 129–31
Prague University, 17–18, 72–73, 109–10
Přemyslid dynasty, 8, 30, 96–99
  Boleslav I, 97
  Bořivoj, 97
  Ludmila, 97
  Otakar II, 98
  Přemysl I, 97
  Spytihněv, 97, 100
  Vladislav II, 97
  Wenceslas II, 99
  Wenceslas IV, 99
Přemysl I, King of Bohemia, 97
Procházka, Ladislav, 154–55
Procopius, Saint, 114
Purkyně, Jan Evangelista, 169

Raabe, Wilhelm, 3
Radetsky, Joseph Wenzel, 4
Rapoport, Solomon L., 51
Rauchmiller, Matthias, 114
Regnard, Jakob, 125
Reiman, Paul, 81
Reimann, Hans, 179
Reiner (artist), 184
Reinhardt, Max, 175
Rejha, Antonin, 162
Rejt, Benedikt, 123–24
Rieger, František, 176
Rienzo, Cola di, 111
Rilke, René (Rainer Maria), 20–22, 24, 54–55
  family of, 54
  Larenopfer, 47–48
  mysticism and, 53
Rodin, Auguste, 4, 18, 194
Rodovský of Hustořany, 61
Roger, Pierre (Pope Clemens VI), 100, 109
Roháč z Dubé, Jan, 66
Rosenberg, Wilhelm von, 58
Rudolph II, of Habsburg, Emperor, 36, 45–47, 57, 90, 98, 124–29
  alchemy and, 57, 59–60
  art treasures of, 125–27, 139–41
  death of, 128–29
Russians, invasions of Prague by, 31–32, 67–69, 211–14, 217
Růže, Hanus, 67

Šafařik, J. J., 205
Šafařik, Pavel Josef, 14
Salieri, Antonio, 167
Salten, Franz, 19
Salus, Hugo, 20, 54, 68
Saporiti, Teresa, 166
Sauer, Franta, 50
Savye, Lambert de, 125
Scamozzi, Vincenzio, 129
Schiller, Friedrich von, 3, 138
Schlick, Joachim Andreas, 130, 133, 134
Schnitzler, Arthur, 48
Schönberg, Arnold, 173, 175
Schönerer, Georg Ritter von, 207
Schopenhauer, Arthur, 33
Schubert, Franz, 173
Schürer, Oskar, 119, 204, 205

Sebastian, Saint, 144
Secharja, Abraham, 39
Seifert, Jaroslav, 63
Seni (astrologer), 147
Shakespeare, William, 15
Siebenschein, Hugo, 69
Sigismund, Holy Roman Emperor, 119–21
Skála, Pavel, 131
Škroup, František, 169
Sládek (writer), 142
Slavata, Vilém, 129–30
Smetana, Bedřich, see Smetana, Friedrich
Smetana, Friedrich (Bedřich), 31, 55, 96, 161, 169–71
  The Bartered Bride, 170–71, 173
  Libuše, 177
  My Country, 120, 161, 173–74
Šnobr, Jan, 63
Sova, Antonín, 1, 63, 142
Spezza, Andrea, 146
Spinelli, Colonel, 132
Sporck, Count, 151
Sporer, Marta, 90
Spytihněv, King of Bohemia, 97, 100
Sramek, František, 23, 82
Stalin, Josef, 9, 79, 183
Stamitz, Johann V., 162
Štech, M., 176
Stefani, Jan, 162
Steinfels (artist), 184
Stella, Paolo della, 123, 126
Stephen, Saint, relics of, 105
Sternberg, Oberstburgrat, 129
Strada, Jacopo, 126, 128
Strada, Katharina, 128
Strauss, Johann, 173
Strnad, Anton, 68
Suetonius, 61
Švabinský, Max, 107
Svoboda, Alois, 60, 116, 135
Svoboda, Ludvík, 32, 158
Syrrus, Claudius, 58
Szell, George, 175

Tchaikovsky, Peter Illich, 175
Teschen, Korálek von, 59
Thèbes, Madame de, 58
Theodoric (builder), 111
Thieberger, Friedrich, 49
Thieberger, Gertrude, 49
Thirty Years' War, 106, 116, 127, 130, 144–45, 161
Thurn, Count, 132, 167
Tirol, Hans von, 123
Toman, Rudolf, 186–89
Tramer, Hans, 52
Tučkova, Anna, 60
Tůma, Franz, 162
Tyl, Josef Kajetán, 2, 21, 165
Tyrš, Miloslav, 176

Ulbricht, Walter, 213
Urzidil, Johannes, 6, 49, 50, 201, 210–11
  on German poets, 24–25
Utitz, Emil, 69, 77

Vaculík, Ludvík, 212, 217
Valéry, Paul, 4
Varnbühler, Karl Freiherr von, 40
Verdi, Guiseppe, 149
Vitus, Saint, 97
  Cathedral of, 102–107, 114, 138
  treasure of, 104–107
Vladislav II, King of Bohemia, 97
Voitěch, Saint, 160
Vrchlický, Jaroslav, 1, 20, 21, 142, 176
  translation of, 54
Vries, Adriane de, 127, 147
Vrtba family, 150–51
Vryda, Stanislav, 204

Wagner, Richard, 4, 8, 18, 110, 171, 175, 176
Waldstein, Albrech von, see Wallenstein, Albrecht von
Wallenstein (Waldstein), Albrecht von, 135, 138–39, 146–47, 204
  palace of, 3, 151, 153
Walter, Bruno, 4
Webern, Anton, 173
Wedekind, Fritz, 43
Weimar, Duke of, 133
Weltsch, Felix, 74
Wenceslas II, King of Bohemia, 99
Wenceslas III, King of Bohemia, 99
Wenceslas IV, King of Bohemia, 32–33, 86, 115, 118–19; see also Saint Wenceslas

Wenceslas, Saint, 30–32, 55, 97, 101, 103, 160; see also Wenceslas IV
  relics of, 105
Werfel, Franz, 20, 27, 50, 74, 75, 120, 199
  first publication of, 53
  mysticism and, 53, 55
White Mountain, Battle of, 131–34, 161, 203
Wiener, Oskar, 26–27, 48
Wilde, Oscar, 18
Wilson, Woodrow, 8
Windischgraetz, Alfred, Prince of Austria, 112, 205
Wirth, Zdněk, 155
Wladislaw I, King of Bohemia, 112
Wohlmuth, Boniface, 123–24
Wolf, Karl Hermann, 23
Wolker, Jiří, 63
Woltmann, Carl Ludwig von, 3
Wřesowetz von Vřesowitz, Wenzel, 58–59
Wurmser, Nicholas, 111
Wycliffe, John, 116, 119

Zach, Johann, 162
Zátopek, Emil, 217–18
Závada, Vilém, 62
Zelená Hora manuscripts, 14
Zelenka, Johann Dismias, 162
Zemlinsky, Alexander von, 175
Ženíšek, Frantisek, 177
Zeyer, Julius, 2, 21, 55–56, 96, 142
Zítek, Josef, 177
Žižka, John, 120–21
Zvěřina, L. N., 142

JUN 23 1971

914. WECHSBERG   119681
3712 PRAGUE
WECHSB
                        7.95

DATE DUE			

78 98 9 94 99 02
8   84   03

South Huntington Public Library
Huntington Station, New York

0652 00 489715 01 3
WECHSBERG, JOSEPH
PRAGUE. THE MYSTICAL CITY
(0) 1971 914.3712 WEC
(CIC=2)
02/25/86

98